The SOCIAL TRADE SHOW

Leveraging Social Media and Virtual Events to Connect With Your Customers

TRACI BROWNE

800 East 96th Street,
Indianapolis, Indiana 46240 USA

The Social Trade Show
Leveraging Social Media and Virtual Events to Connect With Your Customers

ISBN-13: 978-0-7897-4913-0
ISBN-10: 0-7897-4913-0

Library of Congress Cataloging-in-Publication data is on file.

First Printing: June 2012

Trademarks

Warning and Disclaimer

Bulk Sales

Que Publishing offers excellent discounts on this book when ordered in quantity for bulk purchases or special sales. For more information, please contact

U.S. Corporate and Government Sales
1-800-382-3419
corpsales@pearsontechgroup.com

For sales outside of the U.S., please contact

International Sales
international@pearsoned.com

Editor-in-Chief
Greg Wiegand

Senior Acquisitions Editor
Katherine Bull

Development Editor
Leslie T. O'Neill

Technical Editor
Emilie Barta

Managing Editor
Sandra Schroeder

Project Editor
Seth Kerney

Copy Editor
Megan Wade

Indexer
Heather McNeill

Proofreader
Jovana Shirley

Publishing Coordinators
Cindy Teeters
Romny French

Cover Designer
Anne Jones

Compositor
Mark Shirar

CONTENTS AT A GLANCE

TABLE OF CONTENTS

About the Author

Traci Browne has been working in the trade show industry for more than 15 years, beginning as an exhibitor in the technology sector when shows like Comdex were in their heyday. Following that, she worked for a trade show marketing firm managing exhibits for major pharmaceutical and medical device companies.

In 2005, Traci started Red Cedar Publicity and Marketing and continued to consult on trade show strategy for clients in the health care sector. Red Cedar now produces business-to-business (B2B) educational conferences and trade shows. In 2010, Traci also started a trade show production company, Live Well Expos, LLC, with partner Debbie Anmuth-Hunt and now produces a regional consumer health and fitness show. In 2012, they plan to expand the event into three more regions.

Red Cedar Publicity and Marketing still consults to exhibitors on trade show strategy but now has a focus on trade show and conference production. Traci speaks at many industry events, including TSEA's TS2, EXHIBITOR, IAEE's Expo! Expo!, BMA Philadelphia, and SMEI. She also produced a trade show exhibitor peer conference called Exhibit Camp, and was co-producer for EventCamp East Coast. You can find more insights on trade shows on her blog at www.TradeShowInstitute.com.

Traci is a member of the Business Marketing Association and is the immediate past president and founder of the Philadelphia Chapter of the Business Marketing Association. She is a member of the Society of Independent Show Organizers, Senior Planners Industry Network, and the Green Meetings Industry Council.

Dedication

To all the exhibit and brand managers who are asked to do more with less everyday, and who manage to pull it off spectacularly.

Acknowledgments

To Beth Harte, who got me into this mess.

To Emily Breder and Helena Bouchez, who answered desperate calls for help when I could not organize my thoughts.

To Katherine Bull, acquisitions editor, who thought I had something to say and kept encouraging me to say it throughout the entire process. If ever I find myself on a ledge, I hope you are there to talk me down.

To Romny French and Seth Kerney, who somehow managed to keep everything on track and put order to the madness.

To Leslie O'Neill, who made sure all those thoughts in my head made sense on paper—you had your work cut out for you.

To Megan Wade, who corrected more than 7,000 mistakes (let's see if she catches the missing 0).

To Emilie Barta, for being by my side and supporting me through the entire journey.

And finally...to my husband Dean. Without your constant nagging, this never would have been finished—you know me so well—I love you.

We Want to Hear from You!

As the reader of this book, *you* are our most important critic and commentator. We value your opinion and want to know what we're doing right, what we could do better, what areas you'd like to see us publish in, and any other words of wisdom you're willing to pass our way.

As Editor-in-Chief for Que Publishing, I welcome your comments. You can email or write me directly to let me know what you did or didn't like about this book—as well as what we can do to make our books better.

Please note that I cannot help you with technical problems related to the topic of this book. We do have a User Services group, however, where I will forward specific technical questions related to the book.

When you write, please be sure to include this book's title and author as well as your name, email address, and phone number. I will carefully review your comments and share them with the author and editors who worked on the book.

Email: feedback@quepublishing.com

Mail: Greg Wiegand
           Editor-in-Chief
           Que Publishing
           800 East 96th Street
           Indianapolis, IN 46240 USA

Reader Services

Visit our website and register this book at www.quepublishing.com/register for convenient access to any updates, downloads, or errata that might be available for this book.

Introduction

There was a time when the trade show was the place buyers went to learn about various companies' product offerings. If someone was in the market for widgets, he could go to the annual trade show and compare your offering to those of all your competitors.

Exhibitors simply set up shop on the trade show floor for three days and pitch their products to buyers. You were there for one reason and one reason only—to sell more products or services. Buyers were there to research and get the information they needed to make a purchasing decision.

The Internet and social media have created a fundamental shift in attendees' goals and objectives in attending a trade show. Today, buyers are doing their research online and creating a shortlist of vendors based on information available on your website, on industry blogs, and through customer reviews and social media chatter.

They come to your booth armed with information, like a patient who visits his doctor after diagnosing himself with the help of sites such as WebMD. They come to your booth already knowing what your products or services can and cannot do for them. They have researched what your current customers and industry analysts think of those products and services and how they compare to similar offerings. If your booth staff is prepared to teach these buyers only what they already know, you are facing an uphill battle.

So what is the modern exhibit manager to do? First, you must understand why attendees now go to trade shows. They are there to network. They are also there to find new product and service offerings, and they want their specific questions answered by companies on their short list.

By using social media as a communication tool before, during, and after the show, your company can be the attendee's go-to source for networking, industry trends, new product and service information, and information related to his specific needs. Let's take a quick look at how including a social media strategy into your exhibit program can help attendees achieve their goals.

- **Networking**—Social media provides a platform to develop a community that will make it easier for attendees to connect with like-minded individuals who share similar work-related experiences, issues, and problems.
- **Product/Service information**—Social media provides a platform to disseminate real-time information across a wide audience.
- **Relevant information**—Social media provides a platform for companies to listen to what their customers and potential customers identify as their pain points and the solutions they are looking for to solve their problems.

Expanding the Audience

For every attendee who comes to a trade show, there are hundreds just like them sitting back in their offices trying to accomplish the same things—and do so cost-effectively. They are doing their research online, trying to connect with peers in their industry, and scouring industry news for new products and services that will solve their problems. By incorporating social media and virtual event components into your trade show strategy, you can extend your reach beyond just the attendees to those customers back in their offices across the globe.

The current economy has made it difficult for customers to attend industry events. Budgets are being cut, so fewer employees are being sent to industry trade shows. In the past, companies might have sent four or five team members to an event, but these days they typically send only one key member. Shrinking budgets also mean more work is piled on shrinking teams. Customers simply do not have the time to leave their offices to attend trade shows the way they did in the past.

Trade show and conference organizers are tuning in to this and opening their events to a wider audience. They are using social media and virtual events to include those who are unable to travel. Smart show organizers are providing ways for their exhibitors to connect with those audience members who are unable to attend.

Consequently, proactive exhibitors are creating ways to connect with their customers and their potential customers, not just at the event location, but miles away and across time zones.

Expanding the Length of the Show

Just as you expand your audience by incorporating social media into your exhibit program, you can also extend the length of the show. We have to stop thinking of trade shows as just two- or three-day events. There was a time when we would spend a year planning for a show, fly in, construct our booths, sell our products, tear down our booths and stick them in storage, and then begin planning for next year's show.

Event organizers are realizing this, too. Their live events are now just one moment in a year-long continuing conversation. They are providing their attendees with a platform where they can network throughout the year with online communities. Software companies and other solution providers are coming up with new community applications for show organizers every day.

Show organizers understand their attendees' desire to make their time at the show more productive. Because attendees typically want to do their research prior to arriving in the exhibit hall, organizers are providing their exhibitors with robust tools to get product/service information into the hands of buyers before the event. Exhibitors are able to upload brochures, whitepapers, product information, and special offers right onto the event website.

Show organizers also understand that buyers are looking for ways to connect with exhibitors whose products and services will best help them solve their problems. Many shows are now providing tools that allow attendees to preset appointments with exhibitors on their shortlist to maximize their time at the show. More and more trade shows are also showcasing new products and service offerings in the exhibit hall, on the website, and in show directories. Attendees can easily find up-to-date information on industry trends without having to stumble on it when navigating the trade show floor.

Show organizers are beginning to understand that the global marketplace and the current economic budget constraints require that they find ways to reach people in their industry who cannot attend their events in person. Incorporating a virtual component into their face-to-face events is a practice that is becoming more and more necessary. This combination of the two is referred to as a *hybrid event.* While still in its infancy, event organizers are experimenting with different virtual and hybrid solutions to pull in a wider audience.

Exhibitors who do not jump on board with the new opportunities and advantages their show management are providing will be severely limited in what they can accomplish. They will quickly fall behind the competition that is not afraid to thoughtfully experiment and participate in these services. Fear is not an option.

It's Not About the Tools

Tools will come and go, but social media is here to stay. In 2008, MySpace had 300 million accounts and in August of that year, it announced a record-breaking 122 million visitors to the site, according to comScore, Inc. But in 2009, traffic had dropped so significantly that it failed to satisfy a minimum traffic level needed for a three-year $900 million advertising deal with Google. Executives at NewsCorp estimated that MySpace lost about $100 million in that deal.

Twitter is a different story. The micro-blogging service boasted 6 million users in 2008. In 2009, it had jumped to 18 million. On March 11, 2011, the day a tsunami hit Japan, Twitter reported 177 million tweets sent. It also reported that on March 12, 2011, users created 572,000 new accounts. In 2008, Twitter had only 8 employees, and by January 2011, it had grown to 350 employees.

When Facebook was launched in 2004, the social networking site was limited to Harvard students. In 2006, Facebook opened the network up to anyone 13 years and older with a valid email address. As recently as January 2008, Facebook reported just 60 million active users. By January 2009, a Compete.com study ranked Facebook as the most used social networking service by worldwide monthly active users, surpassing MySpace. According to Facebook, it had more than 750 million active users at the time of this writing, making it equivalent to the third-largest country in the world.

Today the blogosphere's newest romance is with Google+. Many social media bloggers are predicting it will be a fierce competitor to Facebook. But keep in mind that much hoopla surrounded Google Buzz and Google Wave, and they are nowhere to be found just years later. For now, Google is quiet about Google+'s actual numbers, but several bloggers who claim to have a formula that will give a close estimate were reporting more than 9 million users by July 2011. That was two months before going public.

So what's my point? If you spend your time jumping on the latest social media tool bandwagon, you will never catch up. If you base your entire efforts on one or two tools, in a year or even months, those efforts may be wasted as the tool becomes obsolete. However, if you create a solid social media strategy that focuses on your audience, you can insert tools appropriate to that strategy to connect with your audience. You can easily upgrade the tools with the latest applications. For example, a plan that involves collaboration between your customers and sales will guide you better than one that is focused on Google Moderator, the tool itself.

Throughout this book you'll find examples of the various tools available today to accomplish your strategy—but the tool is secondary to your strategy. You may be comfortable using a hammer, and it could be your favorite tool. However, you are not going to consider using it to fix a porcelain vase. You must know your goals and objectives before you can decide on a strategy. Only after you are set on your strategy will you begin to choose your tools.

The main focus of this book is on social media in general, including virtual events and how you can harness its power to fulfill an in-depth, robust exhibit strategy. Just as there is no magic booth giveaway that will guarantee success for your exhibit program, there is no one social media tool that will be right for every situation. You will learn how to create a strategy, and then find the appropriate tool to reach the goals and objectives you've defined.

The Social Strategy

Do you know what gets me really jazzed about using social media and virtual events in your trade show exhibit strategy? It's not just the fun games you can play to drive traffic to your booth. It's not Foursquare check-ins or posting pictures on your company Facebook page. To me those things, while a great addition to your exhibit, are still just the same tired strategy of the past but with different tools.

What gets me really excited is the real-time possibilities of social media. The way it allows you to create a community or be a part of one that already exists. It's about leveraging its power to bring you and your audience together. And it's about leveraging that community to reach a wider audience than just those attending the show.

1

Create and Connect Your Community

Social media isn't a campaign or a tool to be rolled out a week or two before a big show. It is a commitment of time and resources undertaken so your company can connect not just with customers and potential customers at an event, but also with your industry's larger community: a community of other suppliers, associations, media representatives, thought leaders, potential employees, mentors, and mentees. But why should you make an ongoing commitment for a three-day event? Being an active member of a community builds your company's reputation as a trusted solution provider and its employees as thought leaders in your industry. People in your community will get to know your company as more than just a brand. Buyers will start seeking you out and listening to what you have to say. Your company will be put on people's "must-see vendor" list for the upcoming show.

I know this because I am one of those buyers at shows. I produce independent, for-profit conferences and trade shows. As a buyer of show services and booker of venues, I attend at least four meetings, industry conferences, or trade shows each year. Like any buyer, I am there to network, find out what's new, and get answers to my specific questions from vendors. I also attend and speak at Exhibitor Media Group's EXHIBITOR as an influencer to learn the current issues of my customers.

Up until 2010, these shows were very lonely events. I would meet other attendees from year to year but never really had the time or the ability to stay in touch. The only vendors I really knew were the ones I had used in the past. I would do my research before the trade show and make a list of vendors I wanted to see on the show floor. There was my A list of must-see vendors, and then a B list of those who looked interesting and might have something to benefit me. If I had time left over, I would wander around and perhaps stumble on something interesting.

In the weeks leading up to the event, I would receive hundreds of postcards and emails. Most were promoting exhibitors' give aways, so I really didn't connect with what they were actually selling or what solutions they were providing. But more importantly, they were not connecting with me as an individual. I was receiving the same solicitation thousands of other attendees were receiving. What was lacking was a rich, personalized experience.

Upon arrival, I would check into my hotel and get ready for the opening reception. Because I do not have an easily recognizable Fortune 500 logo on my business card, I don't have vendors flocking to me. I am exactly like many of the potential customers at your shows who fly below the radar. We are customers who have healthy budgets but who do not appear on exhibitors' wish lists because they may not have heard of our companies. I would arrive at the opening reception and navigate the sea of strangers, desperately hoping that the next person I introduced myself to would be somewhat interesting. After about half an hour, I would head back to my room bored.

The next day, when the show floor opened, I would make my rounds with list in hand. It was very methodical and all business. I would attend a few educational sessions, go to the dinners, pack up, and go home. And then I would forget about it until the next year rolled around. Yes, I may have discovered some interesting products or venues, but there was no personal connection made. Nothing to entice me to purchase from any one exhibitor over another, other than a comparison of features and benefits. Even in a business-to-business transaction, people still buy from *people*—and you cannot build a relationship in a 5- or 10-minute booth visit.

Late in 2009, I discovered Twitter. I was skeptical at first because it seemed like a waste of time. I, like many others, wondered what business benefit was to be gained by people tweeting about what they had for lunch. But friends encouraged me to give it a go, so I did. I stumbled on a small group of event planners who showed me how I could meet and follow along with other event professionals through weekly chats. This group used Twitter to exchange relevant information among the larger community.

This turned out to be a very active community with members who are passionate about events and event innovation. It is made up of event and meeting planners as well as vendors who supply products and services to the industry and members of the media. When a community member comes across an interesting article online, he tweets a link out to the group under the #eventprofs hashtag. Those who have their own blogs tweet links to their most recent posts. Other members *retweet* (Twitter's way of allowing users to share information they see with their followers) the links, giving the original article a much wider audience. After I joined, I learned more in that first month than I had learned in the past year by reading all the information that was being shared.

This particular group also holds bi-weekly tweet chats for members of the community to discuss a particular topic for about an hour. Topics range from selecting a venue, event design, trade show best practices, and brain-friendly learning to creating a thorough risk plan. Mixed in with the abundance of great advice being given is plenty of friendly banter. In no time, I felt like I was getting to know this group of strangers.

I was meeting not only other event planners like myself, but also a lot of vendors. I have been exposed to vendors through this channel I would never have taken notice of otherwise. I was noticing them because of the valuable information they provided, either created by them or forwarded from other sources. They were proving how much they really knew about the industry they served. I could ask a question and within hours I'd have 10–20 members of my community either offering an answer or pointing me to someone who could help.

Many of the vendors in the community, as you can imagine, are competitors. The smart ones embrace one another as part of the community, and it's not unusual to see them joking with one another online. It does not go unnoticed how they conduct themselves. It provides a lot of insight as to what it would be like to work with them as vendors.

But there are those who don't get it. All they do is constantly push information about their company onto the community. They interrupt the conversations taking place with self-promotion. Self-promotion is not bad in itself—it's expected that people are there to promote themselves. It's just good to follow the 80/20 rule. Talk about others 80 percent of the time and talk about yourself 20 percent of the time. Those who do not add value to the conversation but only talk about themselves earn a bad reputation.

Eventually these conversations I was having on Twitter spawned phone and email conversations with people I particularly connected with. As relationships grew with some of the vendors, I began to recommend them to others or hire them myself. I trusted their opinions from what I learned about them through all these conversations. I felt very comfortable making referrals on behalf of these community members.

But What About Face-to-Face Connections?

Soon just talking online was not enough for this group, and a conference was spawned called EventCamp. People wanted a forum to meet in person and expand on some of the new and innovative ideas we were talking about online. What is important to point out here is that the community goes by the name *eventprofs*. There is no delineation between suppliers and planners. Every member is valued because of what he brings to the table. You are not an eventprof planner or an eventprof supplier. You are an eventprof.

The feeling I had when I arrived at this first EventCamp was amazing. I checked in to the hotel, dropped my bags in my room, and rushed down to the bar where everyone was gathering that night. People had arrived the day before just so they could spend more time together. I met people for the first time, but it felt like they were old friends. I actually looked forward to meeting many of the vendors in person and learning more about their products and services. I was not alone in this transformation. Everyone who had gathered there credited their involvement in social media with this sense of community.

The conversations taking place on social media for months prior to the event had already broken the ice. Now attendees were free to spend their time building stronger business relationships. Vendors didn't have to rely on a quick sales pitch. They already had the attention of their potential customers and those customers were ready and willing to listen.

But What About Trade Shows?

Now when I attend my annual industry conferences, my first stops on the trade show floor are the vendors who are part of my Twitter community. They are the first vendors I consider doing business with. I also want to help them spread the word about what they are doing in their booths. I share any promotions or demonstrations they are doing in their booths with my network, and I promote to my community any sessions they are leading. I also bring my peers to their booths and sessions and introduce them to each other.

I used to get ready for a show by using the exhibitor directory to create my agenda, with no personal interaction before the show. Now I am online reaching out to attendees and vendors three to four months in advance to find out if they are going to be attending and exhibiting this year. I am already planning my schedule and want to make sure I have set aside time to meet with these people. It's easy to do because I know where I can find them via social media. I am talking to them almost every week anyway.

Being part of a community can lead to new opportunities. I am often asked to host roundtable discussions and participate on panels. I almost never fill out a speaker proposal to get on the education agenda. I am asked by members of my community who are on the event education committee to participate. I suggest to them vendors who would make great participants in panel discussions or who could lead a discussion on a particular topic.

By being part of a community, you will suddenly find yourself with the wonderful dilemma of not having enough time in a three-day event to connect one-on-one with other members. Social media provides the solution by allowing you to quickly create impromptu gatherings and easily spread the word.

Recently at a trade show, I sent out word to the community via Twitter that we would be meeting in the bar at the hotel an hour before the opening reception. Word passed all through the community, and about 40 people showed up. Personal introductions were made for those who had not met. Some people were invited specifically so they could meet another member of the community we thought they should know. After that we swarmed into the opening reception and dispersed, only to regroup here and there to make more introductions.

Do you want to be the exhibitor who is just sending out postcards and emails hoping attendees will be interested enough to come see you? Or do you want armies of loyal community members bringing people to your booth because they believe in your company and want their peers to know about you?

When I walk on the trade show floor these days, I have very little time to wander around and stumble across someone's booth. Most of my appointments have been set up ahead of time. I still go through the exhibitor list, but now I reach out to my community and ask, "What do you know about this company? Should I visit with them? Is there someone else I should look at?" In my free time, I stop by the booths of those I now consider my friends to say hello—and I bring people with me. I ask them whom I should be visiting with. Often they walk me to the booth and make an introduction. This is not only a much more productive use of my time as a buyer, but it is also more productive for the exhibitor because I am not in her booth just to kick the tires.

How many of your customers are doing this? How many people (who are not your customers) are going out of their way to find people who would be a good fit for your product or service and making the introduction? Are you doing this for your customers? By incorporating social media into your exhibit strategy, you can be sure the answer to these questions are yes. Your booth staff will be spending more time with qualified customers building relationships and less time with the tire kickers.

My story takes place on Twitter. But there are a hundred other stories just like this that are taking place on Facebook, Google+, LinkedIn, Pathable, and many other platforms. Wikipedia has a list of more than 300 of the most active networking sites available at http://en.wikipedia.org/wiki/List_of_social_networking_websites. The point is that you need to find out where your customers' communities are and start interacting.

Failure to Plan Is a Plan for Failure

Anyone can have a similar experience when you participate in a community related to your industry. Companies who incorporate social media into their trade show strategy and are actively involved in their communities can see bigger returns on their exhibit program investments. Social media is not free; there is a cost involved. Sure, you don't have to pay to be on Facebook or LinkedIn, but they do require an investment of someone's time—and that does cost a company money. Although your customers can easily get a benefit just by being part of the community without having a plan in place, you, as an exhibitor, cannot afford this approach. When you decide to invest time in social media, like anything else, you need to have a plan. You need to set definitive measurable goals and objectives. You need to check in often to see whether you are meeting those goals. Where are you exceeding your objectives, and where are you falling short? As an exhibitor, you cannot afford to wing it.

Let's take a look at some possible goals and objectives an exhibitor might have for his social media investment. This exhibitor is a software vendor who has a product used by corporate HR departments and will be attending the annual human resources convention in six months:

- **Really bad goal**—Use Twitter.
- **Bad goal**—Get 100 Twitter followers in one month.
- **Good goal step 1**—Create company Twitter account and find and follow 25 HR directors. Listen to their conversation for two weeks.
- **Good goal step 2**—Get 15 HR directors to follow the company account and connect at least weekly with them by the end of two months.
- **Good goal step 3**—Find appropriate chat for HR directors and participate weekly. At the end of one month of chats, measure the increase in HR directors who follow us.

The first example is a bad goal because there is nothing to measure. The second goal, although it is measurable, is bad because it does not define a specific audience. Getting 100 followers serves no purpose if they are not influencers or purchasers of your product. The last three goals are good because they are specific and measurable.

If you really work this plan and at the end of two months you know only three HR directors, this might not be the best investment of your time. But without setting goals and checking in regularly, you'll never know whether it's working. Trust me, you can be very busy on social media without ever accomplishing anything. You can build up quite a following and suddenly realize that the only people who follow you are people who want to sell you something. That is not what you are trying to accomplish.

There also has to be an end game in sight. I see so many exhibitors creating a Facebook page a month before their show. They encourage people to friend them, and then come by the booth for a prize. In the booth they spend all their time focused on getting more Facebook friends. They forget they are supposed to be selling something. Then, when the show is over they enthusiastically post some show photos on their page to show all their new friends. Within weeks that enthusiasm wanes, and soon it's weeks or months between posts. All their Facebook friends have forgotten about them and their page. When next year rolls around and they consider what booth activity they are going to do, they ditch Facebook because "that didn't work."

That's not a social media strategy. That's a gimmick much like using booth babes, contests, or dunk tanks in your booth. To avoid the trap of social media gimmicks, figure out first what you want to get out of using social media. Defining your goals will help you figure out what your social media strategy should be.

Summary

Social media makes it easy to create and find an active community in your industry. Participating in a community is a wonderful way for customers and exhibitors to get to know each other year round, not just at a three-day event. As an exhibitor, when you are an active member in that community, you reap the benefits of word-of-mouth marketing and loyalty. You also expand your customer base beyond those who are attending the show in person. Now let's get you the support you're going to need.

2

Connect With and
Expand Your Audience

The social trade show is not just a way to get people to spread the word about the promotion going on in your booth. It's a way to discover what your audience wants to know about. Social media can give you insight into the information that you should provide in your booth to draw an audience. This is information not just for the audience at the show, but also for those potential customers who could not attend this year's event. Social media can bring that information to them.

Let's say it's a month or even a week before your trade show. The media breaks a story that impacts your customers' and potential customers' businesses. They want information, and they want it now. It's unlikely show management will be able to address it because their schedule has been planned 6–10 months in advance. You could arrange to have an expert on the topic present in your booth. Have someone from your executive team conduct a relaxed talk show–style interview to help position that exec as a thought leader. Talk about a traffic draw! You can use social media to build anticipation and help you spread the word quickly that you will have that expert in your booth.

And why stop with the attendees who are physically at the event?. Allow the audience unable to attend to still participate in your event by creating a virtual event for them on the most appropriate platform and live streaming your in-booth activities. Then, you can repurpose the content for even more exposure and for an extended period of time by posting videos on YouTube and embedding them into your website for others to view at their leisure. You have successfully expanded your booth's audience from several hundred who may have stopped by at the show to thousands online, and you have extended the length of your trade show messaging beyond the hours the show floor is open for business.

During the EXHIBITOR2011 show, big changes were taking place at Chicago's McCormick Place. There was talk that new work rules implemented in 2010 to make the center more friendly for exhibitors would be overturned. This was something that would affect many of the attendees and tens of thousands of exhibit managers who were not in attendance.

Imagine if any one of those exhibitors would have jumped on the opportunity and quickly rallied to get a representative from McCormick Place and a member of the Chicago legislature into his booth for informational and Q&A sessions. Not only would he have a crowded booth, but he would have a promotion that would draw visitors to his website for days if not weeks or months. It would also have positioned him as a trusted resource for industry information.

If you're an active member of your community, no matter what the social media platform, word will spread like wildfire. There will be no need for an expensive direct mail piece or email list rentals. Just put the word out there and let the community do all the work. If it's something that is truly of value, then word of mouth will take over.

You also do not need a lot of advance notice. If the discussion or presentation really is valuable to your audience, you need only to make the announcement a couple of days in advance on the social media platforms your customers use. Your competition will not have time to come up with their own alternatives.

Other trade show managers who have shows and conferences scheduled over the coming year at McCormick Place might direct their exhibitors to view the video to get more information as it directly affects them and their exhibitors. You would have, of course, branded it with your company name with links to your website. Those other exhibitors could be potential customers, partners, or referrals who further expand your audience.

Before the advent of social media, you would have hoped to get a couple of quali-fied customers in your booth. If people were not attending the trade show, they would not see you. Even if you did decide to live stream the event and make it available online, it would have been difficult to get the word out to the larger audi-ence. You can see by this example that you can now invite thousands of people into your booth regardless of whether they physically attend the trade show.

Where Are Your Customers Hanging Out?

Before you can decide which tools you are going to use in your social media strat-egy, you have to find out where your customers are and what tools they are using. Where are they going to be receptive to your messages? All your customers might be active on Facebook, but are they using it for work or to exchange family news with other family members and friends? Just because they are all on Facebook doesn't mean they want you or your message there. You need to be sensitive to that.

When I refer to *messages* I don't mean just your advertising. Many people are active in social media to be a part of a larger community. They are not there for product pitches—they are there to find support from others in their industry to support others. Your presence and messaging in social media should provide that support and add value to the conversation.

That's not to say advertising does not work in social media. I follow certain brands on Twitter just to hear about their specials or new product releases. I don't particu-larly want to engage in a conversation with @DSWShoeLovers on Twitter. I just want to play along on "Free Shoe Friday."

When you join the community, it is important that you spend time listening. Observe how everyone interacts. Are vendors part of the conversation? Is promo-tion of any kind prohibited? Is the conversation all business, or do members share personal experiences? Who asks the questions, and who's giving out the advice?

Again, it's important you are not spending all your time promoting yourself in these communities. Cull through the trade show event program and find sessions your customers might find valuable; then, point them out to the community. Become the source for tidbits of valuable information. Do you know the best place for sushi near the convention center? Tell people about it. Think of social media as a cocktail party. You wouldn't spend the entire evening telling people about your job. You'd mix in some social things, too.

Your audience is most likely already congregating in several of the world's most popular social networking sites. The following list. will give you a good place to start your search.

LinkedIn

LinkedIn is one of the world's largest professional networking sites with more than 120 million members in over 200 countries and territories. Many individuals use it as an online resume, to connect with past colleagues, and to find new jobs. But LinkedIn is also a great research tool and messaging platform for marketers and exhibit managers via the groups feature.

If you are a business-to-business (B2B) company, chances are that at least one group has been created for your industry. For instance, a quick search on LinkedIn groups for "medical record" returned 51 groups. Another search on "cloud computing" returned 1,302 groups, and a search on "semiconductor" returned 548 groups. "Mixed-signal semiconductor" returned just one, which focused on job opportunities in Japan. There's a void waiting to be filled if I ever saw one.

Join the appropriate groups for your industry and *listen* to what is being said. People reach out on these forums to find answers to their questions. They may be looking for job information, vendor referrals, best practices, or event announcements. These are your buyers, and knowing what their pressing issues are will give you ideas for in-booth activities at your trade shows. Is someone in the group emerging as a trusted source of information? She might make an excellent presenter in your booth. You would not hire her to pitch your product but to provide a mini-session on a topic of high interest that will bring crowds to your booth.

Journalists and industry bloggers also scour LinkedIn groups to find trending topics and experts. Many companies will not participate in discussions taking place there because they do not want to be giving out free advice or showing competitors their secrets. I don't necessarily disagree with this theory; however, if you are not a part of the discussion and your competitor is, who do you think the media is going to call for a quote? Building relationships with the media is very important for the brand manager and exhibit manager. If they are excited about what you are doing in your booth, they will tell their audience, thereby further expanding the reach of your message.

Some of these groups are actually set up by industry associations, and many associations have groups specifically created for their trade shows. Listen to the chatter here to find out what other exhibitors have planned and what attendees are hoping to see. This will give you ideas for your in-booth activities.

Spend time commenting on discussions with helpful advice so the other members get to know you. Jumping into a group and immediately spamming them with, "Come visit us at booth #107 to register for a free iPad," is not going to win you any friends. But if you are an active member of the group and are seen as a great resource for information, the other members are not as likely to take offense when you do promote what you are doing at an upcoming show.

If there is not an active group specifically for your target customer, you can create one. Going back to the mixed-signal semiconductor example, it's clear there is a niche that could benefit by having a group on LinkedIn. If your company sells mixed-signal semiconductors, you might benefit from creating a group with such a narrow focus. What you need to decide is if it should be under your brand or a generic group that you moderate. Will you restrict competing vendors from joining the group or let them in on the conversation? There are advantages and trade-offs for both models, so you have to decide what's right for your company.

Association or Event Community

Many associations and their events have a community that they've established and are hosting on their website. They could be using one of the more popular social networking tools like Twitter, Facebook, or Pathable or an application they've created in-house. The social networking platform they are using is not important. What's important is that it exists, and you need to take advantage of it. Keep in mind that many of these communities are open only to members, so your company will need to be a supplier member to participate.

Note: If an association uses Facebook to connect as a community, you can assume its members are open to talking shop on that platform. The members will likely be open to hearing your company's messaging via the association Facebook page but might not want to "like" your company or want it to connect directly to them.

Associations are using these platforms to connect with their members and to connect their industry members to their supplier members. Members are already familiar with the platform and are receptive to information received there. Facebook may not be your company's thing, but if all your potential customers are hanging out there, why would you decide not to be there? If you found out that all your potential customers went to the local roller skating rink on Friday nights, would you not show up just because you don't skate? Let's hope you'd go out, buy a pair of skates, take some lessons, and then show up at the rink and skate to every song.

Twitter

You might think that you wouldn't be able to spread that much information with only 140 characters. You would be sorely mistaken. Twitter is being used more and more by B2B companies to share pertinent information. It's a platform that makes it easy to locate your audience. It's also a platform that lets you find out about trending topics at the very moment they are trending.

Twitter users started using the # symbol, called a *hashtag*, to mark keywords or topics in a Tweet. It is a way to categorize messages. Let's say your company sells products or services within the cloud computing industry. You can search on the hashtag #cloudcomputing and find out what people are talking about and what information is being shared. While looking through the information being passed along, you can find that the hot topic of discussion is a concern over security. You now have an idea about what attendees at the next trade show are going to find interesting. You could make this the topic of one of your in-booth presentations.

If your company submits a proposal to present at the trade show's educational sessions, you could be sure this proposal would capture the attention of the selection committee. At the same time, you could also use Twitter to reach out to your customers to arrange short video testimonials about how secure your systems are. Those could run on a loop in your booth.

Ideally, event organizers will create a hashtag for every trade show. Check the trade show's website for information on how they will use Twitter to promote and create conversation around the event. If you don't see the information, call and ask. If they don't have one, make one up. Most shows use the show name and year as a hashtag. For example, #EXHIBITOR2011, #FreshSummit, #IOD11, and #CES2012 are hashtags created for specific trade shows.

Although other web-based platforms are great for communicating before and after an event, Twitter's value really shines through during the event. Members of any community can arrange Tweetups (a place or event where Twitter friends come together to meet up in person), let others know which booth is giving away the cool swag, share a sound byte from a session they are attending, share pictures of a cool new product they just saw, complain about the temperature of the room, and much more. The community can easily stay connected throughout the event via their smartphones. Exhibitors can also share what is going on in their booths moment by moment, share pictures of drawing winners, or remind attendees when a special session is going to begin.

Reaching the Media

The media, in particular, has been significantly altered by social media. Traditional media is now online, and journalists are mining social media for trends and stories. You can be sure writers are searching association and event communities on the industries they cover. The more information you are posting in those communities that is valuable, the more exposure you will have to the media.

By valuable information, I'm not talking about press releases. If you are part of the community conversation and sharing timely information (and are available at a moment's notice), you might be tapped for an interview or at least a quote. If you are not the appropriate person to do the interview or give a quote, make sure you know who is and how to reach him. It's not good enough anymore to get back to a journalist in 24 hours. Sometimes a writer has only a half an hour to finish the story, and if he can't get a quote from you, it's easy enough to find someone else.

But traditional media is no longer the only source for news and information. Industry bloggers can be very influential in your community and may cover your specific niche. Your audience could be turning to them for product information, industry trends, and companies to watch. Google has a blog search tool available at http://blogsearch.google.com to help you find bloggers who cover your industry. To find out how much influence a certain blog has, you can search for it on Technorati.com and Klout.com. This doesn't guarantee the blog's influence, but it does give you an indication of whether it has 3 readers or 3,000.

Reach out to these bloggers just as you would to traditional journalists with media alerts about any announcements you might be making at the show or product launches. In addition, actively promoting what you are doing on social media platforms will increase the likelihood of them stumbling across you.

The rule of expanding your audience applies here as well. You are not limited to members of the media and bloggers who are attending the event. By broadcasting your press conference or product launch during the show and making it available to view after the event, you are giving access to these events to writers around the world.

The Three-Day Show That Never Ends

In the past, you worked on a tried-and-true timeline for promoting your presence at a trade show. You rented a list from the organizers and sent out a printed postcard to targeted attendees, enticing them to visit your booth two to four weeks before the trade show. Then came email, and we could really blast our message out at a much lower cost. Weekly reminders became the marketing medium of choice for brand managers. Attendees' email boxes got flooded weeks before a show with hundreds of exhibitors' messages. Standing out from the competition was almost impossible.

You did your best and hoped people paid attention. After the show started, you just hoped your message resonated with the attendees and that they would come by your booth. After the show closed, the sales department would follow up on the leads you collected. You would have months before you even needed to think about pre-show promotions again. What happened in your booth pretty much stayed in your booth. The only people you were exposed to were those who attended the trade show and stopped by to visit with you.

But now, with the advent of social media and event communities, the show activity starts as soon as registration opens and lives on for months after the booths are taken down and put into storage.

You start seeing blog posts about the event popping up days and weeks after the event written by the media, attendees, and exhibitors. The organizers usually post session summaries and release them throughout the year. Video recordings of general sessions and educational sessions are made available online, and people post pictures on Facebook and Flickr to share them with colleagues who could not attend. LinkedIn invitations to connect are sent out. The Twitter hashtag is alive with thank-yous and reflections on the event.

If you have content you've created at the event, you can be part of that sharing. You can keep the excitement of the show alive by slowly releasing session summaries, pictures, and videos to your community over the weeks after the show. And just about the time it starts winding down, you can begin building excitement up for the next event. You will no longer be starting over each year from scratch. You'll be building on an audience you've already established through your community. And that audience will be introducing you to all their new friends.

Summary

Attendees are no longer going onto the trade show floor to only be sold a product or service. They are there to network, find out industry trends, and get specific information they need to make a buying decision. By being a part of the community, you will know exactly what information they are craving and who they want to connect with and can make that part of your trade show strategy.

After there is a community, there is an audience. After you have an audience, you have a way of communicating with them through the community. You are communicating to a receptive audience who wants to hear what you have to say and who wants to share that information with others in the community. You no longer have to rely solely on expensive direct mail campaigns, email marketing, and attendee list rentals to spread your message.

3

Create Company-Wide Social Media Enthusiasm

When I talk to marketers and exhibit managers about using social media in their trade show strategy, they get very excited about its potential. They are able to see the opportunities created by being part of a larger industry community. But I often hear them lament, "We understand how powerful it is, but our boss just won't buy into it." Every time they bring it up they are met with resistance from the executive team. If you are also encountering some skepticism, you'll find the following information helpful in not just getting approval, but also getting full-fledged support from others in your organization.

Some corporate leaders out there still just don't get the power of social media. Consumer brands have jumped on the social media bandwagon and have fully embraced its potential. Many in the business-to-business (B2B) world are still trying to figure out whether there is a place in social media for their brands. These corporate executives who don't see the value hear "social media" and think of people playing Farmville on Facebook or Lady Gaga posting notes to her fans on Twitter. They just don't see a connection to their company and their customers.

Let's face it: It's pretty hard for them to have a serious conversation around getting customers to "friend" you and "like" your page. Then, when you start talking about sponsoring tweetups and tweetchats, counting followers, and checking Klout scores, even you think it sounds a bit silly.

This is why it is so important to start with strategy when trying to incorporate social media into your trade show program. If you simply say, "Foursquare check-ins will drive traffic to our booth, so let's do that," your plan is going to seem frivolous and a waste of resources to upper management. It will confirm their belief that social media is nothing more than a silly distraction. What you must do is show management how it will contribute to the bottom line and help achieve the overall company goals.

To get started on the right path, you need to first create S.M.A.R.T. (specific, measurable, attainable, realistic, and timely) goals for your trade show strategy, and then determine where social media might help achieve those goals. This makes choosing the right platform easy. It also helps you more easily see what is working and what is not and adjust accordingly during the show. You could wait until the end to do this, but it's better and more productive to be proactive and measure and adjust as you go. If part of your objective was to get 100 people to post photos on Flickr during the show but by the end of day one you have just 10, you're going to want to find out where the problem is and fix it for days two and three.

If you want company buy-in on using social media, you need to have a way to measure its success. You need company buy-in because a good social media strategy requires resources and time. Many of these resources are going to need to come from departments other than just marketing.

Find Internal Advocates

If your company is already using social media, you have a big head start. If you're not so lucky and your company actively resists using it, don't be discouraged. You need to find a team of people who are as excited about the potential of social media as you are. These people exist in just about any organization, and the higher up in management they are, the easier your path will be.

Finding an advocate is easier for you because you are just asking the company to take a baby step. Most likely they see your company's trade show participation as a three- or four-day activity. You now know why that is the wrong way of looking at it, but for now let's use that to your advantage. Let them think of it as a limited experiment that will have little impact on the overall company marketing plan.

Social media use could be lurking anywhere. The good news is that it's pretty easy to find by simply doing a Google search, having conversations with department heads, finding out which tools they are using, and if they have plans and policies in place. Their success is what is going to help you sell its use in your trade show program.

Start with a little internal research. Hang on to any and all data you collect throughout this process because you will use it later when you create your social media strategy. Even if social media is not already being used in your marketing department, don't make the assumption that it's not being used anywhere. You just have to know where to look. Try the following:

- **LinkedIn**—Start looking for active profiles of members of your executive team. People often think of social media as just being sites like Facebook or Twitter. They don't realize their activity on LinkedIn is social media activity. Skip over profiles that are only 50 percent complete. You are looking for complete profiles that have an updated status. If someone is using add-on apps like TripIt or SlideShare, he is a power user, and you want to add him to your potential advocate list.

- **IT message boards and LISTSERV**—IT folks were using social media in the form of message boards and LISTSERV long before anyone had even heard of the term. When a programmer runs into a wall, the first place he goes for help is the relevant global community on message boards and LISTSERV. You might have a potential advocate in IT.

- **Customer service department**—Everyone has heard stories about the customer service person who sees a complaint on Twitter and immediately reaches out to offer assistance. You might have even experienced it yourself. It is likely that someone in your customer service department is searching on Twitter for customer complaints and addressing them in real-time before they have a chance to escalate. You can find your advocate here.

Don't be discouraged if you are being told your company does not use social media. It might be a case where they just don't realize they are. Many people have a misperception that social media is only one or two tools. You may be asking about social media, but what they are hearing is Facebook. You need to do some digging around by asking the following:

- Does our company have a YouTube channel?
- Does our company have a Twitter account?
- Does our company have a Facebook page?
- Does our company have a blog? Who are the contributors?
- Does our company have a presence on LinkedIn?

- Is our company creating Podcasts?
- Is our company using Flickr?
- Does our company have a SlideShare account?

Find out who is using which tools and how they are measuring the success of those tools. Take note as to who views it as just another task on their already long list of job responsibilities and who is enthusiastic. Those who are enthusiastic will go on your list of potential advocates. It's important during this research phase that you collect as much data and documentation as you can for use later in your booth strategy.

Getting the CFO on Your Side

The greatest advocate you can have is your CFO because she has a great deal of influence over the budget. I learned early on that the CFO is the hardest nut to crack. If you can pitch an idea to her satisfaction, you can pitch it to anyone. I know what you are thinking. Are you crazy? Our CFO will never be my advocate. She is constantly cracking jokes about the money our marketing department spends. It would probably be easier to get legal on our side. This is exactly why I encourage you to include the CFO in your list of future champions to be nurtured.

Getting the CFO on your side is actually fairly easy if you put in the effort. To get on her calendar, explain that you want to understand what type of measurements need to be in place to demonstrate your program's success or failure. Explain that you want to make sure you are not wasting valuable resources by not having the proper steps in place from the start. That alone will be music to her ears. You should do this for your social media strategy and for your trade show strategy in general. Trade shows often take up a sizeable chunk of your company's marketing budget. Knowing exactly how to justify that expense in a way your CFO will respect is not just the key to getting the resources necessary to add a social media component to your trade show program. It's a way to ensure your exhibit budget does not get cut.

Get the ball rolling by having an honest conversation with your CFO. Show her what your goals are and how you plan on measuring the success of your social trade show strategy. Ask if there is something else you should include that would justify it from a financial aspect. Then, be sure to include that information in your reporting. As a result, you have just made a friend of the person who controls the money in your company.

Create Something They Can't Live Without

One of the tactics car salespeople use to push potential customers over the fence and get them to purchase a car is to let them take the car home for the night. The idea is that after 24 hours you feel like you already own it and don't want to give the car back. You can use this same method to get support and buy-in on your program from other departments in your company.

Trade shows provide a company an opportunity of a lifetime at a very low cost, but you have to be ready to embrace those opportunities. Many companies focus only on sales opportunities at trade shows, but they are missing out on other cost-effective opportunities. When the show organizers put thousands of potential customers at your disposal, your entire company can benefit from the experience. Why just limit it to your sales department? Start thinking of the trade show as an opportunity for customer service, research and development (R&D), billing, tech support, and market research. Use the show as an opportunity to turn your company's leaders into industry thought leaders.

Start interviewing department heads and ask, "If you had a room full of our customers and potential customers, what would you want to ask them?" Let's face it: That's what a trade show is. It is a room full of potential customers, current customers, and competitors. They are all in one place for three or four days. It is essentially a research bonanza. But wait—there's more! By using social media in your exhibit strategy, you'll also be reaching out to a much wider audience than just those at the show.

Companies spend tens of thousands of dollars with market research firms. Yet, when the industry trade show rolls around, the brand manager often stays at the show for just the first couple hours to make sure everything in the booth is running smoothly. This flabbergasts me. Here you have a room full of current and potential customers for three days, so why would you rather be back at the office? What are you rushing back for? To get that request for proposal out the door for a major market research project?

A trade show is a wonderful opportunity to ask customers how they would prefer to access customer support: phone, email, online chat, Twitter, or Facebook. Ask them which features they would like to see on your next product release. Ask them which features they don't use. Ask why they don't use them. Are those features irrelevant, or do they not understand their value? Ask them what their biggest problem is that they wish someone would solve? You never know where your next idea is going to come from.

Let's say you decide you are going to do short "man-on-the-street" video interviews in your booth to post them on your YouTube channel. When you are going over your notes from your department head interviews, you can incorporate these questions into your video interviews. You will get a bunch of great videos to post on YouTube. The customer you interviewed will share the link with all his colleagues and friends and that spreads your message. Your product development team gets a valuable amount of honest feedback about their new product straight from the customer.

Let your product development team in on your plans to collect this valuable information, and let them help you formulate your questions. Now they will have a vested interest in your strategy. Your product development team will go to bat for you to get approval on your strategy because they don't want to lose the opportunity of getting all that information.

Put an End to Common Objections Once and for All

Getting upper management to buy in to your social media strategy can sometimes be a bit tricky. Social media concerns are generally around privacy issues, brand protection, security, and the financial and personnel investment. It's your job to set them straight.

"People Might Say Bad Things About Us"

The common response to this objection is, "People are going to say what they want to say about us regardless of whether we are on social media." By having a presence, you have a voice. You know what they are saying, and you can address it quickly.

What I have found when digging deeper is that the real objection is, "People can say bad things about us on *our* social media platforms." What they fear is having a Facebook page or LinkedIn group where disgruntled employees can post negative comments about the company. They are afraid competitors will post unfavorable remarks about the company or hijack customers or that an angry customer will lash out. All those disparaging comments would be hosted on your company's platform with your logo on the top of the page.

To counter this, you need to have a social media policy that addresses how these issues will be dealt with and by who, as well as outlines the escalation process, should it be needed. Your strategy documents should then address how you will be monitoring comments and how frequently.

By having a policy in place, you can address these issues as they come up. Remember, if it's your brand, you have some control. You can delete comments posted by competitors or counter them by answering with your strengths. Take control and set the record straight. I would discourage you from having a policy that says you delete comments from angry customers. These should always be addressed publicly. If things seem to be escalating out of control, you can then decide to take the conversation offline.

"Our Industry Has Too Many Regulations and Legal Will Never Approve Social Media Use"

This is easily addressed with a social media policy that very clearly specifies what can and cannot be discussed. For sample social media policies, I encourage you to dig through the policies section at the Social Media Governance website: http://socialmediagovernance.com/policies.php. There you will find more than 150 different social media policies from B2B companies, consumer brands, government agencies, nonprofits, financial companies, and healthcare providers. While you are there, print a few out from your industry to show your executives that your competitors have already started without you.

"Our Customers Don't Use Social Media"

This statement has no basis in reality, and it shocks me when I hear people say it. One of the first things a customer will do when researching a company is to Google it. Hopefully, your website will show up on the first page, but many other things could as well—things other people are saying about you. Things other people are saying about you on Twitter, on Facebook, on blogs, and in online magazines are going to carry a lot more weight than what's on your website.

Let's say you sell data management solutions and are not actively using social media. All you have is your static website, but your main competitor has a very active social media presence. Maybe they post troubleshooting videos on YouTube and have a blog that is updated three times a week. They might even post pictures from their last customer meeting on Flickr. When customers Google "data management solutions," the odds of them finding you are pretty slim, especially if your website has not been updated in the last several months. Google likes fresh content. Google likes the company that has three blog posts a week a lot more than it likes you.

So you can see, even if some of your customers are not active users of social media, they are in fact accessing social media all the time.

"We Don't Have the Resources to Start This"

Yes, social media does take up both financial and personnel resources as does any marketing activity. You need to show how costs and resources in other areas will be offset. For instance, perhaps your social media plan will drive traffic to your booth and eliminate the need to ship pallets of give aways to the trade show. Show how you are eliminating the expense of purchasing give aways, shipping, storage, and drayage at the trade show by using social media.

A word of caution here: If you are expecting pushback from your upper management due to a resource issue, make sure your plan does not require a lot of resources from the IT department to make it happen. This is one surefire way to get your plan turned down. You'll need to take baby steps at first and prove your plan works. Before you implement something that requires a dedicated server and a micro site, try posting videos on your company YouTube channel. Have IT look at your plan and get their buy-in before you try to sell it to your bosses.

"Isn't Social Media Just Filled with a Bunch of Chatter and Nonsense about Brangelina and Ashton Kutcher?"

The easy answer to this is "Yes, there is a lot of that. But look at how much activity is dedicated to our industry." Then, overwhelm your executive team with all the research you've gathered on examples of real conversations and online activity taking place in your industry. Show them how the show organizers are using social media and the conversations taking place among the attendees and suppliers. Show them what your competition is doing. Find some case studies online of major successes your competition has had in the social media realm. Demonstrate how your social media program will contribute to the company's bottom line and success.

"We'll Just Stick to Traditional Media Because That Has Always Worked for Us in the Past"

The fact is traditional media now has an online presence. Those who create the content for traditional media are turning to the online world more and more for their information. Also, keep in mind that even traditional media was at one time experimental. According to Wikipedia, "The first television advertisement was broadcast in the United States on July 1, 1941. The watchmaker Bulova paid $9 for a placement on New York station WNBT before a baseball game between the Brooklyn Dodgers and Philadelphia Phillies." Years from now something new will come along, and social media will be called traditional.

How exactly does traditional media use social media? David Meerman Scott tells a story about Eloqua's CEO, Joe Payne, who is active on social media. He was alerted to an announcement about one of his major competitors being bought by another company and that the deal was finalized. He quickly wrote a blog post about it and talked about the impact this would have on the market. Neither his competitor nor the company who bought them said anything of substance. Meerman Scott goes on to say that nearly every news story about the acquisition was quoting Payne's blog post. If that doesn't show the power of social media, I don't know what does.

Summary

Remember that social media can play a role in your exhibit strategy beyond just that of marketing. By making sure that other departments within your company benefit from your efforts, you are more likely to get approval and their enthusiastic support. Be prepared to answer objections and get the CFO on your side. Finding out what the person who controls the money wants to see from your efforts and then delivering that will do wonders for your career.

4

Create a Solid Social Media Plan

When you create your social media plan for your show, you need to first define your goals and objectives. Nothing can proceed until you have defined exactly where you want to end up. Then, you can create strategies and tactics to bring your goals to life. The tools you use should only be considered in the tactical phase of your planning.

After you define your goals and objectives, you can begin looking at your customers and potential customers. Are they active in social media? What tools do they use? What do they think about your company already? When you know this information, you can begin creating your strategy and figuring out your tactics.

As with any marketing plan, you will need to make sure your social media plan aligns with your overall exhibit strategy and with your marketing goals for the exhibit, as well as those of the company in general. You need to include an implementation play book and have a measurement system in place to know when you've hit it out of the park. So let's start at the beginning with goals, objectives, strategies, and tactics and their definitions.

What Are Goals Versus Objectives and Strategy Versus Tactics?

By definition, goals and objectives differ. Goals are broad; objectives are narrow. Goals are vague; objectives are specific. However, when you get outside of academia, the terms *goals* and *objectives* are used interchangeably. The important thing is that no matter which word you use, they are measurable. That means if you have no way of knowing whether you've achieved it, it's not a very good goal. If your goal is to be rich, how will you know when you've arrived? If your goal is to be a millionaire, though, that's pretty clear-cut. An even better goal would be, "I want to have a million dollars in liquid assets by the time I'm 40." Now you just have to ask yourself whether that is realistic.

Strategy and *tactics* are not interchangeable terms. *Strategy* is a story about how you will achieve your goal. It's a conceptualization of how you will reach your end point. A *tactic* is the action you take to get there. My strategy for weight loss might be to exercise three days a week for 30 minutes each day. My tactics will be to walk for 30 minutes at lunch on Monday, go for a bike ride for 30 minutes with my family on Wednesday after work, and to go to the gym and lift weights for 30 minutes during lunch on Fridays.

For many people, strategy is hard and tactics are fun because you can see your plan shaping up. Action is finally being taken. Some people love the challenge of creating a strategy but are thoroughly bored when it comes to the tactical side of things. If you are the kind of person who finds yourself itching to jump into the tactics right away, hold yourself back. You cannot successfully set tactics without a clear strategy—and you can't define a strategy without first setting a goal.

Your trade show program should follow this pattern of setting measurable goals, creating a strategy, and then implementing the tactics. This is true whether we're talking about social media or give aways. You wouldn't base your entire trade show program on giving away flash drives—nor should you base your program on Foursquare check-ins.

Sample Goals, Objectives, Strategies, and Tactics

Goal

Launch our new product and generate new leads at the trade show.

Think of your goal as the reason you are exhibiting at the trade show. This is the big picture that will guide you as you create your strategy and keep you on track.

Some people refer to it as a *mission*, but the purpose is the same. Everything you do from here on in will have to somehow lead you to this goal. If it does not, you need to question why you are doing it. It's best to limit yourself to just one or two goals per show.

Objective

Demonstrate our new product to 500 individuals and collect 200 A leads.

Here you are drilling down to something that is measurable. The overall goal is difficult to measure—it is there to help you focus your efforts. Your objective provides you with a base so that you can determine whether you were successful. Here is where you want to include the *realistic* component of your S.M.A.R.T. goals as well. If you plan on having just 10" × 10" booth staffed by two people, these objectives are unrealistic. Each staffer would have to do a product demo every 3 minutes and 45 seconds during a 16-hour trade show. While they were doing those demos, they'd have to generate one qualified lead every 10 minutes. You would either have to increase your presence at the trade show or scale back on that objective.

Strategies

Allow visitors to test drive our new product in the booth. Give the test drivers a way to share that experience with their colleagues and friends who are either at the show or at home. After the test drive, evaluate their interest, buying power, and timeline for a new product.

Here you are telling a story about how you intend to reach your objective. This is your concept of how you will go about demonstrating your product to 500 people. The strategy is your map that shows the route you will take.

Tactics

Set up seven kiosks for live demos or test drives. Upon completion, each visitor can send a Tweet, Facebook message, text, or email to an attendee at the show telling him about the demo or send a link to an online demo of the product.

Finally, you get into the nitty-gritty of the tools you will use to enable your strategy. The tools you will use are kiosks and social media via Twitter, Facebook, texting, and email. You cannot decide on the most appropriate tools until you have defined your strategy.

I have seen many well-intentioned exhibitors skip either one or two of these steps or perform them out of order. They might set their goal as lead generation and immediately brainstorm ways to get people into their booth. Within minutes, they are searching through the promotional products catalog for desirable give-aways. They are then forced into a strategy that revolves around a tactic.

Aligning with Your Company's Overall Goals

I don't care how cool your social media idea for your trade show is. If it doesn't align with your company's overall goals and objectives, you should not be doing it. The easiest way to get turned down on your idea is not being able to draw a clear parallel. Your social media goal for your trade show should also fit in with your company's marketing goals and objectives.

If your CEO's key objective is for your company to be known as the most innovative leader in the industry and you come up with a bland idea where trade show attendees check in to your booth using Foursquare, she's not going to believe your strategy aligns with the corporate objective. Foursquare check-ins are not innovative. If the marketing goal of the show is to raise awareness of your company among new customers and your plan involves increasing Twitter followers, while only customer service is using Twitter, you're barking up the wrong tree.

If your social media plan and tactics do not align with your exhibit strategy, objectives, and goals, they will be a distraction to your booth staff and to your booth visitors. I have seen too many exhibitors so focused on the tactics that their entire program revolved around a gimmick. I walked into a booth recently that had their tactic so well-branded I have no idea who the company was or what they did. They had a dunk tank, super heroes and villains, QR codes everywhere, and Facebook page sign-up stations. I wanted to ask a booth staffer what he did, but all he wanted to know was whether I wanted a turn at the dunk tank. I could not find one staff member who was not focused on this activity.

That is an extreme example, but many booths are not far from that. I constantly get complaints from salespeople who say they "wasted" the entire trade show trying to teach people how to download a QR code scanner app, and then how to actually scan the QR codes instead of qualifying buyers. This is what happens when you let tactics drive your trade show strategy. This could have been easily fixed by assigning a staff member or hiring temps to help visitors with the QR codes. The sales staff would have then been able to focus on talking to potential customers.

Who Are You Trying to Reach?

After you have defined your goals and objectives, you need to ask yourself who exactly am I trying to reach? Define that audience as if it were a specific person. Do you have more than one audience? Be sure to define each one.

Your goal for the trade show might be to introduce your company to a new market. Perhaps you are well-known in one industry but launching your product or service to a new market at the next show. Taking a careful look at the attendee demographics, you might find that you actually have two audiences at this show. The first is the end user of your product or service. He may or may not have purchasing authority, but he has a vested interest in whether your product or service becomes part of his day-to-day job. Another audience might be a purchasing manager who will not be using your product or service but will have the final decision in the purchase.

These two audiences have very distinct interests in your product, so your messaging to them will be very different. One audience will care about ease of use and implementation, and the other will care about price and ease of purchasing process. These two audiences have different interests, so your social media plan for each should be different. You might decide to use social media only for the end user to generate interest in your product or service and to start a conversation with him. You can focus other booth activities on just the purchasing managers.

What Do Attendees Know About You Already?

Is it likely your prospects have never heard of you? Are you a well-known fortune 500 company that has a known reputation in other industries? If not, maybe people have no idea you even exist. Are you considered the hot new company to watch in your industry or someone who has been around forever?

If you are the hot new company to watch, you might think your job is easy. Everyone will be flocking to your booth. But keep in mind that with the hype comes responsibility to live up to it. If your prospect has no idea you exist, you have the chance to help form her perception of your company, but you first have to get her to notice you.

Any hype surrounding your company is very important to consider when putting together your social media strategy for your trade show program because it can become a resource issue. If you are touted in industry publications a month leading up to the show as the greatest thing since sliced bread, you are going to have attendees and possibly the media flocking to your booth. You're going to be busy enough without adding some complicated social media strategy to the mix.

On the other hand, if no one has heard of you, the resources you invest into a word-of-mouth social strategy might just be the thing that launches you into fame and riches. If you cannot get the media talking about you prior to the show, you can provide incentive for attendees to do the job for you.

What Do Attendees Think About You Already?

This is slightly different from do they know you. Everyone knows who John Deere is, but the question of what they think about John Deere is very different. This is about perception and reputation. You can be sure people are doing their homework and looking into your company online if they are even considering doing business with you. They are also asking peers who have worked with you what their experience was like.

You need to listen to what people are saying, and social media makes it easy to do this. A simple Google search will bring up what the media and bloggers are saying about your company. You can also search on Twitter to see what individuals, organizations, and other brands are saying about you. While you're there, see what's being said about your competitors.

This information is going to be invaluable when you develop your messaging. If you discover before the show that you have a reputation for being very attentive during the buying process but disappear from the face of the earth when it comes to customer service, you can address this in your planning. You can not only prep your staff, but can also use this in your trade show social media strategy. Instead of selecting a strategy that broadcasts your message, you can focus on tools that give customers a voice and a direct line to your company.

Where Are Your Customers?

Your strategy is going to have to take into consideration where your customers are hanging out online. Think of this as you would a traditional media plan. You might love *Cat Fancy* magazine and read it every month, but if your customers are not reading it, it doesn't make sense to take out a full-page ad in the magazine. Many times companies fall into the trap of falling in love with a particular tool because of all the great things it can do to help them meet their objectives. But, you can't force your potential customers to use a tool they have no interest in.

I find this happens a lot in the trade show industry. For a while the Twitter backchannel (a conversation about the topic or speaker) was the hot thing that every conference organizer had to have in 2010. We would set up huge screens next to or behind the speakers. While the speaker was giving her presentation, the audience could follow along with all the conference tweets as they were broadcast.

Aside from being obviously distracting—too many comments about what the speaker was wearing combined with a steady stream of, "It's too cold in here," messages—there was an even bigger problem. Many organizers did not take the time to find out whether their attendees were big Twitter users. This "tweet thing" put off many attendees, and conference organizers ended up alienating their audience.

At a recent conference I attended, a game required attendees to engage with the conference, exhibitors, and other attendees via Facebook to earn badges. On our team of 12 players, all but 1 refused to do this. We all said unequivocally, "Facebook is for personal only—I don't mix it with business." It's important to consider where your customers are open to your message.

Finally, do your research to see if your customers are really active on a particular platform. I'm a member of several association LinkedIn groups where it seems the only people participating in discussions are suppliers and the organization itself. Very few members are actually active in those groups. This could be because, without good moderation, these groups tend to become just another advertising directory for suppliers pushing their products or services.

Have a Purpose

One of the dangers of not clearly defining your strategy and jumping into tactics is you get caught up in just one step of achieving your goal but not getting any closer than that first step. When I hear people tell me their grand plan is getting 500 people to join their Facebook page, I always ask why. I get anything from blank stares to "exposure" to "so they will see our messaging."

I'm not referring here to the benefits or disadvantages of using Facebook in your marketing plan. I'm specifically talking about your trade show program and how this part of your strategy may or may not fulfill your goals. I do not make the connection on how getting 500 people to join your Facebook page gets you closer to your goal of 200 qualified A leads.

If your answer is, "Our goal for this trade show is to expose our company to a new industry and a new customer base," then I'm interested in hearing more. I want to know what your plans are for your Facebook page after the show. If you do not have a strategy beyond getting fans, your strategy is a waste of time.

I've come across many Facebook pages that were very active prior to a show, garnered many likes during the show, but were abandoned anywhere from days to weeks after the show. What was the point again of getting those likes?

One tech exhibitor had what seemed like a good idea for her show. The attendees were the end users of her product; they were what we call *influencers*. Influencers are people who do not make the final purchasing decision but have influence over the decision. They were also geeks. This company knew its audience was tech savvy and familiar and comfortable with social networks. The exhibit manager devised a contest that would run in the weeks leading up to the show to name the booth mascots. This was done via the Facebook Questions polling feature.

During the trade show, booth visitors would receive a stuffed animal mascot and be encouraged to take photos of their mascot posing all over Las Vegas, and then post them to the company Facebook page. The strategy was that the company would gain exposure throughout the user community via these end users' Facebook friends liking their photos.

Sounds fun, no? Let's take a look at what actually happened. After this four-day show, the company had just 233 likes despite 19,000 people attending the show. I do not know how many they had before the show, but there was activity on the Facebook page for months leading up to this particular show. Only about 20 people participated in the mascot-naming game. Only about six people took pictures of the mascots throughout the trade show and posted them to the company's Facebook wall. Occasionally, someone got a like on his photo. This was clearly not the viral fun they were anticipating.

Upon closer inspection, I found some disconnects. First, nothing explained why people should post photos of stuffed animals on the company's Facebook page. There was no obvious mention anywhere of a contest. The company was not commenting on any of the pictures or giving words of encouragement. Occasionally, they would post information about product demos taking place in their booth. And, there was complete silence on their side when it came to the photo contest.

From the end-user standpoint, he posts a photo to this company's page, and his Facebook friends see that on his Facebook updates. If his friends decide to click on the photo, they are taken to the company's Facebook page. After they are on the company page, there is no explanation of the contest and what the picture is for. Some of the photos were very creative, but the fact that no one took the time to comment on the friend's photo or even click the Like button means they completely lost interest in what they were looking at and moved on.

The plan should have been reevaluated at the first sign of trouble at the trade show. Only 20 people participated in the naming contest. Why was there such a low response? Was the contest promoted adequately? Was it promoted on the right channels? Were people sharing with their Facebook friends? If they were not, why weren't they?

Then, there was the problem of the lack of information and interaction on the company Facebook page during the show. This makes me think they either did not have a good plan in place to follow up on this activity or did not dedicate the proper resources to manage this contest. Any social media plan you implement must have one key element: It must be social. This company was not being social. It takes resources and a thorough plan to be social.

Specify When and Who in Your Plan

When you create your social media plan, you should include a timeline for exactly when each piece will be implemented. Also include in that timeline check-in dates. *Check-in dates* are intervals where you will evaluate how your plan is progressing. Making minor changes and fixes early on can save the entire plan from failing in the end.

You need to plan for the before, during, and after elements of the trade show. How will you promote what you are doing in your booth to both the trade show audience and the wider virtual audience? How will you get them interested and involved in what you are doing? How will you instruct people how to participate? If visitors are unfamiliar with the tool or platform you are using, you will need to have personnel available to assist them. But the last thing you want is for your salespeople to spend all their time teaching visitors how to set up their own Twitter accounts and explaining what "*retweeting*" is.

Also, specifically plan who will keep your audience engaged and how he will do that. It is clear in the mascot photo plan that no one was assigned to keep the online audience engaged or to build excitement. You could assign this task to someone in the office or to someone at the show dedicated to this task. At least one booth staffer should have been assigned the role of helping booth visitors with the contest. That way, the sales and support staff could focus on their assignment of promoting the company's products.

What if someone posts an inappropriate picture on your Facebook wall? Remember when we discussed getting company buy-in and common objections? This is where you are going to need to have a social media policy in place for what is acceptable and what is not. Appropriate is not subjective—not in this case. If you clearly define what kind of photos will be deleted (and post these policies on your Facebook page), those responsible for monitoring the photos will have an easy job. Include in your plan who exactly is responsible for this task and how often the photos will be checked. This not only will help you sell your strategy to management, but will also eliminate the "I thought you were going to do that" discussion.

The plan does not end here. You need to specify what will happen after the trade show as well. How will the program you are running at the trade show be used in future marketing or messaging? If it is a one-time event, how will you close it out in a way that will make sense to people who stumble across it months later? Remember, social media doesn't go away.

What if, in a few months, a new customer searches on the previous example company's products and up pops a wacky photo of a stuffed animal sitting by the pool having a cocktail. She looks at the link and sees it goes to that company's Facebook page. "That's odd," she thinks. She then clicks on it and sees many photos of stuffed animals in various locations. There is no explanation to these photos any-where. That customer is certainly not going to go searching for one. At best, her reaction is, "That's fun." But it could be, "What does this have to do with anything? Are these people serious?"

Now if this company had archived this information on a separate area on its Facebook page with a clear description of what the contest was and when it was, the purpose of these wacky photos would be clear to people stumbling across them. This way, that potential customer might think, "Oh, I get it; that's fun." If I'm a stick in the mud I might think, "I knew these trade shows were a waste of time... all my employees do is run around taking photos of stuffed animals, and this is the company responsible for it."

Hmmm...what was that original goal again?

Measure the Results

One of the wonderful things about social media and the digital age is that results are so easy to measure. We can see moment-to-moment how many likes, followers, hits, forwards, and retweets we get. As long as you set good measurable objectives early on in the process of planning, you can easily measure whether you hit your goal.

Without spending much money, you can measure traffic to the platform you are using and pinpoint specific times of day traffic is either heavy or low. If participa-tion goes way up during booth hours, you know your instructions and promotion are working. If you get people signing up for your contest before the trade show even starts, you know you are doing a good job promoting it. Tools are avail-able that allow you to track who is spreading the word for you. Some are free like Google Analytics; some carry a fee, like Radian6. You can even set up a reward sys-tem for those people who are sharing your content.

But, you need to take it a step further. This is where that conversation with your CFO is going to come in handy. You can take these social media measurements and figure out where they fit into the overall return on investment (ROI) or other measurements your company is using. You will be able to assign a weight or influ-ence your social media program has on sales as a result of the show. This is impor-tant information when looking for support to expand or keep your trade show budget.

It's important to remember that not every strategy is going to be a big winner. As with any marketing endeavor, some will fail horribly. What is important is to be able to evaluate what worked and what did not along every point in the plan. Careful measurement will tell you exactly where failure occurred. You can use this information to tweak and fix your trade show program in the future. If it can't be measured, it cannot be determined whether it's a success or a failure.

Summary

When creating a social media plan for your trade show program, always keep asking yourself, "How does this help us reach our goal?" If you don't have an answer to that question, it is likely you are going down the wrong path. Only look at tactics after your strategy has been clearly defined, and all the planning in the world means nothing if you cannot measure its success or failure.

5

Choose the Right Social and Virtual Platforms

Only after you have your strategy in place can you start to work on the tactics you will use to see that strategy through. It is during this tactical phase of your plan that you will take into consideration all the information you have gathered about your audience and the needs of various departments in your company and start looking at social media and the companion virtual platforms.

Some of the tools or platforms you use will be free and easily available; some you will have to pay for. Some will be off the shelf; some will need to be customized just for you. Each will come with its own advantages and disadvantages.

Do You Have Internet Access? Are You Sure?

Social media tools require the Internet, not just for you in your booth, but also for those attendees playing along. You need to find out what access is available at the trade show. Here is where I issue my biggest warning: If your plan relies solely on the Wi-Fi available through the venue, you may want to rethink your plan. The Wi-Fi available at many convention venues is very unreliable at best or is unable to accommodate the number of devices that are connected. The more people accessing Wi-Fi, the worse the reliability. I have been to trade shows where free wireless access was available to all attendees. Exhibitors and attendees were using it alike, and I could not for the life of me get a signal. There were so many people at the event that I could not even make a phone call on my mobile phone. The only thing that would work was texting.

Find out from show organizers how many devices the Wi-Fi that will be available can accommodate. If they have done their job, they should have this information. If they don't, ask them to find out for you. If the organizer is expecting 10,000 attendees but the Wi-Fi accommodates only 5,000 devices, you should expect problems. These days many attendees will each have two devices connected at times. They might have a smartphone and a laptop or tablet with them and have both connected to the Internet via the wireless access. This means that that two-thirds of the attendees will likely be unable to connect.

This is one reason mobile apps are becoming more and more popular on the trade show floor. The user can download them before the show and update them nightly from the more reliable Internet service at the hotel. If you need to access the Internet in your booth, you will have to suck it up and budget for the more expensive delivery methods, such as dedicated or shared Ethernet service. Hopefully, we will see these often-exorbitant fees drop in the future as more and more exhibitors and organizers are crying foul. But, for now, they come with a hefty price tag you will have to budget for.

Another alternative available is cellular Internet services. More and more providers focused on the trade show industry are popping up every day. I've talked to exhibitors who've used these services, and they have been very happy with the reliability. Companies like Trade Show Internet provide self-contained, easy-to-install kits you rent for your trade show booth space. Your kit will include a signal booster antenna, a modem, network cable, a router, and easy-to-follow instructions that will have you up and running in five minutes. A three-day rental will cost about $300; one-week rentals are available for about $600. The number of devices you can connect varies by provider and the available add-on components. A reputable company typically guarantees the device based on the venue you are showing at. These services are also great for in-booth mobile lounges where you can provide free Wi-Fi and charging stations for your visitors.

But you need to make sure this service will work at the venue you are exhibiting at. If the provider is not familiar with your venue, either find one who is or have a backup plan in place.

I am not a lawyer and am not giving legal advice here in any way, shape, or form. The information that follows is based on my experience, research, and conversations with experts and lawyers. It is likely that if you choose to set up your own Internet service such as the one mentioned previously, you will eventually be told by show management or venue management that it is not allowed. They will tell you that you must use their service or provider. This simply is not true. Know your rights. As a consumer, the Federal Communications Commission (FCC) protects your right to use compliant wireless devices in hotels, conference centers, and convention centers. I carry a paper that explains my rights that I pulled directly from the FCC's website and dare anyone to defy me. The following excerpt is from the FCC's website:

> Over-the-Air Reception Devices (OTARD) rules preempt and prohibit lease contract provisions and building regulations that restrict the use of wireless devices. Specifically, 47 CFR 1.4000 (a)(1)(A) provides in relevant part that:
>
> "Any restriction, including but not limited to, any state or local law or regulation, including zoning, land-use, or building regulations, or any private covenant, contract provision, lease provision, homeowners' association rule or similar restriction, on property within the exclusive use or control of the antenna user where the user has a direct or indirect ownership or leasehold interest in the property that impairs the installation, maintenance, or use of:...(ii) An antenna that is: (A) Used...to receive or transmit fixed wireless signals other than via satellite...is prohibited."

In a nutshell, as the exhibitor, your space contract provides you with sufficient rights to characterize your leased space as within your exclusive use or control. If you are challenged on this, you should request the person's full name and contact information and continue using your federally protected equipment. You can then submit information relating to violations of federal wireless spectrum laws to the FCC as evidence in the commission's ongoing investigation of in-house Internet service providers.

Here is another excerpt from the FCC's website. This one is my personal favorite:

FCC Clarifies Consumer Protection Extends To Hotels, Conference and Convention Centers (FCC Public Notice DA 04-1844)

"...in response to questions from the public regarding the use of unlicensed devices, including customer antennas [... used] in **hotels, conference and convention centers** [...] we reaffirm that, under the Communications Act, the FCC has exclusive authority to resolve matters involving radio frequency interference when unlicensed devices are being used, regardless of venue. We also affirm that the rights that consumers have under our rules to install and operate customer antennas one meter or less in size apply to the operation of unlicensed equipment, such as Wi-Fi access points—just as they do to the use of equipment in connection with fixed wireless services licensed by the FCC."

You have my permission to rip these pages from the book and laminate them.

Live Streaming

Wikipedia defines *streaming media* as follows:

"**Live streaming**, more specifically, means taking the media and broadcasting it live over the Internet. The process involves a camera for the media, an encoder to digitize the content, a media publisher where the streams are made available to potential end-users, and a content delivery network to distribute and deliver the content. The media can then be viewed by end-users live."

Live streaming comes into play when you incorporate virtual events as a part of your social media engagement strategy. First, let me address what I'm not referring to, as there is often confusion. I am not talking about virtual trade shows and the platforms on which they run. In my opinion, virtual trade shows are not a viable medium. They attempt to mimic a traditional trade show but fall desperately short. At this point in time, virtual trade shows are merely a repository of web links and white papers. How is that an "event"? Virtual trade shows need real-time, two-way human engagement to provide information sharing and question answering for them to truly become a virtual representation of what occurs on a physical trade show floor. Until someone stops trying to mimic a trade show and comes up with something completely different, I will consider them a waste of time and money.

Many virtual trade shows will guarantee you a number of qualified leads. Very few marketing and sales departments within the same company can agree on the definition of a *qualified lead*, so I am completely stumped as to how this can be guaranteed. If you are considering exhibiting in a virtual trade show, I encourage you to ask how the organizers are defining a qualified lead. Attendee names and contact information is not a qualified lead—it's a directory. But enough about that, as I could go on all day on that subject.

The type of virtual events I am talking about are interviews, product launches, demos, Q&A sessions, and other "mini events" taking place in your booth or at the trade show that you can make available in real-time to a wider audience around the world. By live streaming your product launch, you make it available to attendees and media at the trade show, as well as to potential customers and media outlets worldwide. Some exposure is better than none.

Q&A sessions are a wonderful way to fulfill the buyer's need for information, and by live-streaming them, you can open the session to those who are unable to attend the trade show. You are providing that all-important real-time, two-way engagement between your company and the in-booth attendees and virtual audience. By using tools like Skype and Google Hangouts, your virtual audience can also engage with your in-booth attendees, thus providing a networking opportunity as well.

A Word About Free Live-Streaming Services

Several free live-streaming services are available, such as Livestream, Ustream, and Justin.tv. You could broadcast right from your smartphone, and viewers with a viewer app can receive it on their smartphones. This can be a fun and easy way to broadcast impromptu videos to friends. In 2010, a snowstorm in Washington, D.C., caused the organizers of the American Society of Association Executives (ASAE) to cancel their ASAE 2010 Technology Conference & Expo at the last minute. Some of the attendees who had already arrived banded together and carried on with an unofficial meeting using Ustream to broadcast their version of the conference to attendees stuck at home. The event was a huge success. However, no one was expecting much, so if it failed, it would not have been a big deal.

I was a virtual attendee, attending via my office computer, of another conference where the organizers cut corners and used a free live-steaming service for half of their sessions. The wireless service they were running it on was overloaded, so no one in the virtual audience could get a feed on the first day. The second day the feed was available but was choppy at best. This reflected poorly on the professionalism of the organization. The question is: Do you want to rely on a free service for your product launch?

In contrast, I had the opportunity to be a virtual audience member of a product launch and demo. The demo had a live audience and online viewers across the United States. The company this exhibitor contracted with to broadcast the event provided the platform for viewing and interaction, the broadcast, production services, registration, attendee tracking, reporting, and proactive technical support. I almost forgot I was not a live attendee. I was able to ask questions and chat with other attendees, not to mention the quality of the presentation and viewing platform was flawless.

Do your homework when finding a provider for your live steamed event. Ask to participate in an event the company is providing service for or test it in an environment similar to what you will be using in your booth. Let's face it: You get what you pay for, so you must weigh the risks involved in using a free live-streaming service to broadcast your message to the audience unable to attend.

Video and Photo Hosting

When the booths have been all packed up and shipped back to storage, it's time to extend the length of your message through repurposed content. You have the option to host your videos and photos on your own website or post to other platforms such as YouTube, Google Video, Vimeo, Flickr, Photobucket, or Shutterfly. There are several things to take into consideration. Each platform has its pluses and minuses. Which one you use depends on what your needs are.

Hosting on your own site—positives:

- Unlimited number of videos and photos you can post
- Unlimited length on videos
- Unlimited size
- Dimension flexibility
- Detailed viewer statistics
- Ability to incorporate advertising
- Full control over content protection
- Control over brand image
- Potential for revenue generation
- Ability to provide continuing education credits

Hosting on your own site—negatives:

- Cost
- Ability to have concurrent users depends on capacity
- Limited ability to embed on other platforms
- Resources and expertise needed to incorporate effective SEO strategies

Hosting on third-party sites—positives:

- Free
- Unlimited number of concurrent viewers
- Unlimited number of videos and photos
- Easily embeddable

- Effective SEO
- Broad reach
- Easily sharable

Hosting on third-party—negatives:

- Limited video length
- Limited size and dimensions
- Limited interactivity and customization
- Limited statistics
- Limited control over content protection
- Possibility of brand image being hurt by association with hosting site
- No control over advertisements affiliated with your content

Personally, I like posting as many photos and videos as possible on third-party sites because the exposure is greater, and it's set up to be easily sharable. Unless your company already has the capability of posting this content on your own website, you may have to wait a long time for your IT department to be able to dedicate their resources to accommodate you. Free hosting sites are available right now. The main negative to hosting on third-party platforms is the loss of control over your brand image. As I listed, you do not have control over which ads or other content could appear right next to you.

Be Careful What You Post

Aside from the obvious—don't post inappropriate videos and pictures and ask for permission before posting a picture or video of someone—there are a few less obvious guidelines to take into consideration.

Before you post pictures and videos of your customers and employees for the entire world to see, give them a quick review. Even if you have permission to post a photo, no one wants an unflattering picture of himself on the Internet. If it's an obviously bad photo, don't post it—same with video. I like to go so far as to let people know if I'm using high-definition video cameras because it can be very unforgiving of the condition of the person's skin tone and makeup application. Providing a mirror for people to get themselves camera ready will be greatly appreciated.

Also keep in mind that the employment of those you are taking photos of lies in someone else's hands. If you are hosting an evening entertainment event and are serving drinks, be considerate of what you are putting on the Internet. Companies spend a lot of money sending their employees to these shows. They might view an innocent picture of their employee enjoying a beer in the evening as funding a bac-chanal. Also, beware of what is going on in the background of the picture. Be sure nothing appears that could be damaging to someone's reputation. When in doubt, don't post it.

Social Platforms

There are hundreds if not thousands of social media platforms and tools. Some are well-known, and some cater to a very small niche audience. Which you use depends on your audience and what you are trying to accomplish. The following are some examples you can use categorized by how you intend to use them. This will help you narrow down your search based on your trade show engagement strategy.

Communication Platforms

Consider a communication platform when you want to have a conversation with your customers. You can let them know what's going on at the trade show and what is taking place in your booth, as well as get their feedback. Communication platforms are often what people think of first when they think of social media.

You might already be using some of these type of communication platforms: blogs, microblogging sites (Twitter, Posterous, Tumblr, and so on), location-based social networks (Foursquare, Facebook Places, Gowalla, and so on), event-based social networks (Eventful, Meetup, Yelp, and so on), information aggregators (RSS feed readers, iGoogle, and so on), and online advocacy and social-based networking (Facebook, Yammer, XING, Google+, LinkedIn, Plaxo, and so on).

Collaboration Platforms

Consider a collaboration platform when you want to go one step beyond just com-munication. A collaboration platform allows customers or teams to work together to create something bigger. At your next trade show, you could easily get your customers to collaborate on a new product or service. Let them design the perfect product or service offering. A collaboration platform allows everyone to participate whether they are present at the show or not. A tool like Google Moderator enables participants to vote on which of the suggested components they like best.

You might be familiar with some specific collaboration platforms, such as Wordpress, Dropbox, Google Docs, Google Moderator, Delicious, StumbleUpon, Social Media Gaming (Empire Avenue), Social News (Digg, Reddit), and Wikis (PBworks, Wikipedia).

Entertainment and Educational Platforms

If you are looking to entertain and educate your customers, you can create proprietary applications or make use of some of the platforms already utilized by your customers. I say *entertain and educate* because I think, in business, entertainment is not enough. But at the same time, education can be fun.

These platforms work well for both entertaining and educating people and include media sharing (such as YouTube and MySpace) and virtual worlds (such as *The Sims Online*, *World of Warcraft*, and *Second Life*).

Multimedia Platforms

I covered some of the multimedia platforms earlier when I talked about live streaming as well as video and photo hosting. But multimedia is not limited to pushing your message out there. You can also use it to communicate and educate both your customers at the trade show and those who are stuck at home.

You might not have the budget to live stream all your booth presentations, but you could create a video and podcast. You could then post these on the Internet via video and audio sharing sites where your extended audience could view or listen to them any time they want.

These multimedia platforms might already be familiar to you: livecasting (such as BlogTV), music and audio sharing (such as Playlist.com, iTunes, and Audible), presentation sharing (such as Prezi, scribd, and Slideshare), video sharing (such as YouTube and Vimeo), podcasts, and BlogTalkRadio.

Reviews and Opinions

I have seen some pretty confident exhibitors use review and opinion tools in their booth. People don't want to take your word that your product or service is awesome. They want to hear it from your customers. Why not incorporate live reviews as part of your product demos?

You might have heard of these tools: business reviews (Customer Lobby and Yelp), community Q&A (ask.com, Quora, and Yahoo! Answers), and product reviews.

Virtual Event Platforms

A web-based seminar is more commonly referred to as a *webinar*. These are educational seminars delivered to a viewer or group of viewers over the Web. Webinars can accommodate two-way communication between the speaker and the audience and between audience members via polling, Q&A sessions, and chat windows. The audience can communicate via their phone lines, voice over Internet protocol (VoIP), or even a webcam and microphone.

You can use webinars in your plans as teasers for what the audience might expect from presentations in your booth. These could be recorded and made available for viewers to watch at their leisure. Keep in mind that the recordings would not have any interaction between the speaker and the viewer.

Webcasts

Webcasts are different from webinars in that they do not provide the collaboration that a webinar can have. They are essentially one-way communication from a single source to an audience over the Internet via streaming media or more simply a broadcast over the Web. When people think of a broadcast, they think of their favorite television or radio station. A webcast can be distributed live or on-demand. Common uses are investor relation presentations and e-learning.

You can use a webcast in much the same way as a webinar or even to create a presentation with step-by-step instructions for a social media contest you might be running as part of your trade show.

2D, 3D, and 3D Immersive Environments

Wikipedia defines *immersive technology* as "technology that blurs the line between the physical world and digital or simulated world, thereby creating a sense of immersion." An immersive environment is one that makes the participant feel as though she is part of the online environment. Some examples of immersive environments you might be familiar with are driving simulators and the games *World of Warcraft*, *Second Life*, and even *FarmVille*.

You could create some type of game or simulation that your live and virtual audiences could participate in. This type of activity, when done well, generates a lot of buzz. Janssen Pharmaceutical had a very well-received exhibit at the 2002 annual convention of the American Association of Psychiatry. It featured "The Bus Ride." Attendees entered a module where they got the opportunity to spend four minutes "feeling schizophrenic." At that same show, Eli Lilly had its "Journey of Hope," which took doctors through a tunnel with different stops in a young schizophrenic's life. Its purpose was to let doctors, through the immersive environment, get a feel for what their patients experience.

What Is the Trade Show Using?

The other things you want to take into consideration are the tools or platforms the trade show organizer is promoting and using. If they have a Twitter hashtag, you should take advantage of that. But please, don't just tweet, "Come see us in booth 1234." Add value to the tweet stream. Why not recommend some good restaurants in town or the closest place to grab a great cup of coffee? Cull through the session schedule and tweet about sessions your customers might find valuable. You can decide later if you want to keep the Twitter account active based on the number of followers you have, whether they've been actively engaging you, and whether you have the resources to continue.

If the trade show has a Facebook page, you might decide you want to participate in that. But Facebook isn't like Twitter. If you create a Facebook page, you cannot just abandon it after the show. Well, you could, but that won't look good. If you don't want to continue using it, you can delete the page completely—but keep in mind that this means you will have to re-create it if you want to jump back on Facebook again. A better alternative would be to indicate clearly on the page that you are not actively using Facebook at this time and refer visitors to where you do want to communicate with them. Otherwise, it's like having a storefront that's never open—and no one knows if you are out of business or just on vacation.

Many trade shows are using different geo-location services like Foursquare and Gowalla to enhance the attendee experience and up-sell the exhibitors. The idea is that when attendees check in to certain booths or sessions, they earn points. This is the high-tech version of the "passport" we used to see at trade shows. I hated the passports because exhibitors were so busy stamping people's passports as they were thrust in front of them that they had little time to talk to serious buyers. Most of these stamp-hungry attendees rushed into the booth, got a stamp, and rushed back out again. It did the exhibitor no good whatsoever.

However, the geo-location games, if set up properly, can require that booth visitors actually get information or sit through a presentation. It's a little better but not ideal. You're still going to have people taking up space in your presentation just so they can be entered into a drawing to win an iPad or whatever this year's Apple object of desire is. But if you make learning fun and that game-playing audience gets involved in your presentation, they will be much more likely to retain your message, and your brand will be much more likely to have left an impression on them.

You might not need to implement a complicated and intensive social media strategy. Piggybacking on what the trade show is doing can be a great solution. It also might help you get approval if your management is still not totally on board or worried about the resources it will take up. A small step could end up jumpstarting your company's social media participation. Then next year, you can really have some fun!

Summary

I did not spend a lot of time here talking about specific tools. New social media tools are launching every week, and others are dying just as frequently. What you need to do is decide how you want to communicate. Do you want to talk to your customers? Do you want to collaborate? Do you want to do that via text, podcast, or video? For example, if your social media plan is based on collaboration, you can find the tool that's right for your goal and your audience. If that tool goes away, you can easily adjust.

Make sure you have the Internet availability in place to properly accommodate your social media plan. Check with the venue to be sure it can accommodate the number of devices that attendees will be using. And, of course, when in doubt, have a backup plan for Internet access. When it comes to choosing your social media tools, you must first know what you are trying to accomplish. Are you looking for collaboration or communication? Do you want to educate or entertain your audience? Only choose a tool after you have decided what you are trying to accomplish.

Prime the Pump

Pre-show promotion efforts used to be pretty easy. Exhibitors would create a direct mail campaign, usually post-cards, inviting people to their booths. Then they added email to the mix. Exhibitors loved that because it was so inexpensive. Using their own databases and a list they could buy or rent from show management, exhibitors would begin promoting their presence at the show a month or two out. That was about the extent of pre-show promotion. All that was left to do was hope it was compelling enough to draw traffic to the booth.

Now we have social media. While it opens up so many more channels to get your message out, it also means a lot more work on your end. This isn't another avenue to just push your marketing message. The social media audience does not want to be bombarded with your marketing. People want to have a conversation. They are becoming more and more immune to advertising and are learning to tune out the clutter.

Show producers are starting to protect their attendees from the deluge of exhibitor marketing as well. Many shows no longer rent their email lists to exhibitors—or, at the very least, organizers require that attendees opt-in to receiving pre- and post-show promotions from exhibitors. Attendees want to choose how they receive information and whom they are willing to receive it from. Attendees are tired of their email inboxes being flooded with hundreds of pre-show promotions in the weeks leading up to a show and have demanded that shows put a stop to this practice. The era of "spay and pray" is ending.

One might be discouraged by this news, but I see it as a huge opportunity to fix what exhibitors have been doing wrong for so long. It's a chance for savvy exhibit and brand managers to take their physical presence at a show and extend it to a much wider audience via social media. Instead of using give aways to entice as many attendees as possible into your booth, you are forced to create a message that attracts the real, qualified buyers. With social media, you are participating in conversations with attendees and providing them with information they need—instead of just shouting a marketing message at them. The result is walking away from the show with better-quality leads and, at the same time, getting your message out to buyers who cannot attend the show.

You might be thinking, "But I thought the whole point of a trade show was to connect face-to-face with my audience. What is the value in reaching out to an audience that will not be present to experience what we are doing at the show?" Or, "Why not just skip it all together and participate in a virtual trade show?"

Nothing can replace the value of meeting face-to-face. In a down economy and even in a recession, buyers still go to trade shows. While the quantity of attendees at the show has dropped, the quality of attendees has gone up. Those who go are there to buy. Buyers still see an advantage in having all their potential vendors in one spot over a few days to shop and compare products and services.

But the fact remains that not everyone who wants to attend a show can. This might be because of budget cuts, time constraints, or an inability to travel. The same social media strategy you've added to your exhibit to enhance the value of the face-to-face event will also open your exhibit up to a wider audience.

More and more show organizers are realizing many of their potential attendees cannot make the trip to the show and are incorporating virtual components into their show. By doing this, they are creating hybrid events. A hybrid event is one event that reaches both the in person audience and the audience unable to attend, otherwise known as a virtual audience. You, as an exhibitor, regardless of what the show organizer is doing, should be extending your presence beyond the show floor and reaching out to that virtual audience as well. Your booth strategy should create one seamless hybrid event that reaches these two audiences and even allows them to connect with one another. By doing this, you can connect with both audiences through one cohesive exhibit marketing campaign.

6

Use Social Media to Generate Awareness

During the days when direct mail was your only option, you would wait until mere weeks before the show to begin marketing to your audience of attendees. You had to wait until most of the people registered to get the most value for your money spent. Now you can use social media to start marketing months before the show opens, and you are no longer dependent on a registration list to get your message out. Using the power of social media, you can expand your reach beyond just the people who will be attending the live event.

You can now start marketing your exhibit at the same time the producers start marketing the show. While they are generating interest for the show, you can get a head start generating interest in your exhibit. Remember, attendees are going to the show having already done their research and creating a short list of which exhibitors they want to see. By starting early in your marketing, you can ensure you have secured a place on their lists.

When you start your social media outreach, remember what people want. They want to find new products and services, they want information and education, and they want to network. They want these things a lot more than they want the stress ball or flashlight you might be giving away.

Your social media marketing is going to have to be a lot subtler than your direct mail campaigns were. Social media is social. It's a conversation. It is possible to promote your company and your message without cramming it down people's throats. Your goal in social media is to stay on top of people's minds. You want them to remember who you are and to be open to your message when you deliver it.

One of the easiest ways to do this is to be a great source of information. Any information that might be valuable to your potential customers is fair game. You need to know the show program inside-out, backward, and forward. Be on top of any announcements the show producers are making. Share that information via the social media channels you identified in Part I, "Creating Your Social Strategy." Be sure to do the following:

- Post information on the show with a link to the registration page as soon as registration is open.
- When the show announces its keynote speaker(s), share that information with your online communities.
- Post reminders of when early bird registration is coming to an end.
- Let your audience know which social media platforms the show will be using to stay informed.
- Cull through the show program and point out educational sessions you think your customers would find beneficial.
- Tell your community about any sessions the show is live streaming, the agenda, and how they can participate.
- Point out any sessions you will be presenting.
- Share reviews or tips on the official show hotels.
- Share restaurant recommendations or things to do in town while attendees are there.
- Tell them about special events that are taking place in your booth.
- Ask attendees to connect with your staff members who will be at the show.

Don't pick just one or two of these things. Do all of them, and do them often enough to stay at the top of people's minds. This way, when they are starting to make that list of exhibitors they must see before they leave, they will be thinking of you as the company that has already provided so much valuable information. If you are pointing out many worthwhile presentations to attend, no one will mind when you throw in a few you are presenting as well.

If you do this, you will be far ahead of the curve and of your competition. Most exhibitors are not making the effort to do this. Look at just about any show's hashtag on Twitter or its LinkedIn group a few weeks or a month before a show. Aside from information the show's producers are putting out there, the only thing you usually see from exhibitors is, "Come visit us in booth 184 and register to win an iPad." They are not part of a conversation. They are simply using the social media channel to broadcast their message.

You, on the other hand, by offering information useful to the attendee, will find yourself quickly becoming part of the conversation. Attendees will start relying on you for up-to-date information. They will start reaching out to you and engaging with you. They will start telling their colleagues to follow you. You are essentially creating relationships and warm leads.

Later, we'll talk about why it's important to maintain this conversation during the show, but for now, let's focus on promoting your presence at the show to both the face-to-face audience and the audience unable to attend. While everyone else is focusing only on those who will be actually attending the show, you will be opening up your booth to a much wider audience.

Integrating Your Social Media

It goes without saying that your exhibit design and marketing across all channels, including broadcast, print, and social media, should align. No matter where people encounter your messaging, they should instantly recognize it. There should not be any disconnect. Message wording can be customized to each particular audience, however; you don't want to come across as serious and business-like on LinkedIn and trade publications, but then have a fun, quirky style on the show's Facebook page. So, if your booth is a little on the wild side, your traditional marketing and social media can be as well. Be consistent across all channels.

But remember, your social media strategy is not just a trade show effort. You are building relationships online between your company and the community. The community does not see your presence on social media as a four- or five-week effort around the trade show. They are going to want to hear from you long after the show. They've come to rely on you for information, and your company should be taking advantage of that relationship all year long. You need to integrate your social media efforts throughout your trade show program, in all of your marketing efforts, and across your entire business.

Every company wants to be seen by its customers and potential customers as caring about their needs. Every company wants to claim great customer service. By using social media to educate, inform, and connect, you are reflecting those values. If you are using social media just to push your message on them, you are telling the world you only really care about you and are not interested in building relationships.

Creating a Message for Each Audience

When creating a pre-show marketing strategy, your goal is to get people to come to your booth. This does not fundamentally change when you incorporate social media and virtual events into your exhibit program. But now you are not just inviting people into your physical space; you are inviting them into your online space as well. You are also adding new ways to reach out to your customers and potential customers by using the various social media platforms you've identified.

The look and feel of your message should be consistent across all mediums. Your print and broadcast marketing should appear similar to your social media marketing. You don't want to confuse your audience with inconsistent design. The colors you use, your logo, and design style should remain the same across all platforms. It should not matter if I, as an attendee, come across a printed piece, an email, a tweet, a blog post, or a YouTube video. I should immediately be able to recognize it as yours.

What should be customized is the content of that message depending on the audience you are trying to reach. You can have one message when reaching out to the media, one message for potential customers, and yet another message for current customers.

Similarly, you will have a different message for in-person attendees and the audience unable to attend that you are reaching online. You might not know who fits into which bucket just yet, and that's okay. Your audience will sort that out themselves and filter out messages that do not match their needs. In some cases, you will be able to identify those who are attending and those who are not, but the nature of social media makes your messages viewable to everyone. Again, the social media audience is very adept at filtering out messages that are not relevant to them.

How Do You Create Different Messages?

Let's say you plan on tweeting about relevant sessions to your community on Twitter. You also plan on summarizing the sessions on your company blog. You know that several LinkedIn groups your company participates in would also find the content relevant. Some members of your community will be attending the trade show, and some will not. Others have never even heard of this event but might become interested in attending. Here are some examples of how you can tailor messages to each different audience in your community.

Tweet for those who are attending:

> Attending Widget 2011 #widget11 and struggling w/procurement? Be sure to check out Session 142 on Monday http://bit.ly/a2lT1K*–Booth1473

> *Here you are linking to a session description on the show website*

Tweet for those not attending:

> Not attending Widget 2011 #widget11 but want to catch "How to Fix Procurement"? Check out our blog summary at http://bit.ly/mZmT1K**–Booth1473
>
> **Here you are linking to your company blog*

LinkedIn Group post:

> Do you struggle with procurement? We noticed a few sessions taking place this year at Widget 2011 (*link to event*) that might interest you.
>
> Monday – Session 142 – "How to Fix Procurement" by Dan Lewis (*link to description*)
>
> Tuesday – Session 287 – "Procurement—Working with Small Businesses" by Susan Hoffman (*link to description*)
>
> If you are unable to attend Widget 2011 or cannot make those sessions, we'll be posting summaries on our company blog that can be found at www.widgetthingamajig.com.
>
> Widget 2011
>
> http://www.widget2011.com
>
> November 4-6, 2011
>
> Las Vegas Convention Center
>
> Booth Number1473

The first tweet targets attendees of the show by giving them a link to the session summary on the show website. You are being social and helpful to your potential customers by pointing out sessions they might find useful. You are also including your booth number. Whenever possible, I suggest including your booth number in your tweets. The last thing you want is for someone to decide that *@yourcompany* is incredibly helpful and has his best interests at heart, yet he has no idea where to find you at the show.

The second tweet targets those who are not attending the show in person. Even though they are not attending, they could still benefit by reading your summary of that session. You are also driving them to your website. You should be sure you prep your audience for how the session summaries will be posted. Create a special trade show landing page or blog post ahead of time that clearly tells people when they can expect the summaries to be posted. Provide an option for your audience to opt-in to receiving notice of them via email or RSS feed when they go live. You should still include your booth number in these tweets because those who are attending the event will see them as well.

Having that landing page is very important. If I click on your link a month before the show and I don't see anything at all about procurement, I might be confused. And if that's the case, I'll just back out and move on to something else. If, on the other hand, your link takes me to a landing page that clearly explains what information you will be providing there and when, I'll know exactly what to expect. The email or RSS feed sign-up is important because your reader is unlikely to remember any of this 30 minutes later and will never remember to come back on her own.

The posts on the LinkedIn group let you provide more information than the 140-character limit on Twitter. You can craft your message in a way that is appropriate for those who are attending the show and for those who are not. Here you can also give people information about the show with a link to the show website, so those who were unaware of the show's existence can find more information. People who are already planning on attending will make the connection that you will be exhibiting at the show. Be sure to include the web address for the appropriate landing page and sign-up form on your website.

Is this information appropriate to post as a discussion? Different LinkedIn groups will have different rules that you need to abide by. Personally, I do not see this as self-promotion. You are providing the audience with information that is both appropriate and valuable to them. The content of the post referenced here includes sessions at an event your audience would find useful, so it's not just driving traffic to your website. If you sent them to your website home page, then I would argue that you are only baiting the group to visit your website and not providing relevant information.

Posts similar to ones made to the LinkedIn group can be used on Facebook as well. But again, you should drive traffic to your website because it is owned by you and accessible by everyone. Putting all of your content on Facebook exclusively means that people who don't use Facebook will not have access to it. You should be posting links to your content on each social media platform you are using. The actual content should be on your corporate website or blog. Duplicating that content across several social media sites just creates too much work for you and is a drain on resources. I also caution against putting content on sites you don't ultimately own or control because all that content can be deleted or repurposed at someone else's whim.

Whichever social media platforms you choose to use depends on where your audience is, what the trade show organizers are using, and what you are comfortable using. The following are what's important:

- Your message is consistent.
- You are informing and educating your audience.
- Your messages are customized to each audience.

Stick with that plan, and you can't go wrong.

Personal Connections

One of the benefits of email and social media is that they allow us to reach a broad audience with one push of a button at a very low cost. One of the downsides of email and social media, however, is that they allow us to reach a broad audience with one push of a button at a very low cost. We can get very lazy and begin talking *at* our audience and trying to make our message be all things to all people. Even by creating messages with a specific audience in mind, we are missing out on the value of the personal touch.

Many social media platforms provide the option to message individual users. The whole world might see the message, but if you are addressing one person specifically, he is likely to take more notice of the message.

Every Wednesday at 3 p.m. I moderate a Twitter chat called #expochat. This Twitter chat is an hour-long conversation that takes place 140 characters at a time. By adding a hashtag (#) to the tweets, participants are able to follow along with the conversation. I get a lot out of these chats and want to make sure people remember them. It's not enough to hope people remember that the chat takes place every Wednesday at the same time and that they show up to participate.

So, I send tweets throughout the day that will be seen by all my followers announcing the chat time and topic. However, that does not have a personal touch. It's an announcement, not an invitation. Each Wednesday morning I start sending private direct messages to past participants with a personal invitation and a reminder to attend. I also reach out to people I think would benefit by attending with a link to instructions on how to participate. As a result, I get a good turnout for my chats and have built a stronger connection with dozens of people whether they were able to participate or not.

Your trade show participation is no different. Don't rely on broadcast messages to drive traffic to your booth or increase your online participation. Your staff should use social media to reach out to individuals they are connected to with a personal invitation. This is why it is called *social* media and not *just-another-broadcast* media.

Think of your booth as an event. Post an agenda on your website that includes what you are doing each day at your booth throughout the show and include the link in tweets. Create a LinkedIn event and invite the people in your network. Or create an event on Facebook and invite your friends. Don't just rely on the broadcast features or hope that people stumble across it in your status updates. Take the time to make a personal touch.

A colleague of mine recently did this to invite her network to an event I was producing. The people she thought would be interested and that she normally communicated with on email got a personal invitation or recommendation to attend the event via email. Those she normally communicated with on Twitter got a short note via direct message that read, "Thought this event would be interesting to you...how have you been?" with a link to the event website.

Almost everyone responded due to the personal nature of the message. One client whom she had not spoken to in a long time responded with something to the effect of "Thanks for the information; it looks very interesting. By the way, you reminded me that I need to talk to you about an upcoming job we need you for. When can you talk?" I am not sure the person is coming to the event, but my colleague is thrilled because she was able to get back into her client's appointment book.

The benefits of this approach are contained in layer upon layer of touch points. Information can spread beyond just my colleague and her contacts. Each of her contacts might spread the information about the event to their colleagues as well, multiplying its reach each time it is passed along. It's also information that is shareable because it gives those passing it along an opportunity to get in touch with customers and prospects in a way that is helpful and not "salesy."

Direct mail and email blasts are certainly less time-consuming ways to communicate with our databases, but they cannot ever replace the value of a personal invitation. Over and above your marketing efforts, your sales force should be reaching out to their customers and potential customers with a personal invitation. Why not include customer service reps in this mission as well? Be sure to give the people who cannot attend in person ways to follow-along from their office.

VIP Program Invitation

VIP programs are like personal invitations on steroids. I love it when people reach out to me before a show and personally invite me to stop by their booth. I find it hard to decline the invitation and thus would feel guilty if I didn't actually stop by. What I really love is when people invite me to a special event or party they are hosting for VIPs. Everyone wants to be a VIP.

You're probably already used to hosting VIP events at your trade show and sending personal invites. Nothing here really changes; you're just adding another way—via social media—to reach out to your selected attendees. But I want to issue a couple of warnings here. If you are having an invitation-only event during the show, be careful not to broadcast the event on social media. Otherwise, you might have more attendees than you planned—a lot more—as social media can spread the news like wildfire.

The other warning is that, again, social media is *social*. Word spreads quickly within a social media community. At a recent event, a Twitter friend asked me if I was attending an exhibitor's "secret party." She had received an invitation, and I had not. I was actually looking at that vendor's product to use for an event I had coming up, so I could not help but wonder why I wasn't important enough to invite.

I'm not saying that you have to invite everyone to everything you are doing. I am saying be prepared to slight someone—and have a response ready. I got my invitation two days later, and I have no idea if I was on the original list or if my friend gave them a heads up. I decided it was better for my ego not to know and RSVP'd immediately.

Summary

Social media is a great communication tool you have in your pre-show toolkit. Because of its capability to spread your message far beyond the show's attendee list, you are reaching a much larger audience. You are generating awareness of your presence at the show to your entire community and potentially to the networks of each community member. I would not suggest you abandon all your traditional marketing and only use social media. Keep doing what has given you the best results in the past and add social media to that marketing mix.

Make sure your social media efforts are integrated with your traditional trade show marketing and booth and fits with your company image. Customize that message to those who are attending the show and those who are not but still want to be a part of it. But don't just customize to a wide audience—personalize your invitations and reach out to individual customers and attendees. And be sure you give VIP invites special consideration.

7

Find and Engage Your Champions

We talked earlier about champions internal to your company, but now we get into the nitty gritty of reaching out to your potential customers. Just exactly what do I mean by champions? A champion, according to Alice in Wonderland, is someone who would be willing to die for you. That's a little dramatic for what we're talking about. It's very unlikely you will come across someone willing to put his life on the line for what your company is selling. That's a stretch even for your CEO. Although reflecting back to a holiday dinner with my brothers-in-law and a discussion revolving around NASCAR, perhaps there are those willing to die for their favorite brand. At the least, they were willing to come to fisticuffs for it.

What Is a Champion?

When I'm referring to champions, I'm talking about people who would shout your company's message from the mountaintops. They are the people who are in your corner no matter what. They are the first people to jump in to defend your brand when your name is being drug through the mud.

Think about it for a moment. Is there a company out there you feel this way about? Either a business-to-business (B2B) company or a consumer brand? Maybe even a band, an artist, or an author. My husband brews beer for a local brewery. There are a lot of online forums where beer lovers (a.k.a. beer geeks) hang out and discuss the intricacies of their favorite brews. When someone slams a particular brewery's beer, the brewery doesn't even need to defend itself. Some folks will argue the merits of the beer in question. But there are others—champions—who will basically rip the complainer to shreds, carefully dissecting each point of the unsuspecting poster's argument.

Have you ever been present or taken part in a discussion on the merits of one operating system over another? Bring up a discussion with your friends about the advantages of Windows versus Mac. Many won't have a preference, but some will argue passionately for one over the other. Throw a Linux user into the mix and things begin to get really interesting.

Champions are not just fans. They are not people who simply prefer one product over another. Instead, champions will passionately come to the defense of the brand. They often hang out on the Internet for the sole purpose of saying nice things about you. These are the people who will create YouTube videos, basically commercials about you, and post them online. Sometimes they are a bit overzealous, but that's okay. Everyone knows they are just passionate fans, so don't try to reign them in.

In 2010, Doritos recognized passion and creativity for what they were worth and created a contest in which fans got the chance to submit Doritos commercials. One lucky winner was chosen via Internet voting and received $5 million. Plus, his ad ran in one of Doritos' three Super Bowl ad spots. But it's not just a fun contest for Doritos. These consumer-created TV commercials achieved the highest net improvement score of any Super Bowl advertising.

Why Do You Need Champions?

In the beginning of this book, I talked about the reasons people go to trade shows. They are there to network, find new product and service offerings, and get specific answers about products and services provided by the companies on their short lists. Using social media and virtual events can help attendees meet these needs, and your champions can help you do it.

Networking

Ask yourself whether your champions are people your customers want to meet or are people who want to meet your customers or other industry leaders. They could very well be both. They might make great VIP guests for a tweet-up you are having at the show because they would draw other attendees.

Your champions might be people who would treat an invitation to a dinner with industry experts like it was a VIP ticket to the Super Bowl. At the very least, they should get one of your free passes to the conference. Go a step further and ask them if there are any industry big wigs they want to meet with while at the show and arrange the meeting if possible. You might have to reach out to your executive team if you yourself are unsuccessful. Invite them to attend a networking event with someone from your executive team so you can be sure they have the opportunity to be introduced. This doesn't have to be a big formal affair. Just simply making the introduction with a little background information is often all it takes.

If your champions are active on social media, they'll promote a tweet-up to all their followers telling them to come. They'll tell everyone about their dinner with the industry expert and publicly thank you, their host. Yours will always be remembered as the company that cared enough to introduce them to the person they most respect in the industry.

You have to trust that if your gift to them was good enough, your champions will spread the word about it themselves. There is a fine line between a charming host and an overbearing one. Constantly asking if someone is going to tweet about his experience will only make him feel as though you are trying to buy his allegiance. If instead you've earned it, he will acknowledge it without being asked.

Take an active interest in the wider audience your champion exposes your company to. Treat these introductions as you would if your best friend introduced you to someone at a cocktail party. They have both your best interests in mind and the interests of the person they introduced to you. If they feel it's a good match, it deserves special consideration and attention.

Finding New Products and Services

If you are planning to hold a press conference for a new product or service announcement, be sure to invite your champions. Treat them as you would a member of the traditional media. After all, what is a journalist but a trusted source for information? Your champions, active in social media, are viewed in the same way by their followers.

If you are not holding a press conference at the show or making a formal announcement, give your champions a sneak peak at the products or services you will be presenting at the show. These are people who love to get a scoop, and their followers turn to them because they are tuned in to what is new and different. When you tell people to come to your booth to see your new offering, it's marketing. When they tell people to go to your booth to see your new product or service, it's valuable information from a trusted source.

Information

People are shopping much differently these days. They are turning to the Internet to find solutions to their problems. Social media makes it easy to get a second, third, and fourth opinion. Often your champions will be a source for that information. It's not just product information customers and prospects are looking for. They are digging deeper. They want to know what it's like to do business with your company. They wonder about the ease of your products' implementation, the level of customer service you provide, and whether you'll be around for the long haul.

Make it easy for your champions to provide that information to their followers. Reach out to them before a show and set up appointments for them to meet with people from your company. Give them one-on-one meetings with your engineers, customer service reps, product managers, and executives. But don't just use these meetings to push information on them. Listen to what your champions say because they have a finger on the pulse of your customer base and can be a valuable source of information as to what your customers' true needs are.

Where Do You Find a Champion?

"But I'm not making beer or snack chips," you say. "No one is passionate about disc brakes." Really? Safety experts are. Parents are. Certain mechanics might be. Is there a race car driver or cyclist who swears by them? I hope you are sponsoring him if he is.

Just out of curiosity, I googled "passionate about disc brakes." Then, I looked at the first two references of about 20 million hits. The second link sent me to a site called Two Wheel Blogs and an entry titled "Avid BB7 Disc Brake Set Up and Tuning." The writer, Ken, states, "I am passionate about brake performance, and if you are not also passionate about it, please don't read this." It took me all of about 60 seconds to find a potential disc brake champion.

You just need to go out and find where your champions are hiding. You might be able to get help from your customer service, research and development (R&D), or business development departments. You would be surprised, but passionate customers call customer service a lot. They take it personally when something is not working the way they want it to. And why not? They consider your product or service theirs. It's not just something they use; it's something they are invested in.

It's something they tell all their friends and colleagues to buy. If something is not working, it reflects poorly on them.

R&D or business development is a good place to look because your champions will often offer unsolicited advice on product or service enhancements. Their conversations usually start with, "You know what you should do?" and then they tell you in detail. They may have even already drawn up schematics for you.

Talk to booth staffers who've worked past trade shows. Champions come by your booth several times during the show just to talk. They love being there. Heck, if you let them, they'd probably work your booth and be the best booth staffer you ever had. Your staff will likely describe them as "that person who never goes away." What you need to do is harness that passion and make it work for you.

Champions don't have to be customers. Sometimes they are people who will never have a need for your product or service. Your greatest champion could be a supplier, a retired industry thought leader, a blogger, a hobbyist, or even an employee. You need to dig through online forums and communities and see whether you can find your champions. But remember, they're not just people who mention your company here and there; they actively promote what you are doing or selling. A champion might be writing a blog that is solely dedicated to one of your products or services. It can take work finding them, but it's worth the effort.

Other times finding your champions is as simple as doing a Google search for your company's product. People try to make things more complicated than they really are. There are days when I wonder how on Earth we ever functioned before the World Wide Web and Google. I would likely never have been able to find my disc brake champion in the *Encyclopedia Britannica* or by looking through miles and miles of microfilm and microfiche.

To show you how simple it can be to find these champions, I randomly chose products and services that would fit into our B2B discussion and then did a quick Google search. The first thing that popped into my head was a Xerox printer, and I stumbled across Michael Josefowicz's blog ToughLoveForXerox.blogspot.com.

He starts his "About Michael Josefowicz" page with, "I can't remember when I fell in love with print." Seriously, how big does the clue stick need to be to pick up on the fact that this guy may be a potential champion for your printer? On that same page, one anonymous commenter asked, "I am confused, if you bash some of these companies why are they in your IRA?" Michael's response is, "For the same reason that I used to 'bash' students in my classes...I love 'em, but sometimes they do such stupid things."

From what I can see, Michael has never worked for Xerox. He owned a print brokerage for a long time and now is a teacher. Michael is a great example of a champion—he's online, he's passionate, and he's talking.

Moving on in my challenge to find champions of just about any B2B product or service that jumped into my head, next up was the "unsexy" school bus. After about 10 minutes of searching, I came across a couple of potential champions. The first is a site called School Bus Rulz. On this site, created by a part-time school bus driver and retired ad executive, you can find some fun t-shirts for sale, personal stories written by other bus drivers, and advocacy for the "Stop the Bullying" campaign. People who use their free time to create websites and write about what they do are potential champions.

I also came across an article in the *Lewiston Sun Journal* about a 12-year-old who is so passionate about busses that he has dressed as a bus for Halloween three years in a row, has redecorated his bedroom with a school bus theme, and has amassed a miniature collection of 93 school buses. Clearly, little Carter will not be purchasing any new buses for a school's fleet any time soon, but don't be so quick to dismiss him. He'd probably do a much better job starring in a company video than your CEO would. In a sense, he is the true end user of your product. Before you get too excited about looking young Carter up to make a job offer when he's out of college, he says he wants to be a bus driver only when he retires from a career in architecture. But how great would it be to capture his spirit and enthusiasm and use his story in a marketing campaign and also in your booth?

Do your own search and start finding your potential champions. Treat them as you would your best customers, and invite them to the show. Include them in your media campaigns and invite them to meet with key people in various departments of your company. Word-of-mouth is and will always be your most effective marketing. Social media takes word-of-mouth marketing to a whole new level. Your customers have learned to tune out what you, as marketers, say about your own company and instead focus on what others are saying about you. Your champions are your best advocates, making them more valuable than ever.

Engaging Your Blogger Champions and the Media

I'm going to let you in on a little secret here. You don't have to be a trained PR professional to reach out to bloggers, journalists, or writers to pitch a story. I don't care if you are a little girl selling lemonade on the corner or an exhibit manager of a Fortune 500 corporation who is doing something really cool in her booth, you have the skills necessary to pitch your story. Here is the secret—just pick up the phone, send an email or tweet, or post on the person's Facebook wall if that is how he wants to be reached. You don't have to know any PR jargon to make this call. As a matter of fact, it's probably better if you don't. You just need to have something interesting and relevant to say that his readers will want to hear.

PR agencies will tell you that you need to have established relationships with journalists and bloggers to get your story written. That's just a load of bunk. Sure, relationships never hurt, but bloggers and journalists are always interested in a great story or a tidbit that will interest their readers no matter who it comes from. There are only two things you need to know to do this right. First, know what the person writes about and be sure your pitch is relevant. If you sell automotive products and she has never written about cars, don't waste her time even if her readers all own cars. If she is a mommy blogger and your automotive product is relevant to child safety, then you are on to something.

Second, know how to open the call or email or whatever form you use to make initial contact. Be courteous, short, to the point, and relevant. Here's an example: "Hi Joe, this is Sara Smith from ABC Company. We have an industry expert presenting on the reductions in child accidental deaths through the installation of back-up cameras in vehicles in our booth in November at XYZ show. I think your readers would be interested in this based on other articles you have written on child safety. Do you have a minute to talk, or is there another way you prefer I tell you about this?" This is short, to the point, relevant, and courteous.

It never hurts to specifically name the stories the person has written that relate to what you are pitching. This shows writers that you have done your research and actually read what they have written. To them that's a big flag waving above your head that says, "I actually put some thought into calling you specifically." There is nothing bloggers or journalists hate more than someone pitching an irrelevant story. Well, possibly worse is getting a call from someone saying, "Did you get my press release?"

If the writer gives you the go-ahead to pitch your story, stick to just the who, what, where, when, why, and how. Don't ramble on and on; be brief and to the point. Let him know you have a press release you can send him with all the relevant information and whether it includes videos, audio, and images he can use for the story. Trust me, if you've gotten to this point, you are already well on your way to getting your story published.

What shouldn't you pitch to a writer? Anything you would put in an ad. While a 50 percent off sale at Cole Haan is certainly of interest to me as a reader, it's not a story a journalist wants to write—unless it's the only time Cole Haan has ever had a sale in its history of doing business. Even then, the story isn't that the store is having a sale, but why it is having a sale.

The moral of the story here is that if you truly have something that is of interest to a blogger's or journalist's readers, then don't be afraid to pick up the phone, even if you stumble a bit for the right words. Make sure it is really story worthy and not just an ad, and don't be discouraged if you get a "no." Just move along to the next contact on your list, knowing you have something valuable to offer.

Social Media Releases

A well-written press release is a great way to get word out about what you are doing in your booth at the trade show. Once upon a time, you would send your press release directly to your media contacts or send it via a wire service and hope someone would pick up the story. Even more recently, wire services such as PR Newswire, Marketwire, PRWeb, and Business Wire provided effective services to disseminate your release online. Even if no one picked up your story, it was widely available on websites like Yahoo News, Reuters, and Google News. With careful placement of key words, anyone searching the Web for those words could potentially stumble across your press release. People started not just writing the release to capture the media's attention, but rather directly for their audience who might be searching the Web.

We now have what are called *social media releases*. They are essentially the same as the press releases we are all familiar with. The difference, though is that these social media releases are made to share. They contain embedded video, audio, and images. They have Real Simple Syndication (RSS) feed links and buttons for readers to share the releases via various social media networks like Facebook, LinkedIn, Twitter, and Google+. They even have a way for readers to email the releases to a friend or colleague or post them to a blogging platform.

Like a traditional press release, the secret to a good social media release is in the writing. A good, well-written release is informative without being overly promotional. It doesn't shout your marketing message; it speaks directly to the interests of your reader. It captures a reader's attention by giving him information he finds valuable. It's not just information that only makes your company look good. I once had a dear friend who said, while we both admired an elegantly simple handbag, "It doesn't say nothing." What he meant was that it didn't need to have its designer logo stamped all over it. By simply being what it was, it made the shopper say, "It is beautiful." A well-written press release provides the reader with information that is valuable to him and that he wants to share. It doesn't matter if the reader is the buyer or the media, it is valuable and shareable because it is intended to inform.

Why is it important to know how to write a good press release or know about social media releases? Maybe you have a PR department that handles these things. But perhaps they have a lot of work on their plate, and it's difficult for them to find the time to do little more than one or two releases about your presence at a show that they send to their standard media list. Or, maybe you have a PR department but they don't understand the needs of your trade show attendees. They do not truly understand what is important to this audience. Or maybe you do not have a PR department so you need to handle these things on your own. Knowing how to create a social media press release will give you the flexibility to get your message out directly to your audience.

There are a plethora of social media press release services out there that you can find with a simple Google search. Prices range from free for the basics to hundreds of dollars per release and include rich analytics and tracking features. Whichever service you decide is right for you, it should include the following:

- A template to guide you
- The capability to include multimedia (pictures, audio, and video)
- The capability to include links to appropriate content
- A sharing feature for readers to spread your story through social media sites
- An RSS feed subscription link
- A space for general company information
- A place for readers to comment
- The capability to track who has referred to your release

Anyone can write a good press release that readers will find valuable enough to share. Write the press release the way you know a journalist would write your story. That means keeping the self-promotion, over-the-top claims, and bias out of it. Stick with the facts, but make sure they are interesting facts. Write something that if you were the customer, you'd want to read. Every good social media press release contains the following elements:

- **Attention-grabbing headline**—Keep it brief and to the point without being too creative. Your company name, the show name, and a few key words is enough. Refrain from using the following terms anywhere in your release (or your marketing for that matter): leading provider, unique, state-of-the-art, revolutionary, award-winning, and the like. They are meaningless and overdone.
- **Secondary headline (optional)**—Only include this if you have something that will really hook the reader and encourage her to read on; otherwise, skip to the next step.
- **Summary**—Keep this to a paragraph or two summarizing what your release is about. This paragraph is where you want to really hook the reader. Here is where you will either get her to read on or lose her. Keep this area rich in key words (including the show name) and carefully craft each sentence.
- **Body**—This is the meat of your story. Write it in a way that a busy journalist could just cut and paste it into her story. This means keep the bias out of the story and stick to the who, what, where, when, why, and how.

- **Facts/sound bites**—These are short-and-sweet bullet points that back up the content of your press release and that people may find shareable. It's good to include your company, product, or service name within the fact. Also incorporate the show hashtag and your booth number if possible. Try to keep these to 120 characters, so people can share them on Twitter and add a personal comment.

- **About your company**—People often refer to this as *boilerplate text*. This is a short paragraph about your company that should include a link to your website and any social media sites your company participates in (Twitter, LinkedIn, Facebook, Google+, YouTube, and so on). It should include general information on what products or services the company provides, where the business is located, when it began operations, number of employees, and anything else that might tell a reader what exactly the business does. It should not contain words like "revolutionary" and "leading provider of."

- **Multimedia**—This is all that cool, sharable stuff. Include any videos, images, audio clips, and RSS feeds.

- **Relevant links**—While you have readers' attention, why not include a few links to some of your other products and services? Also include links to sessions you might be participating in at the trade show or invitations to social events you are hosting.

- **Social media sharing buttons**—Make it easy for the reader to share your information by embedding key social media tool and bookmarking site buttons right into your press release.

- **Contact info**—Whatever you do, do not forget this very important step: Include any and all contact information just in case someone is motivated to seek out more information. Just be sure you are including contact information for someone who can address the issues brought up in your press release and that she is not caught off guard. I also like to include a specific contact number for the media. This should be someone who is ready to answer questions at a moment's notice and not just between the hours of 9 a.m. and 5 p.m.

I don't care if you use a wire service or just post the social media release on your own company website. What is important is that this keyword-rich, informative information is on the Web, is searchable, and is sharable. It's another way to be found by anyone remotely interested in the show you are exhibiting at and maybe some potential customers who just find themselves interested in what you are selling.

Summary

Customers are turning to the Internet to get information on products or services they are considering buying. Your website is not the only place they are looking. Your customers and prospects are turning to industry thought leaders, bloggers, and traditional media outlets on the Web for opinions they trust. You improve your chances of being seen by delivering that information to bloggers and the media in a format that is rich in multimedia and easily shareable.

Your champions are not just writing about you themselves; they could also be referring readers to articles written about you that are favorable. They know what your customers are looking for and will go out of their way to point them in the right direction. Provide them the information they want to share, and they'll do much of the work for you.

8

Pre-Show Social Media Tactics

After you've captured the attention of your audience, you need to keep them engaged during the time leading up to the show. What better way to engage them than by getting them involved in the activities that will be taking place in your booth early on? Pre-show activity is not just about invites and press releases. It also involves developing stronger relationships with your community members and getting them excited about your booth.

It's a time when you should be prepping attendees with instructions for how they can participate in various booth activities. Clear instructions and communication up front will give you and your booth visitors, either online or in person, a great start for your conversations.

Crowd Source Activities and Contests

The best way to find out which booth activities and contests would be of most interest to your potential customers is to ask them. Here's where the power to reach out to a mass audience via social media comes in handy. You never know how many people are listening. Creating simple polls or crowdsourcing your plans is an easy way to get input from your social media audience, and it won't cost you a dime.

Polling

Whether you are trying to decide which speaker to bring to your booth, which promotional item would have the most effect, which contest would generate the most interest, or which products to showcase, a simple poll is your answer. Services, such as PollDaddy, Zoomerang, and Survey Monkey, are just a few of the inexpensive or even free services that are easy to set up. There are even widgets available to embed a poll right into your website.

Let's say you are considering topics for an in-booth presentation, and you're not sure which of two or three topics will resonate the most with your audience. You could create a simple poll and distribute it using all the tools available to you. Send it to your marketing database via email, post on your website, and post it on different social media platforms such as Facebook, Twitter, LinkedIn, YouTube, community platforms, and so on. Be sure to encourage people to pass it along to their coworkers and friends. This will give you broader and more diverse answers.

Of course, it's not necessarily going to be a scientific sample size, but it could act as a flip of the coin for you. Or, it might keep you from going down the wrong path. Just be realistic as to what you are asking people. If you are asking which give-away they would choose, such as "a $20 gift card or a white paper," your responses will be skewed. Of course, people will choose the gift card. They know all they have to do is ask for the white paper, and they'll get that, too.

Maybe you have two ideas for a contest that will drive booth traffic and can't decide which one your audience would prefer. A quick poll will show you what your audience is more interested in. Just be careful where you are asking the question. If you are thinking of doing some kind of contest that relies on Facebook as a platform and another that runs on Foursquare and you post the poll only on Facebook, your results will probably be skewed toward Facebook. Had you also asked your LinkedIn connections, the results could be very different.

Keep your polls short, sweet, and to the point. Don't try to get answers to every question you ever wanted to ask on one poll. You are more likely to get better participation with three separate polls that take five seconds to respond to than if you had one poll that took 10 minutes to complete. Why not add a bit of an incentive to get people to take your poll? Let people know you will be choosing one lucky winner from those who participate each day to win a gift card. If it only takes a minute of my time *and* I have a chance of being rewarded, I'm more likely to participate.

Crowdsourcing

Crowdsourcing is slightly different from just getting a quick response to a poll. When you crowdsource ideas, you can actually get attendees to help strategize your ideas with you. *Crowdsourcing* is putting out an open call to an undefined group to perform tasks, submit ideas, and solve problems. Although the term is new, the concept is decidedly not.

One of the earliest examples of crowd sourcing is the creation of the *Oxford English Dictionary*. An open call was put out around the world, and volunteers took on the task of indexing every word in the English language and providing sample quotations of each of their usages. Seventy years and six million submissions later, we have the most comprehensive dictionary of all time.

Another more recent example of crowd sourcing is the United States Department of Defense's Adaptive Vehicle Make (AVM). This is actually several programs, overseen by the Defense Advanced Research Projects Agency (DARPA). This agency is using crowdsourcing to come up with a next-generation combat vehicle. And, of course, let's not forget Wikipedia, one of the first Internet crowdsourced projects and a great place to find many examples of crowdsourcing.

Google Moderator is a great tool you can use for your own crowdsourced project. Google Moderator is social media *agnostic*, meaning anyone is welcome on the platform—even people who are not into the whole "social media thing." Although you can use Facebook to invite people to your Google Moderator activity, if you were to use Facebook as your platform for collaboration, you'd eliminate all the people who don't use Facebook or who have accounts but don't want to use it for business. Use all the communication tools available to you to invite people to participate.

Instead of coming up with a contest that you think would resonate with your audience, why not just have them collaborate and create it for you? All you need to do is provide them with a platform to communicate with one another, and you can sit back and let your audience create the best contest ever. You can even give them a budget. Do you have to pay your collaborators? It"s not always necessary, but a reward could draw more participation. It could just be recognition, or it could be a coveted prize. (Why not do a poll and find out what prize participants might want?)

The crowdsource project could be the end goal in itself. Your company might want to try crowdsourcing a new product or feature with the winning product being announced at the trade show. Invite the crowdsource project teams into your booth to show off what they've created. Talk about viral! How many people do you think the final contestants are going to tell about their success? It has great potential for press coverage as well.

Webinars and Webcasts

You can incorporate webinars and webcasts into your pre-show promotion in several ways. A *webcast* is a broadcast over the Internet where the presenter is dispersing information to the audience through audio and/or video via streaming media. A webcast can be distributed either live or on demand. A *webinar* is a web-based seminar that can be delivered the same way a webcast can be but is instructional by nature.

How might you incorporate a webinar or webcast into your pre-show promotions? Let's remember why buyers are coming to a show. Some are there to get specific information from vendors they have pre-vetted. Why not do your product demo via a webinar or webcast before the show, and then let busy buyers come to your booth to ask more specific questions about what they've seen? This lets your booth staff know these buyers are quality leads as they have taken the time to view the demo before even showing up to your booth. In addition to the live webinar or webcast, you can record the product demo and offer it for on-demand viewing.

You could also use webinars or webcasts in conjunction with sessions your company might be presenting in the conference portion of the trade show. Your webinar, delivered prior to the conference, would give attendees extra meatier content prior to the session allowing for more interactive Q&A time with your experts during the session time slot. This content can be made private and available only to session attendees or be made public so that anyone can view them.

You could also use a webinar or webcast to instruct attendees on how to participate in any social media contests you will conduct in your booth. This will take some of the pressure off your booth staff during the show and generate buzz prior to the show for contest participation.

If you are live streaming presentations in your booth at a specific time, you could create an instructional webcast for the remote audience with step-by-step instructions on how exactly to access the virtual event and how to navigate the platform you will host the event on. I cannot stress enough how important this step is to the success of your virtual event. The last thing you want is for remote attendees of your product launch or big announcement to have no idea how to access it. Clear instructions on how to communicate with the virtual emcee or moderator should be included.

Instructions for the Virtual Event

Live streaming your in-booth product launch or presentation can extend your audience beyond those attending the show and open it up to the entire world—but only if they know how to get there, how to get there on time, and what to do once they get there. We cover in detail in Part III, "On With the Show," how to live stream your booth activities, but here we cover what you need to do pre-show to ensure you can get the most online participants for your virtual event.

How many times have you signed up for a virtual event, such as a webinar, months in advance, only for the day of the webinar to arrive and you're left trying to find that two-month-old confirmation message for the instructions or link to log in? You've searched under the company name that is sponsoring the webinar with no luck. You finally find it from a generic info account of the platform provider in your junk mailbox.

Or, you do get the instructions the day of the webinar, only to find out you need to download a bunch of software updates to access it. After 20 minutes, you finally get access but find you've missed the majority of the content and now they have gone on to the Q&A portion.

You want your attendees to have an easier time accessing your live-streamed virtual event. You need to create easy-to-follow instructions on how and when to access your live-streamed event. Make it clear during the sign-up or invitation process what hardware and software your audience will need to participate. Include a system check to test their computers upon registration. Are you taking questions from the virtual audience during the presentation? Explain how audience questions will be handled. Do participants need a headset and microphone? A webcam? Should they dial in via phone? What phone number should they use? Don't forget to include the country code for those accessing the event from out of the country. Also include a time-zone converter so attendees can easily see what time a 9:00 a.m. EST start time is in their own time zone.

I once was on a live webinar but joined in late because it took several minutes to install some software that was needed. I missed some very important information relevant to the content of the webinar. I used the platform Q&A feature to ask my questions, but the answers coming back were vague and didn't make much sense to me. Finally, the person answering my question about the content admitted that he was a tech support person with the webinar platform provider and didn't know the answer. He suggested I email the company doing the webinar to get my answer. That would be too late.

Near the end of the webinar, the moderator opened it up to questions from the audience. I had absolutely no idea how to ask my question. There was a screen up that said, "And now we want to hear from you," with no instructions as to how to participate. This made me even more frustrated because I did have questions, but as I discovered earlier, the Q&A box was not the right place to ask them. Much of the actual content of the webinar was lost to me because I was too busy trying to figure out how I could get my questions answered.

I gave them constructive feedback and the company's next webinar went much more smoothly. The presenter posted a Twitter hashtag people could use to ask questions during the presentation (always use more than one communication tool so all audience members can participate). The presenter reminded us throughout his presentation what the hashtag was and encouraged us to ask questions. He did an excellent job incorporating comments and questions from the tweets into his presentation. As a result, I felt much more engaged, and the presentation held my attention.

Both topics were relevant to me, and both presenters had great content. The only difference was the clear instructions on how to participate prior to the second presentation. I was able to focus on the content of the second presentation and the interaction helped me retain much more of the information. Because I could communicate with the speaker and other participants, I stayed engaged throughout the presentation, and my mind did not wander.

The More Information, the Better

Make all this information available in the reminders you send leading up to the event and give your audience a way to test their equipment to ensure it will work with the virtual event platform you are using. I also suggest you send these reminders from your corporate email accounts, rather than from the virtual platform provider's email account. I cannot possibly be the only one who goes hunting for start times and instructions for logging in before an event. Make sure you are not putting your audience in the same frustrating position.

Communications and instructions should include the following:

- Date and time of the event (include time-zone converters)
- Presenter's contact information (include the presenter's Twitter handle if Twitter is being utilized as a communication tool)
- Software and hardware requirements
- System check prior to the virtual event
- Access instructions (include how long it will take to load everything and connect)
- Instructions on how to interact with the speaker and other audience members during the virtual event
- Details on how to get technical assistance during the virtual event)

- Any social media tools you will be using during the virtual event and how they will be used (such as a Twitter hashtag)

It's important to include all instructions and communications, including who your virtual attendees should contact in the event of technical problems. Do not leave them hanging out there and don't put your speaker in the position where she is being asked these questions. The last thing you want to have happen during a product launch live-streamed worldwide is your CEO turning it over to the audience for questions and immediately facing, "Yeah, I'm not getting any images on my screen, and the sound is fuzzy. What should I do?"

Be sure to keep all the instructions in one place, such as in one document or on one web page. I recently attended a hybrid event where I received a link to the virtual event platform from the organizer and two additional links from individual speakers to various tools they were using. I had such a hard time figuring out where I was supposed to be and when I was supposed to be there that I just gave up. This could have easily been solved if everything was in one spot on the event website.

Don't just send these instructions once—send them repeatedly. Email a confirmation with instructions after someone has registered to attend your virtual event. Post instructions frequently on the various social media platforms you are using specifically for your event. Email a reminder with complete instructions a week or a few days before your event. Finally, email them again about four hours before the event begins. Remember to keep all pertinent information in one place for easy access by your audience!

Creating Videos to Generate Excitement and Teasers

Videos are a great way to tease your audience and generate excitement about what you are planning for a trade show. Are you demoing a new product or service? Why not give attendees a video sneak peek at what you will present?

Have you ever seen the "Will it Blend?" videos created by Blendtec? They were a series of infomercials created by Blendtec featuring owner Tom Dickson and its line of blenders. Since 2007, Dickson has blended more than 100 different items, including a Chuck Norris action figure, a Thanksgiving dinner, a toilet plunger, and an iPhone. All these videos are available via YouTube, and they are a viral sensation. The early videos were not overproduced but each were viewed by millions of people and shared. All Dickson was doing was putting things no one would expect an average blender to survive into a Blendtec blender and letting it rip.

What could possibly be more mundane than a blender? Let's take a look at Big Blue, IBM, and the mainframe. In 2006, the hardware vendor released *Mainframe:*

The Art of the Sale." This series has been described by many as *The Office* meets corporate sales training videos. These videos were voted by Comedy Central as a "staff favorite" in its comedy test-pilots contest. These tongue-in-cheek videos were sponsored by IBM and used to recruit new customers and employees to their mainframe division. According to IBM-the videos increased traffic to their "mainframe blog" by 1,000 percent.

Does a video have to be funny to be appealing? Comedy does help to turn a video viral, but it's not necessary to generate interest. Samsung released a teaser video (http://bit.ly/samsungsts) for its product launch at International CTIA Wireless 2011 (the International Association for the Wireless Telecommunications Industry's annual convention). The video received more than 2 million views yet the show had just 40,000 attendees.

This video works well because it gives the viewer all the information about the where, when, why, and how of the event, but it only includes a hint as to the what. It leaves viewers desperately wanting to know what product they will be launching. The video is not a big production number—it's basically clip art but is branded with the bold colors featured in the event logo. It also contains a call to action inviting viewers to download their Samsung Mobile Unpacked app for Android, so you can be kept up to date with the latest announcements. Speaking of the app, how cool is it? Well, you can now view the live stream of all Samsung Unpacked events right there on your Android mobile phone using the Unpacked app.

"But I'm not IBM or Samsung," you say. "We're a small company without a huge product launch. We're just having an industry expert presenting in our booth, and we would be happy drawing a crowd of just 100 people or so." Here is where the teaser video is so worthwhile and economical. Have the presenter create a 30–60 second video presentation stating the takeaways the attendee will get out of the presentation. Upload the video on YouTube and embed it on your website. Then, start distributing it throughout your social media channels—tweet the video link, post the video on Facebook, and include it in your LinkedIn status with the show name (and hashtag if on Twitter). After the video starts getting views, it will also start getting shares. Include the presentation times and booth number so people know when and where to find your booth at the trade show. If you are planning on live streaming the presentation, be sure to include a link to your instruction page as well. Don't forget to include key words in all your descriptions and copy so the video is easily found in Internet searches.

Videos are becoming a more popular way to access information on the Internet. Many people find them more entertaining than just reading text on a screen. With the increase in the use of mobile devices, such as smartphones and tablets that popularity will only keep increasing. According to a Nielsen study, 40 percent more Americans were watching video on mobile devices such as smartphones and tablets in 2010 versus 2009. ComScore reports that 176 million U.S. viewers—83.3 percent of the country's Internet audience—tuned in to watch video online in May 2011. Even the U.S. government is jumping on the YouTube bandwagon. The Commerce Department's FedFlix channel (http://bit.ly/fedflix) on YouTube has had more than 9 million views of more than 8,000 videos.

Teaser videos are a great and inexpensive way to tap into all those online viewers and generate interest in what you are doing in your booth. You can also use them for a session you are presenting or participating in and even parties you are hosting during the show. If you post videos on sites like YouTube or Vimeo, viewers will have a way to easily share them with colleagues, and the media can include them in stories they publish online about the show. Make sure you include contact information, the show name, and your booth number in your video description. Also, be sure to embed your videos into your own website if the videos are hosted on a third-party platform.

Summary

Use social media, not just to invite your community into your booth, but also to engage them throughout the time leading up to the show. By using social media tools such as polling and crowdsourcing, you can get your audience actively involved and invested in what is taking place in your booth during the show. Make it easy for both the in-person attendees and your remote audience to participate in the activities going on in your booth by providing them with clear instructions. Don't forget to have some fun with it. People love to be entertained.

On With the Show

So far I have talked about setting a strategy and discussed preshow activities that generate awareness and create an audience. Now I focus on what activities will be taking place during the actual show. These are going to be activities that address the attendees physically at the show while also expanding your audience to those who might be stuck back in the office.

Trade shows are a big part of your marketing budget, so I want to make sure you get the biggest bang for your buck. Associations report that only a small percentage of their memberships actually attend their annual trade shows. That means there are tens of thousands of potential customers you could be reaching by adding social media and virtual event components to your booth strategy. That doesn't even include the thousands of potential customers the show organizer does not know about but who might stumble across you online because of those add-ons.

In this part, I tackle driving both the in-person attendees and those listening in from around the globe to your booth. You'll learn about the various types of content you can create at the show to become a trusted source of information for your customers and potential customers. You'll also find out how to get your company on the radar of bloggers who will be at the show and how to make it easy for them to write about you. You'll discover ways you can create a hybrid event—one that turns an in-booth presentation into an online show that engages a remote audience and immerses them in the live experience. I also discuss how to listen to what is happening all around you and use it to your benefit, as well as the mobile options you can incorporate into your program.

As in previous chapters, we'll be focusing more on the strategy and less on specific tools. I want you to be able to walk away with a sound understanding of how these practices might fit into your strategy, so that when new tools come on the market and the old ones fade away, you won't be scrambling to adjust. You'll simply insert the best tool available into your existing strategy without ever missing a beat. Now, let's have some fun at the show!

9

Drive Traffic
to Your Booth

What is the best way to drive traffic to your booth? What could you do that would almost guarantee that every person at the show came to your booth? That's easy. Give away $100 bills.

But you don't want everyone in your booth—you want just the right people there. First, you have to define who you want to come to your booth. Before you say, "I want everyone to come to my booth. I can qualify them once they are there," really think about it. Do you realistically have the manpower to deal with 4,000 attendees streaming into your booth? In some cases, depending on the show, 40,000 attendees? What if you have a 10×20 foot booth at the Consumer Electronics Show? Can you handle 140,000 people coming to your booth? While you're sifting for gold among the crowd, how many potential customers do you think you will lose because it was too hard for that customer to get to talk to one of your staffers?

I'm being extreme now, right? Not really. Even if you have just 20 people crowded around your booth because you are giving away something in demand or have a fun contest, that could discourage a real customer from stopping by. I'm not saying that having people flocking to your booth is a bad thing. Crowds generate buzz, and buzz generates more crowds. I am saying that you need to make sure you are prepared for those crowds and have the systems and staff in place to handle them. I have seen many a company go home with very few good quality leads even though their booth was packed for three days.

On the other hand, maybe your show goal is not to generate leads. I've seen companies who show up year after year just to support the industry association event. It's more about good will than marketing. Sure, they are there to sell too, but really it's to maintain their top market share position in the industry. If that's the situation you find yourself in, perhaps meeting up with 140,000 people is what you are hoping for. As long as you have the budget for the 10,000 square feet of booth space with money left over to send an army of staffers.

Perhaps yours is one of those companies with the hot new product of the year, and you don't have to worry about driving booth traffic. You just need to worry about staffing. Even those customers who could not get through the mob will reach out to you when the show is over, so collecting leads is the least of your worries. If you are that company this year, I suggest you keep reading because you might not be so lucky next year. Whatever your goals for the show, you still want to attract the right audience to your booth.

Driving Traffic for Brand Recognition

If your main goal is generating brand awareness or goodwill and not collecting leads or making sales, there are a lot of fun things you can do with social media. But you also have to be especially careful because it could backfire. To create a positive brand image, it is so important that you meticulously plan your strategy and tactics. Follow these strategies:

- Make it easy for people to participate.
- Make it easy for people to share.
- Be sure to have staff on hand to handle the crowds.
- Be sure the staff is trained on all aspects of your plan.
- Be sure people are assigned to keep the buzz alive.
- Be sure it's legal.

To brainstorm ideas for using social media to drive booth traffic for branding purposes, think of ways you already do that via traditional methods. Social media is going to be very similar. Your goal is to get as many people as possible at the show to think of your company and to see your company.

I worked with a client way back before many companies even had websites. This company would ship pallets of umbrellas to every show on the off-chance it might rain. Let me tell you, when it did rain, it was a wonderful thing. The umbrellas would be ordered from accessible storage and quickly brought to the booth. Word spread like wildfire throughout the exhibit hall that this one particular exhibitor was giving away umbrellas. We would go outside and stand across the street from the convention center practically weeping at the awesome sight of thousands of bright yellow umbrellas imprinted with their brand logo clustered tightly by the front doors and then spreading out for blocks. That is exactly what you want to do with your social media campaign. You want to get everyone to your booth, and then you want to see your message spread.

We'll assume you already did your pre-show promotion. You've sent invitations, posted information about your promotion in all the appropriate groups online, and garnered some media attention. You've even mixed in some traditional marketing by making use of the show's branding opportunities and have possibly even taken out a few ads in the show daily.

Now you are onsite and need to keep driving that booth traffic. Social media efforts to drive traffic to your booth should be accessible by attendees' smart phones and other mobile devices. Do not require attendees to be connected to their laptops in their hotel rooms to access your company website. Twitter is great for this as is the use of geo-location tools, like Foursquare, because they take seconds to update and are easy to use while you are moving. They also work well with a slow Wi-Fi connection because they don't require a lot of bandwidth. Stick with social media tools that are easy to use on the go and those that have an easy-to-use mobile device app.

Make It Easy For People To Participate

A social media promotion that's too complicated will make attendees throw up their hands in frustration. Worse, it will leave a bad taste in their mouths when it comes to your brand. Make sure it is easy for people who may be unfamiliar with the social media tool you are using to play along. If it takes you longer than one or two minutes to explain how attendees can access the tool, how to participate, and what will happen when they do, your plan is too complicated. A great promotion is as simple as having users check in to your booth using Facebook or Foursquare to get a giveaway, a special offer, or an invite to a private event. These tools are simple to install and set up on a smartphone or other mobile device.

Make It Easy For People To Share

Be sure you are using a tool that is already popular among your audience and enables them to share with friends. Foursquare allows users to share their check-ins with their Foursquare, Twitter, and Facebook. The ability to share with friends beyond those just on Foursquare will help spread the word to a larger audience. Encourage people checking in to post what they've won on their favorite social media sites. Another idea is to have a photo booth where attendees could have their pictures taken with a celebrity. Pictures can be instantly available via kiosks that allow access to any of their social networks and let attendees post the pictures immediately. These pictures should, of course, be branded with your company logo.

Be Sure To Have Staff On Hand To Handle the Crowds

Unless you work for Google, Twitter, or Facebook, it is unlikely that you are exhibiting at the show to teach people how to use social media. Most of your booth staff should be talking to customers and prospects about your product or service. Your best salesperson should not be spending all her time showing booth visitors how to upload a photo on Twitter. You should have a few booth staffers going to the show who are responsible for assisting people with the social media tools you are using.

Personally, I like to get as many people in the company involved with the show as possible. It's a great experience for new hires and entry-level employees to learn more about the company and the industry. Assigning them with the social media helper task is a great way for them to experience the show and isn't as scary as being a full-fledged booth staffer. If your budget does not allow you to send a few more employees to the show, you can always hire temporary staff from the city you are exhibiting in. These staffers don't need to know more than the basics about your company, as their sole responsibility will be to get people involved in using social media and assisting them if they are having difficulty.

Be Sure Your Staff Is Trained On All Aspects Of Your Plan

I encourage you to have specific people trained to handle your in-booth social media activities or any contest you are running. This allows other staffers to focus their time on talking to visitors about your company, products, or services. However, every person staffing your booth should understand how the contest works, what participants receive, what the rules are, and how prizes will be awarded. The last thing you want is an excited visitor coming to your booth and waving his smartphone in front of a staffer to claim his check-in prize, only to have that staffer look at him blankly and say she has no idea what he's talking about. It's just as bad for that staffer to tell him to go and ask one of the people managing the contest. Congratulations, you've just burst that visitor's bubble—or at the very least, lessened his excitement about your brand and his willingness to spread the word about it.

Be Sure People Are Assigned to Keep the Buzz Alive

Remember the story of the Facebook contest that had visitors taking pictures of the company mascot all over Las Vegas? The contest likely never built up any steam because the only people who seemed interested were the few who were participating. No one from the company even acknowledged that a contest was taking place. No one from the company commented on photos or encouraged those who were playing along. Nothing is more discouraging than thinking you just posted the most creative picture ever, something that the company would just love, and then getting absolutely no reaction at all. "What is the point of even doing this anymore?," an attendee might think. Or worse, "Screw them and their stupid contest!" At the very least, those who jumped on board at the beginning of the show will quickly lose interest and word will cease to spread, rendering your promotion completely ineffectual.

The people you assign to encourage those playing along do not even have to be present at the show. They can be back at the office following along online. Just be sure that the employee is enthusiastic about the promotion. His enthusiasm will shine through in his comments. It doesn't even have to take up a lot of his time. You can just ask that employee to log in every couple of hours for 10 minutes and comment on any new pictures being shared. Encourage him to banter back and forth with the participants about their photos in a fun, conversational way. This will keep participants interested in what they are doing and spur them to continue sharing with more friends, so they can show off all the great comments they are receiving for their work.

It is also important that your staff at the show keep the buzz alive by showing enthusiasm in what you are doing even when not working in your booth. Although responsibility should be assigned to specific people, everyone should be encouraged to get involved and the rest of your staff should be having fun with it as well. They are much more likely to be enthused if you show them what you are doing is connected to your goals and objectives, and that it won't interfere with their booth and show responsibilities.

Be Sure It's Legal

What you call your promotion is very important. A *sweepstakes* and a *contest* are legally two very different things. A *sweepstakes* promotion is awarded based on random chance. In a *contest*, though, prizes are awarded based on skill. If booth visitors must first carry out a set of tasks to be entered for a drawing, that is a contest—not a sweepstakes. If you are doing a true sweepstakes drawing, you will need to make sure you have "official rules" in place as required by law. Laws vary from state to state as to what is a contest or a sweepstakes. What is considered a "skill" in California may not be in Pennsylvania. This is not something to be taken lightly. Getting this wrong could put you in violation of the law. Check with your show management and see whether they have any advice or information available. But, as with anything that has legal implications, I suggest you seek the advice of council if you are not absolutely sure about what you are doing.

Rules of the Platforms

When you are using social media in your promotions, it's not just the state and national laws you need to take into consideration; you also need to consider the rules of the social media platform you are using to promote or run your contest. Facebook has specific rules laid out in its Promotions Guidelines (www.facebook.com/promotions_guidelines.php) that prohibits one of the most popular promotions I've seen exhibitors doing—giving out prizes for simply "liking" a page. Facebook guidelines state, "Promotions on Facebook must be administered within Apps on Facebook.com, either on a Canvas Page or an app on a Page Tab." Basically this means, you must use a third-party application to administer all your Facebook contests. You can restrict your contest to those who have first liked your page as long as the promotion is administered through a third-party application. An example of one such app is Wildfire.

Google+ is much stricter. Its rule is basically that you can't conduct contests. Google+ Pages Contest and Promotion Policies (http://bit.ly/googlests) state, "You may not run contests, sweepstakes, offers, coupons, or other such promotions ('Promotion') directly on your Google+ Page." You can, however, post a link to another website or social media platform that is hosting a contest.

Twitter's guidelines (http://bit.ly/twittersts) are definitely more guidelines than rules. In a nutshell, Twitter doesn't want you to encourage people to tweet the same message over and over again. Twitter is trying to prevent spamming. So, you can't tweet, "Get registered to win a free iPad by stopping by booth 182...every RT gets you another entry."

Remember, if your goal is simply brand visibility, then a fun, simple contest that is easy for people to share with their friends is a great way to accomplish that goal. This will drive traffic to your booth, leave a positive impression on your visitors, and spread the word beyond the show floor thanks to the very nature of social media.

Driving Traffic for Qualified Leads

When you are attempting to drive booth traffic to generate qualified leads, your goal should be quality of visitors over quantity. Of course, a large quantity of qualified leads is even better. Creating a strategy that addresses not just an audience at the show but also those not able to attend is well worth the effort. Just keep in mind that these are two different audiences with different needs that you must take into consideration.

In-booth presentations and industry-specific information relating to your product or service will help keep the riffraff out of your booth. Give away an iPad and everyone will show up. Give away a research study released only at the trade show and you'll draw only those interested in that information. If your company sells a product that secures cloud-computing services, a study on security issues in the cloud, and how to avoid them delivered either through a white paper or an in-booth presentation will appeal to your potential customers. Or, you could say someone who finds this information appealing would be a potential customer for your company.

Hands-on product demos will also attract qualified leads to your booth. After all, who's going to spend time on a demo if they have no interest in purchasing that product or service? Don't just talk about your product or show it to booth visitors; let them experience it for themselves. You can say your software is easy to use, but how better to prove that than by handing control over to the prospect?

Let visitors qualify themselves by making a game of it. Create a short game that tests the knowledge of your target audience. Have a series of increasingly difficult questions that only a person with the role you are targeting would know the answers to. People love to show off what they know, and you could easily incorporate a way for them to share their results with others via social media.

Addressing Both the Show Attendees and Your Online Audience

I do not advise making attendees who are interested in this information jump through hoops to get it. To spread the word as widely as possible, you should use multiple social media platforms for your messaging. For research purposes, you should track how people are finding your message. For example, if you are using Twitter, Facebook, Foursquare, YouTube, and your company blog to invite attendees to stop by your booth to get your white paper, you'll want to know which platform is the most effective, which is repetitious, and which is not an effective resource to reach your target audience. This information will tell you a lot about which social media platforms your customers are using; then, you can apply this knowledge to your future efforts.

Do the same thing for the online audience that is not physically at the show. You could make the information available for download after the show opens. Have a way to track where those leads are coming from as well. Of course, it goes without saying that you should collect any information you need in exchange for the information you are passing on to a potential customer.

Whenever you send a tweet encouraging attendees to stop by your booth for access to the information or to see a presentation, be sure to use the show hashtag. Potential customers trying to stay in the loop while not physically present will be following along on the hashtag. You're also going to reach an audience you didn't know existed by tweeting on the show hashtag. Include a link after the show starts for people not at the show or those who just could not make it to your booth to download the white paper or watch the presentation. You could also include your virtual audience members in your game that tests a visitor's knowledge by making it available online. Tie the two together, and those at the show can compete with your virtual audience.

If you are promoting an in-booth presentation, you need to make sure you include presentation times and expert availability in the information you send during the show. If you intend to have a presentation every hour on the hour, then don't tweet that you are having a presentation at 1:00 p.m. in your booth. People might have missed the earlier tweet that had all the times and only see the tweet that says 1:00 p.m. They might have something else going on at 1 p.m. and assume they will have to miss it and move along. However, if you tweet that your next hourly presentation will be at 1:00 p.m. and then again at 2 p.m., 3 p.m., and 4 p.m., those same visitors will know they can catch a presentation that fits in their schedules.

If you are using Facebook or Google+ to pass along information, you'll need to post frequently here as well. Just like Twitter, some people are following hundreds or even thousands of people. Fifteen minutes after you post your message, it is buried in their busy news feeds. Post often but mix in other pieces of valuable information about the show as well. You want people to see your stream and think, "I have to pay attention to these guys; they know what's going on at this show," rather than "Wow, these guys are pushy salespeople who are shoving their product down my throat."

Each social media tool will have its own requirements for posting strategy. Observe how quickly the stream moves along to decide how often you will need to post your information. Think about what your schedule will look like both to attendees who follow many people and those who follow very few. This is why it's important to mix up the information you post. If someone just got on Twitter to follow the show hashtag and is following only a handful of people including your company, what will she see when she views your Twitter stream? Will it be one promotional post after another as far as the page can scroll, or will there be a mix of valuable information along with the promotion?

Engaging Your Live Audience

To make it just that much more enticing to draw people to your booth, have experts on hand in the booth to answer any questions or have a discussion on the topic presented. Remember, two of the reasons people attend a show is to learn new things and to network. Education should not be limited to sessions that might be occurring off the trade show floor. You can educate your audience right in your booth. Having experts available in your booth or an industry thought leader presenting information also satisfies visitors' need to network.

You might not think meeting some of the head programmers or the product manager of one of your software products would be a huge draw, but you'd be surprised. Some programmers are practically rock stars to your customers, and they'd love a chance to meet with them, ask questions, and offer input.

Turn these presentations and Q&A sessions into networking opportunities by promoting them as a time to get together with others in the industry that share their same interests. You could arrange an in-booth tweetup, a LinkedIn event, or a Facebook event for CIOs struggling with data security issues right after a presentation on that subject. Encourage people to drop by and not just hear your solutions to the problem, but learn about what's worked for their peers.

These types of activities don't just attract qualified leads to your booth. You are showing attendees at the show that you are not just there to sell them something. You are there to educate them and help identify and solve their problems. You are also there to connect them to others at the show who might have already walked in their shoes and be able to guide them to a solution to the problems that keep them up at night.

Engaging Your Virtual Audience

Why limit access to those experts to just the attendees visiting your booth in person? Assign someone the role of virtual emcee or moderator and funnel questions from your online audience to your in-booth experts. Or, have experts back at the office answer those questions. I will be covering virtual events in detail a bit later, and talk about just how you enable your virtual audience to ask questions. But for now, I just want you to understand that you are not limited to driving only in-person attendees to your booth. You can also attract those people who could not attend the show to your booth in much the same way. You never know—that person viewing from their office could be about to put together a list of vendors for an upcoming contract. By giving them access to these experts even though they could not attend the show, your company could be included in the bidding process.

If you are going to open questions to your online audience, you need to have someone assigned to monitor whatever platforms you are encouraging people to use to ask questions. Nothing is worse than putting a question out there and having no one hear you. Just like there are slow traffic times on the show floor, there will be lulls during your virtual event. You wouldn't tell your booth staff it's okay to close down early for the day because there are only a few people trickling by. The same goes for your online efforts.

Let's say that during the first four hours you opened questions to your online audience no one asks anything. That doesn't mean that during hour five, one or two questions won't come trickling in. After you've put it out there, you must commit to the program. You're going to hear this repeated often when I talk about the virtual audience. That is because it is something so many companies screw up or don't plan for. It can make or break your online efforts.

You should provide clear and concise instructions for your online audience about how they can access the information or live-streamed presentation. Provide one location where the online attendees can get these instructions, perhaps a page on your corporate site or blog post; then include that link in communications. I find it helpful to include tools that convert time zones so attendees in Kuala Lumpur do not need to figure out what 3 p.m. EST is in their time zone.

Create communications specific to your online audience. Although these communications will likely be seen by all, they will not confuse people who are present at the show. Those at the show just might share them with their co workers who are stuck back at the office and might return to see what they missed if you record the content and offer it on-demand.

Here's a sample tweet:

> Couldn't attend the XYZ show? You can still attend our "cloud computing security" booth presentation via our virtual platform: (*link to instructions*) *#insertshowhashtaghere*

Remember that people who are not attending the show are not just doing so because it's not the right fit for them. There are many different reasons they cannot attend, but they wish they could be there. By bringing a little bit of the show to them, you show that you have not forgotten about them. You will be seen as the company that values its community members even when they are not standing right in front of you. You are recognizing their need for information and the need to connect with others in the industry, and you are providing them access to it.

Summary

Always make sure your show goals inform your strategy for driving traffic to your booth. Don't get caught up in quantity if it's quality leads you are looking for. Think about who your customers are and what you can provide that would be valuable to them. A research study might not be sexy, but if your potential customers put a high value on that, then it's the right thing to give. Using social media as part of your strategy will help increase the number of leads you get both at the show and from those who were not able to attend but were also interested. Create experiences that get the attendees actively involved in qualifying themselves. Create experiences they want to share with others at the show and those who are back in the office.

One of the biggest reasons leads are not followed up on is because they are poor-quality leads. Try to imagine yourself as the salesperson assigned to follow up on 75 leads after a show. You call the first 10 and find that they are bad leads. The people you've called were only interested in entering your contest to win an iPad. The "lead" has no use for your services or product. The other 65 leads will go on the back burner while you get back to calling on your real potential customers.

10

Be THE Source
for Content

The best networkers are the ones who can provide valuable information to others. They are the ones who can connect people to what they are looking for. Good content is nothing more than valuable information. Trade shows are filled with valuable information, and social media allows you to share that information in real time with show attendees and those who could not attend the show. While you are sharing information, you're constantly driving traffic to your site or social media platforms and keeping your company's name at the top of live and virtual attendees' minds.

A year ago, I very much wanted to attend an industry event but could not because of another obligation. The conference used a hashtag on Twitter, so I followed along whenever I could via the hashtag. One person tweeted snippets of information all throughout the conference sessions. Even though I wasn't in attendance, I got the highlights of many of the speakers through these tweets. He was doing such a good job of summarizing, I paid attention to only his tweets. I found his information so helpful that I started telling others to follow him to stay informed. See how information spreads?

I was impressed but unfamiliar with this person, so I checked his Twitter profile and then followed the link to his company's website. Tweeting great conference content compelled me to dig deeper and find out who he was. When I checked out his website, I found that his company provides services I might be in need of one day. I reached out to the person tweeting to find out more about what he does. Jump ahead a year later and I am contracting with him and his company on a conference I'm producing. It's not because he tweeted, but it's the content of his tweets that caught my attention.

What Is Content?

Wikipedia defines *content* (in reference to media) as

> **Content** is information and experiences that may provide value for an end-user/audience in specific contexts. Content may be delivered via any medium such as the Internet, television, and audio CDs, as well as live events such as conferences and stage performances. The word is used to identify and quantify various formats and genres of information as manageable value-adding components of media.

Personally, I prefer the simplicity of the *Oxford English Dictionary* that defines *content* as "what is contained." Anything and everything that is information can be content. Social media is just providing us with more and more ways to deliver that information than we've ever had before. Social media also makes it easy for others to share your content.

Think about your favorite magazine, newspaper, television show, or radio broadcast. There was a time when we had very limited ways of sharing our favorite stories. We could clip an article from a magazine and mail it to co-workers. We could record a favorite television show and invite friends over to watch the recording. If something interesting on the news had not been recorded, you had to rely on others to summarize it for you.

Today, even your local news channel does not rely on its live broadcast to deliver the news. You can go online to the station's website and watch or listen to live news coverage. The website delivers stories via text, video, and photos. I no longer have to turn on my TV to catch the weather and traffic reports. I can access that information any time I want online. If I'm reading an article I think others might find interesting, the news outlet has provided me with several ways to share it with a simple click of the mouse. I can follow the channel on Twitter and Facebook to get the latest news. I can easily email the writer of a story and tell her what I think. Sometimes I can even share my opinions with anyone else reading the story through a comment feature. I can not only look up stories I missed on this morning's broadcast, but can also find stories that are months or even years old and watch them for the first time.

So don't think of content simply as a blog post or white paper. Don't think sharing is limited to one or two social media platforms. Content is delivered via pictures, tweets, video, and the spoken word. It can be shared via a link in an email, which gets posted on Facebook as well as tweeted. The more forms you create your content in, the better because everyone has a preferred format. I love to read and prefer text to audio and video, while others find they retain information better when it's delivered via video.

During the strategic planning process, you may have decided to limit your social media outreach to just LinkedIn because that's where your audience was—and that is perfectly fine. But make sure you are not just posting text. Mix in some videos, photographs, and even podcasts. This way, each person in your community will be able to access your content in the way she most prefers to consume it.

Show organizers love when exhibitors and attendees create and share content gleaned from their show. Every time you post a video or write a blog post or tweet, you're spreading the news of their show and are helping them build a wider audience. I often feature exhibitors' blogs, photos, and podcasts on my event sites, which in turn gives them a wider audience.

What's In It for You?

Every single thing you do on social media needs to have a purpose. But not every single thing you post on social media will result in a sale, and that's okay. But it is a step in the right direction. Someone who reads your post on gluten-free dining options might not pick up the phone and buy something from you. But, he may be compelled to take a closer look at your company and stop by your booth. With everything you post, you are building your online reputation and creating touch points with your customers and prospects. People begin to form an impression of what kind of company yours is, one that is interested in its customers. Will all this get more people to your booth?

Maybe it will and maybe it won't. Again, today's trade shows are not just a shopping mall that is open for three days each year. It's not just a place where sales are made and contracts are signed. It's a place where you build relationships and educate your customers and potential customers. No longer are today's attendees confined to the space of the convention center. Your potential customers can be popping in and out of the show via social media from hundreds of miles away.

Sure, part of what you are doing is in an attempt to drive traffic to your booth, but in the bigger scheme of things, you are driving traffic to your brand and then hopefully making a sale. All eyes are on you, looking to you for information. All ears are on you, listening for what is going on at the show and in the industry. And it's okay to have a little fun, too.

Local Inside Information

Attendees at a trade show are usually in town for a few days. They might need to know things like who has the best coffee around, where they can get a new shirt because they spilled their coffee on the one they packed, where they can find gluten-free meal options, the best places for dinner, the best karaoke bar, at what time the hotel fitness center is the least crowded, and more. While these things have absolutely nothing to do with your company or your customers' day-to-day job, they do have something to do with your customers' personality and needs.

I cannot say enough to emphasize that social media is social. Throwing in a tip on where to get gluten-free muffins or dinner recommendations only takes a few seconds but could make you some new friends among your community. It also gives your company's Twitter account some personality. It shows attendees that your company is worth following for good information that's not just self-promotion.

Trade Show Floor Reporting

Your staffers are going to be walking the show floor, so why not have them tweet information on what they are seeing. Obviously, you'd prefer they not tweet what your competitors are doing, but there are plenty of vendors who are not competitors that your customers might find valuable. If you see something new and different, why not share it? Even those not able to attend the show can find this type of information interesting, especially if they consider you, or are beginning to consider you, a trusted resource.

If your company has preferred partners who are also exhibiting at the show, share information about what they are doing in their booths. This not only builds your reputation with your customers, but your partners as well. If exhibitors are doing presentations in their booth that your customers should see, share the presentation times, topics, and the booth number. Suggest they stop by your booth before or after that particular presentation.

Session and Speaker Highlights

Tweet reminders of session times and locations for topics that might be of interest to your customers. You should definitely tweet reminders of sessions your company will be participating in. This kind of information can be shared in the weeks leading up to the show to help attendees plan their day. It can also be shared during the show as reminders of where they need to be and when.

Also be sure to have someone from your company in those sessions tweeting pertinent pieces of information that are being shared. Just pick someone who can listen and type at the same time. Personally, I'm hopeless at this. I blame my age. Attendees who had an interest in that session but could not attend because of a conflict will be thankful for the information. Those not at the event but following along via social media will appreciate these types of highlights and the benefit you are providing.

I specifically mention using Twitter because more and more shows are promoting their Twitter hashtags. But this same information could be posted on a show's Facebook page and LinkedIn group.

Blog Session Summaries and Posts on Company Site

Session summaries are valuable to people both attending the show in person and virtually. People often have to miss sessions they want to attend because there's another session at the same time. Assign someone or a couple of employees to sit in on sessions you think would be most interesting to your customer base. Have them take notes of the sessions' highlights and key ideas and then post them on your company's blog, Facebook page, and Google+ account. These don't have to be lengthy commentaries; simple key thoughts and takeaways are good enough. No one has to have any particular training to do this. All a person needs is login information (in some situations); a template to follow is helpful (specify what info is needed, such as session title, speaker's name or panelists' names, session date and time, and blogger byline). Get these posted as soon as possible to maintain relevancy, and spread the link to the information through all the social media channels you are using.

Share Through Podcasts

One of my favorite podcasters is Mike McAllen from Grass Shack Events & Media (http://bit.ly/grassshack). He interviews people in the events industry, and his podcasts run anywhere from about 10 to 30 minutes long. The vibe that comes out of his podcast interviews is of two people chatting over a cup of coffee or, in some cases, over a beer. They are not performing so much as you, the listener, is eavesdropping on a conversation. How does he do it? He asks great questions that hit on the inter-viewee's passion and then lets her talk. He often interviews conference organizers about upcoming events or does an event wrap-up once it's over.

You can do the same thing as an exhibitor at an event. Trade show organizers are always looking for ways to promote their event, and I think you'll find them very willing to record a podcast with you. But don't wait until a week before the show when they are way too busy—and so are you, quite frankly. A podcast can be recorded months in advance and posted whenever you want.

You could also do short interviews with your customers who are attending the show, asking them what they hope to get out of the show. Or if they are return-ing from last year, ask them why. Take a look at the education agenda and con-tact some of the speakers. You can do quick teaser interviews with them on what attendees can expect to learn during their sessions. You should do this with any sessions your company is presenting.

You don't have to focus only on the show in general. Why not do some podcasts with members of your company talking about what visitors to your booth will get to see or people they will get to meet?

You may be asking what's in it for me? Why should I put all that time and effort into promoting the show or various sessions? Shouldn't I be focusing on my booth? Remember, you are not just doing this as a one-time marketing push. You are in it for the long haul to get the best return on your investment. You have to get the push advertising mentality out of your head. Instead, see what you are doing as becoming a go-to-source for information that is relevant to your booth visitor. And not just any booth visitor, but potential customers and current cus-tomers you don't want jumping ship to your competition.

And if you can't see the value in that, there is always the numbers game. More qualified attendees at the show means a bigger pool of attendees whom you can convert into booth visitors. Ask just about any trade show organizers and they will tell you that some of the best quality attendees come from exhibitor referrals.

Also keep in mind that if your content is good and considered valuable to your target audience, they are likely to share it with people who are just like them. If you host those podcasts on your website, Facebook page, or LinkedIn group, more eyes and ears are going to be heading there for a look or listen. They just might get curious and stick around to see what else you have to offer. More importantly, they might put you on their must-see exhibitors list for the show.

Tell a Story Using Aggregated Content

During an event, attendees, exhibitors, the show organizer, speakers, bloggers, and the media are all sharing content using many different social media platforms. But not every person you are trying to reach is on every social media platform that is being used, and they might be missing out on great information. To ensure that no one misses out on the most valuable information, you can pull it all together and put it in one convenient place—your blog or company website.

You can summarize the highlights of the day's events or narrow it down to just your company's information. All day long people are tweeting, uploading pictures to Flickr and videos to YouTube, writing blog posts, and updating their Facebook statuses. Most of this great content gets lost because of sheer volume. You can create a day's summary by aggregating the best content across many forms (photos, blog posts, videos, status updates, and so on). Think of it as the event highlight reel that you share with your community, which your community is likely to spread.

It seems that as more and more companies are jumping on the social media bandwagon, more and more people are creating great applications that enhance social media. Some of these applications make aggregating content a breeze. One example is Storify, an application that lets you easily create a story by pulling in information from many social media channels. You simply drag and drop content into place and add some text around it. Storify pulls from public content and attributes the creator so there are no copyright worries. It's very important that you give attribution to the creator of the original content. It's not just the right thing to do; it also entices the original creators to share your story with their social media connections.

Tell a Story Through Video

I love the potential of video content because it can be entertaining or informative, and it can be both at the same time. People love videos, and they are very sharable via social media. The key to creating a good social media video is an infectious and engaging personality that comes across on camera. Videos are conversational and should feature someone your audience can relate to. If you have a product you want to demonstrate, you should show, not tell.

A great demonstration of show not tell is the Gibbon Slacklines video created at the Outdoor Retailer show in 2010. Gibbon's website describes slacklining as "the act of balancing along a narrow, flexible piece of webbing usually low to the ground." It started as balance training for climbers but is growing in popularity as an activity on its own.

You will notice three distinct things in the video. One is that no one is speaking. It is simply a series of product demonstrations that are more descriptive than any words can be. Second, it features real people performing on the slacklines; some are really good at it and some are not so good. Some people fall off the slackline, and that's okay. That's going to happen in real life and it's pretty funny, so they don't just feature the perfect runs. Third, it's short, clocking in at less than three minutes long. This is exactly the kind of video that people love to share because it's fun, entertaining, and a bit unusual. Check it out at http://bit.ly/slacklines.

Maybe you sell a product or service that is not quite as exciting as a Gibbon Slackline. You can still create a compelling video that speaks to your audience both at the show and with viewers at home. Kodak did just this at Graph Expo 2011. Their video, "Kodak at Graph Expo 2011—CompuMail Wins Benny Award for Dimensional Print Application," (http://bit.ly/compumail) is a great example of creating a customer testimonial video.

This two-and-a-half-minute video has key components that have nothing to do with production cost and can be re-created with an inexpensive video camera. The first component is that the customer is real and someone the audience can relate to. The customer is doing all the talking, and it sounds genuine and non-scripted. Second, the video shows not tells. When the customer refers to the printed piece he created, the video camera focused on that printed piece. Third, the customer is not talking in general terms about the Kodak product. He is specifically talking about how he used it and how it helps his business grow. He tells stories about what his customers say about the product he produces as a result of using Kodak's printer.

Finding good examples of video content at a trade show is not easy. I searched for an hour and a half and suffered through some of the most boring self-promotional videos I've ever seen. I watched product demos in which the cameraman kept the lens on the demonstrator's face instead of the product. I saw many key executives talking about "me, me, me" instead of their customers. I heard more marketing speak than anyone should be exposed to. I saw videos that claimed to be hilarious but instead were just extremely boring. I watched customer interviews that looked promising but were pointless because the sound quality was so poor. Many were nothing more than a commercial.

A good video should have the following attributes:

- It should be representative of your customer.
- It should engage the viewer and be informative.
- It should be shorter than five minutes (break it into sections if it is longer).
- It should feature the product if it is a product demo.
- It should show, not tell.
- It should have a clear call to action at the end.
- It should include keyword tags so people can find it when searching the Internet.

I stumbled on a video about six months ago that was produced by an exhibitor using his smartphone video camera or Flipcam. It was a video of a very enthusiastic customer who stopped by the booth to tell them how much he loved their durable phone cases. This customer improvised a testimonial and dance right there in the booth, and it was not staged (http://bit.ly/otterboxvideo). It's important to mention that I came across this video when I was searching for cases for my iPhone. I was not an attendee at that show, yet their repurposed content reached me a year after they posted it.

What other types of content make great videos?

- Attendees talking about why they decided to attend the conference.
- Attendees talking about what they are learning and the value they are getting from the conference.
- Attendees discussing why people not at the conference should attend next year.
- Exhibitors or partners discussing what their companies can do for attendees and how they work with each customer.
- Speakers sharing additional details, insights, or thoughts about their presentations.
- A "question of the day" that attendees answer—you can then use it to create a montage of all the answers.

Remember, it's okay to have fun—especially with that last suggestion. You can ask people which session was the best or who their favorite speaker was. You can also ask people what the best meal was that they had during the conference. Ask them what kind of pet they have and post a psychographic profile of your industry leaders and their pets. I would suggest tacking this question on at the end of an interview or at the very beginning because you'll probably want to get more information from them than just their pet preference.

A note about comedy: Comedy is very difficult to pull off. Many companies that try to produce something comedic end up with content that falls flat. But then other companies nail it and their videos go viral. I wish I had the secret formula to what is funny. If you're not sure, then it's best to stick with fun and forego funny. I recently received an email from a company announcing five hilarious holiday messages. Each video was a "funny" message or skit from one of their employees. The employees could barely get through the two-minute video without bursting into laughter. I didn't even chuckle. You cannot make a viral video; you can only make a video that might or might not go viral.

Create a Photo Log of the Event

Photos might not help position your company's executive team as thought leaders, but they will add a bit of fun for everyone. People who are attending the show can check to see whether they are in any of your photos, and those not at the event can live vicariously through them. Creating a photo log of an event is as simple as posting pictures on a photo sharing site like Snapfish, Flickr, Photobucket, or Facebook. This can be a good tactic if you are doing a booth activity that involves photos because you'll already have attendees actively sharing them and spreading the word.

Many people love sharing photos of themselves with friends, so make sure when you post them that it's easy for viewers to do this. Photo sharing sites already have sharing tools or the ability to "tag" people built in to them, which makes your job much easier. After you've uploaded the photos, let people know through the social media channels you are using with a simple, "Hey, check out some fun photos from last night's opening party! Do you recognize anyone?"

Give these photos a once-over before posting. Just as you probably don't want unflattering pictures of yourself floating around the Internet, neither do your customers. Stick to the rule of "when in doubt—leave it out." Because photos are so widely shared, two things you need to take into consideration are permission and branding.

Permission

In these days of social media, everyone is taking pictures and posting them everywhere and anywhere. People assume now that any photo is fair game. How many times have friends posted pictures of you on Facebook that you wish they would not have posted? I like to err on the side of ultra-safe when posting event photos. If I have a photographer taking close-ups of people I intend to post, I ask the photographer to tell her subjects what the photos will be used for, ask for verbal permission, and then show the photos to the person right then and there on the digital camera and get his okay. I also ask her to delete the photo on the spot if it is not okay. If I am posting the photos online, I have the photographer pass out cards with the web address of where the photos will be posted.

Taking pictures in your own booth is one thing, but taking them at sponsored events or elsewhere on the show floor or conference space during the trade show and posting them online is another thing. A convention center or event space being rented by the show organizer is considered private property. You need to ask permission of the show organizer before taking photos and posting them online.

Let the organizer know exactly how you intend to use them. Want to turn the show organizer into a good friend? Offer to let him use any photos he particularly likes for next year's promotion.

Branding

If you want all those great pictures you took to be associated with your company no matter where they end up on the Internet, you should use a watermark. A *watermark* is a faint logo or text that appears on the photo. If used properly, it will not take away from the photo itself.

You can use programs like Photoshop to put watermarks on your photos. There are also inexpensive plug-ins for Apple's iPhoto and Windows Live Photo Gallery that let you add watermarks in batches. You can find several good, inexpensive software programs that let you add watermarks to 100 photos in just five minutes.

Include a Call to Action

Every piece of content you create must have a clear and concise call to action. It can be as simple as "Come visit us at booth #182" or "Visit us on our website.com for more information about our Widget 2000." A great call to action at the end of a customer interview would be, "If you'd like information about how you can receive the same benefits that John at XYZ Co. got from partnering with us, contact one of our customer service representatives at 800.888.1234 or visit us on the web at website.com."

But note that if you are asking for a specific call to action, you need to send people to a specific place. If you want them to contact a salesperson or pre-sales support on a specific product, don't just send them to your home page. Send them to that product's info page on your website or a special landing page you have created just for that particular call to action. This will help you track how effective the content was in compelling people to take action.

Do not make the mistake of thinking that everything you do should be done only if it drives traffic to your booth. Getting visitors to your booth is not the end goal. Getting visitors to become customers is why you are at the show. Your trade show program is just one piece of your company's marketing mix. What is important is that everything you do takes you one step closer to a sale. Sometimes that step is just getting your name out there and making people aware of who you are. The content you share via social media allows you to create a personality for your company and it builds trust.

Summary

When creating content, mix it up. Content isn't just text on a page; it's video, audio, and pictures, as well. Content can be in-depth coverage of a session or just a few tweets of key sound bites. It can also be entertaining, for educational purposes, or even both at the same time through the use of podcasts, video interviews, and photo logs. By aggregating content, you can use what others create to tell a story of the event. Content can also be helpful as we saw with local inside information.

Social media is all about sharing information. By creating information that others want to share, you extend your presence beyond your booth. You are creating an opportunity for those unable to attend the show to catch a glimpse of what is happening.

11

Capture the Bloggers' Attention

It's time to put any misperceptions you might have about bloggers aside. There was a time when bloggers were generally thought of as out-of-work twentysomethings living in their parents' basements typing away in their pajamas. I'm sure there are some of those people out there, but it does not accurately represent the majority of bloggers today. Today, bloggers cover all industries and are of different, ages, education levels, and skill levels. Some are unemployed, some get paid for their blogging, and some are employed full-time and do their blogging on the side. Many have built very successful businesses from their efforts.

Sure, some bloggers might be opinionated whack jobs, but others are highly respected in their communities. I laugh sometimes at my husband when he says "bloggers" with distain. I laugh because he's constantly referring favorably to things he has read on The Huffington Post. The Huffington Post is one giant blog with many, many contributing bloggers. I also like to remind him that I have a blog and am therefore a blogger. But I have to admit at times I do roll my eyes when I hear "I'm a blogger"—after all, isn't everyone these days?

And therein lies the great news. So many people are blogging and every industry segment has a blog or two or three or a hundred. You don't just have traditional media to turn to; to get your word out, you have all these bloggers as well. Don't dismiss bloggers as not worth the effort because you think they don't have the reach that traditional media does. Why would you not pay attention to someone who wants to write about your new product because he only has 50 loyal subscribers? Are you doing so well that you don't need those 50 people to buy your product or service? I cannot think of even one salesperson who would not want 50 new clients.

The number of subscribers means less and less on the Internet. Although only 50 people might get that blog delivered to their inboxes or RSS feeds, the content is on the Web and searchable indefinitely. Subscriber numbers become irrelevant because the true reach is so much more than a few dedicated readers.

How Do You Get Bloggers to Your Booth?

We've already talked about reaching out to the bloggers you are targeting by contacting them directly and through the use of social media press releases. The social media press releases might even fall into the hands of interested bloggers you didn't know about. But remember, some bloggers do this as a hobby, so they don't have the financial backing of a large media empire. They might not be in a position to fly all over the country to cover industry trade shows. If there is someone you really want at the show to cover your product launch, you might consider paying her way.

There is absolutely nothing wrong with doing this. The Federal Trade Commission (FTC) blog disclosure regulations require those who write articles or reviews of products or services on the Internet to disclose, in a "clear and conspicuous" manner, any free products or payments they receive for these reviews (http://www.ftc.gov). This means that if you pay a blogger's way to the show and she writes a review about your product launch, she will have to disclose the fact that you paid her way. Personally, I don't have an issue with this. Basically, you have a financial agreement that you are paying for a blogger to attend an event and in exchange she will write about you and your company.

What I do have an issue with is demanding the blogger write something positive about you. The loyal following that blogger has that you want access to is loyal because her followers trust her. They trust that she is going to give her honest opinion. This isn't unbiased investigative journalism trying to get at the truth. This is a blogger with an opinion and an audience, and that's why you invited her. Let her give her opinion. If you have a good, quality product or service, you shouldn't have to worry about what she'll post in her blog.

Her post might not be all sunshine and roses, but what counts is the overall content. Just make sure your boss understands there are no guarantees and gives his consent based on that fact up front. Get management to sign off on the deal, understanding that there is the potential for this blogger to write something less than flattering. You can always turn posts that contain criticism into a positive by commenting on the post, asking the blogger and her readers how you can improve. If your bosses can't deal with the possibility of negative comments or criticisms, then don't pay for the trip. That could definitely come back to bite you.

Also, other bloggers will be wandering around the trade show who you never knew existed. Reaching out to them is easy. As bloggers, they are sure to be active on social media. Just include them by creating specific messaging that speaks to them. When you tweet about your product launch at the show, tack on "bloggers welcome." But don't just invite them to the educational stuff you are doing in your booth. Invite them to the parties you are hosting as well. When bloggers write about an event, they don't take the evenings off; they love to write about everything. I would encourage you to add "bloggers welcome" to any message you send whether it be via social media or print.

Checking Blogger Credentials

Journalists are used to this procedure. Almost all shows require journalists and now bloggers to apply to receive press credentials. Keep in mind you're not putting on a concert here, so don't worry about swarms of bloggers taking up all your space. You're inviting attendees who happen to blog into your booth to view a demo, presentation, or product launch. You'd most likely want them there anyway. But, perhaps you are hosting a party for qualified buyers and it's by invitation only. Opening that up to anyone who's a blogger might get you a lot of people there you didn't really want, including people without purchasing power or purchasing influence or even some of your competitors.

Instead, you could announce that your company is giving out a limited number of passes to industry bloggers. You can make your credentialing process as simple as asking the blogger to send you links to his three most recent posts. Or just ask him to submit the link to his blogs and have someone look it over to see whether inviting him is worth it. I would avoid doing this piece-meal. Give a date when all submissions must be in, and then let the bloggers know the date when they will be notified. Emphasize that you only have a limited amount of media passes. This way, when you notify someone that she is not getting a pass, it's not so much you rejecting her as it is her not getting lucky.

How do you handle someone who shows up at your booth at the last minute and says he is a well-respected industry blogger and he'd love to have a pass to your party? Again, I don't like rejecting people straight out. You don't want to get flamed on someone's blog because you told him he couldn't come to your party. Ask him for the name of his blog, tell him you're going to have to check whether there are any more passes left, and suggest he return in an hour. Now you have time to check out his blog and find out whether he is a key opinion leader in your industry with thousands of loyal readers. On the other hand, he could write one post every four months that only his mother comments on. When he comes back, you can either tell him he's in luck and you can get him in, or tell him you're completely out of media passes—if only he'd submitted earlier.

Making the Bloggers Comfortable

You've welcomed the bloggers into your booth; now you have to make them *feel* welcome. The best way to do that is to provide them with their basic needs. For most people, that is food, water, and shelter. For a blogger, that is power—the electrical kind. And maybe even a place to set down their laptops so they can take notes. Remember, not all bloggers at the show will have access to the media room set up by the trade show organizers. By providing them with a place to charge up during your presentation, you are making a huge gesture of respect and of welcoming.

The Blog Bar

If you are doing in-booth presentations and want to accommodate the press and bloggers, then you need to include them in your booth design. They do not need much. A 14-inch deep bar that accommodates four or five laptops is a great start. Build it at the right height so that an average person can stand and type. Make sure you have power available for bloggers to plug in and recharge their equipment while they are at your booth. Having an assortment of phone chargers and an iPad charger never hurts either. This is another goodwill gesture that will be noticed. And it's not good just for the bloggers coming to your presentation. It's great to offer other visitors a charging station. I'll talk to anyone about their service offering for 10 minutes if it means I can get an extra boost of battery life.

Don't put your blogger bar at the back of your presentation area. Place it close to the stage so bloggers and media delegates can get a good view of everything. Be sure to have good lighting so they can shoot any pictures they might want during the presentation. I personally don't believe you need to make sure your logo is everywhere just in case a picture gets taken. Your booth is there for your visitors, not for the camera. Cluttering your booth with your logo everywhere looks desperate and will distract from what you are showcasing. Don't worry, though, your product and company will be mentioned in the writer's blog post and most likely in a photo caption so there will be no confusion.

Press Material

Be sure to provide the media and your bloggers with all the information they will need. I like to give them a packet that includes a small headshot and a short bio that includes the presenter's name, title, and role in presentation. This information is on a printed sheet and can be very helpful to the blogger. This way, when the expert is speaking, the bloggers can quickly refer to their sheet and get the pertinent information they need to make notes or send a tweet. I can't tell you how many times I wanted to tweet what someone said during a presentation, but I either couldn't remember his name and title or didn't know how to spell it. Having that sheet is a huge help, though most people often won't realize it until they actually need it.

That packet can also contain some print material for reference, but remember that these folks will be using computers so printed pieces are just for reference. Create a special media page on your site that you can refer them to specifically for information for each presentation happening in your booth. Include the link to that page on your printed materials.

That web page can also include links to anything else they might need from other parts of your site, but they should be able to start in one place to find everything. Writers might want access to:

- Boilerplate company information
- Company logo (low- and high-resolution versions)
- Executive team bios and pictures
- Product photos (low- and high-resolution versions)
- Social media press releases
- Product or service videos
- Fact sheets
- Relevant quotes from experts or company employees
- Contact information for specific staff members and their areas of expertise
- General press contact

By putting this information all in one spot, the writer—whether blogger or traditional media—does not have to hunt anything down and can get the story out quickly.

What information should you provide? Use common sense. I'm sure you've read blogs and know what you like to read. Would you want to read two pages of someone's marketing brochure? I didn't think so. So give these writers the meat of the information. Give them information on how your product or service is going to actually change your customers' lives. That's what they want to write about.

Prepping the Speakers

Let's say you are doing a product launch at the show, and it's a pretty big deal. You're likely to have several bloggers and journalists there as well as a nice crowd of show attendees. If you are expecting a big crowd, I suggest you assign someone the job of press handler if your PR department has not already taken care of this. After the announcement, the writers are likely to have a lot of questions—but so do your customers. And you never want your customers to take a back seat to anyone.

If you know your announcement is going to be huge, then you should have a separate press conference just for the media to avoid this circus. But, if your announcement does not fall into the same category as the launch of the newest iPhone, then a press handler and some speaker instruction might be all you need.

Let the speaker know where the press will be located if they have a special area. Let him know that bloggers might be there live blogging, and tell him where they will be. In addition, tell him not to speak to the media but to his audience of customers. I see a lot of speakers get overwhelmed when they see a camera in the room and start talking directly to the person with the camera, forgetting to look at the audience. Your announcement, if on the show floor, is to your customers first and foremost. Don't worry—the press is getting what they need. The speaker need only treat the camera as another audience member and make eye contact occasionally. There's plenty of time for photo opportunities after the announcement.

Give the media representatives a heads-up before the presentation or announcement that the speaker will be taking questions from the customer audience first. That information packet is a great place to put this tidbit. After that, the press will have the opportunity to ask any questions they might have. You could also take the press to a space away from your presentation area where they could address their questions to other staff members. Then you can bring in your executives for the photo ops after the audience questions are finished.

Product Demo for Bloggers

If a blogger or member of the press wants to get a private hands-on demo of your product or talk at length about your service, you might want to schedule it before the show floor opens or after it closes. Although the blogger's attention is desirable, you never want it to come at the expense of quality time with your customer or prospect.

An even better alternative would be to get that writer to observe a demo you are giving to a customer. Ask that customer to give her consent to the writer to be photographed and quoted for the article. Any good writer would prefer to write about the customer's experience over his own.

Blogger Bar in Sessions

If you are presenting any sessions or participating in any panel or round-table discussions as part of the conference education, be sure to invite your blogger friends there as well. Again, you want them to feel welcome. I like to bring a power strip or two with me to any sessions I am conducting and give them to bloggers to use. This shows them I'm open to the idea of them live blogging my presentation. If the room is set up with rounds, half-rounds, or classroom-style, I turn the back row of tables into the blogger zone. Sometimes I'll even post a sign that says "reserved for bloggers." If I have to do my presentation with a theater or auditorium setup, I always ask for at least one table in the back of the room to accommodate the bloggers' computers and mobile devices. If you want to try this out at your next session, be sure to let the show organizer know how you want the room set up. You can't expect them to bring in tables five minutes before your session starts.

Your presenters should mingle with the bloggers prior to the session just as they would the rest of the audience members. Have your speaker tell the bloggers that she will be available to answer any questions they have after the presentation. Remember, the presenter's main focus is not the media. It's the people who paid a lot of money to attend the trade show, including your company's customers. Their questions should be answered first. Mingling with the audience before your presentation will let you know whether a blogger is also a potential customer.

Have your company's presenters include a slide with a link to their LinkedIn pages. This way, any bloggers in the room will be able to access the correct spelling of their names, their titles, and their bios as well as a picture if they want it. Sure, they can go to your company page, but the specific presenter information might not be there or could be hard to find.

If your presenter is part of a panel, be sure to hand out this information to the bloggers in the room. Let's say one of your company employees is on a panel with several of your competitors. The printed session guide might have your presenter's name and title, but that's about it. All the blogger has at hand to write is "James Smith, VP of Research and Design of XYZ company, said..." Now imagine if he has access to Smith's LinkedIn profile at his fingertips, but none of the other speakers' profiles. There is a chance James Smith could be featured more prominently in the article.

Sponsor a Show Blogger Zone

Consider sponsoring a blogger zone on the show floor. This is a win-win for everyone, and the show organizer will love it because it draws more media attention to their show. It's also added value for all their exhibitors so they can use it as another benefit when selling booth space. It gives your company even more exposure to bloggers because now you are the company who is making their job easier. Your company will be seen as one who is friendly to bloggers and treats them with respect.

The sponsorships that are available at a trade show are not just the ones listed on the sponsorship marketing information. I guarantee that if you have a good idea for something you want to sponsor, the show organizers want to hear about it. Don't be afraid to reach out and pitch your idea. Show them how it benefits not just your company, but the attendees and the show as well.

The blogger zone could be plush, or it could be just a larger version of your in-booth blogger bar. The show will have a press room for credentialed press, but what about all those attendees who have blogs but who might not be credentialed? This area needs only a few things to accommodate bloggers:

- Set it up in the middle of the show floor. Bloggers don't want to be off in a corner; they want to see what's going on all around them.
- Provide plenty of power outlets.
- Provide Wi-Fi access. Make sure that when the space is designed, it can accommodate a large number of devices all at one time. Bring in special equipment and provide the bloggers using the area with their own password to access the Wi-Fi connection.
- Provide a few hardwired Ethernet drops as well in case anyone is uploading a larger amount of data. Streaming media and video is popular with bloggers. This can take up a lot of bandwidth and overload the Wi-Fi option.
- Provide plenty of different seating and working options. An area with couches and chairs and low tables as well as stand-up bars works very well.

- Include a Twitter wall/fall for up-to-the minute information about must-see events happening on the trade show floor (a flat-screen displaying the Twitter feed of the show hashtag) is a great idea.

Because you are sponsoring the area, your branding should be prominent. But this might or might not be your own private area. Other vendors may have access to it. The show might even want to use this area for presenters and other sponsors and exhibitors to meet with bloggers. The point of this area is to create an environment beneficial to bloggers. Demanding that no other vendors have access to this area can backfire on you and might not be something the show is interested in providing.

You might wonder why you need to let other vendors have access to an area you sponsor. A sponsorship must do three things. It must first benefit the sponsor and give the company exposure to its desired audience. Second, it must be a benefit to the show organizer by enabling them to do something special their audience will appreciate. Third, it must enhance the show experience for the attendees. You can work out the logistics of who will have access to the area and when with the show organizer. My recommendation would be to set up a reception desk (which could be staffed with a representative from your company in a logoed shirt) where you check credentials of bloggers. Bloggers who want to invite vendors and attendees into the area would have to sign them in at specific times. This would eliminate your competitors from hanging out in the blogger zone all day.

What About Microbloggers?

The statement "everyone is a blogger these days" is a slight exaggeration, but not so much if you add microblogging to the mix. Microblogs such as Twitter and Tumblr, and even Facebook with its status updates and Google+, leaves out almost no one. During any presentation your company is giving—whether it's in your booth or in a session—someone might be microblogging.

It's good to get in the habit of including short sound bites that are 140 characters or less. I know many presenters who create special slides which include a quote they want the audience to tweet during their presentations. They put the quote, hashtag, and their name on the screen just the way they'd expect someone to tweet it. Speakers will also place their Twitter handle and the show hashtag on the bottom of every slide so everything they say has the potential to become a tweetable moment.

Example: "Include your Twitter handle and show hashtag on the bottom of every slide" @TraciBrowne #thesocialtradeshow

Example: "Social media is not a marketing tool—it's a communication tool" @TraciBrowne #EXHIBITOR2012

But it's not just Twitter. Some audience members include information like this in their Facebook status updates, and some write mini posts on Tumblr or in Google+. So, why not make it easy for them to get the correct information? It reduces the chance you will be misquoted and helps spread your message accurately.

Summary

The good news is that social media gives everyone a voice. (In some instances, that's also the bad news of social media.) Social media and bloggers will spread your message throughout the show and beyond to those who are not attending. Have a system in place to verify media and blogger credentials to weed out the freebie seekers who do not have an audience you want to reach. If you want to make sure a certain blogger is in attendance, consider paying her way to the show.

Make it easy for these bloggers to spread the word about your company and products and services. Invite them into your presentations and make sure they have what they need to do their job. Supply them with electrical power, Internet access, and your blogger-enhanced media kit in your booth for presentations, but also in any session rooms where you are presenting.

Bloggers crave the same respect and attention traditional media gets, and they often deserve it. Don't try to control what they write because that could come back to bite you.

12

Create Engaging
Video Interviews

Video interviews create tons of valuable content that can be repurposed in many ways and shared via social media to a wider virtual audience to extend the length of the show. One interview can be cut and edited to serve many purposes, and a trade show is a treasure trove of interesting interviewees. You can interview customers, potential customers, your key executives, employees, other vendors, association representatives, industry thought leaders, and even the media. Informational interviews will help satisfy the attendees' desire for information and education and can also expose them to new industry trends and products.

A three-minute interview with a customer can be broken down into ideas for future products that can be passed along to research and development. Passing on valuable information to other departments in your company creates internal advocates for your trade show program. An interview with a customer might also generate rave reviews of a recent purchase that can be posted on YouTube and embedded into your company website. That review could be what leads a potential customer to sign on the dotted line. Ask interviewees on the show floor why they think other attendees should come visit your booth. Those clips can be quickly posted on YouTube and sent via social media channels during the show. But before we get into the interview content, let's talk about the physical piece of the puzzle.

The Right Equipment

These days anyone with a smartphone has the capability of producing videos. Some work much better than others. My old iPhone 3GS did not shoot great videos. The lighting had to be very bright, and even then it was quite grainy and the sound quality was bad. My husband's Android shoots surprisingly great video (for a phone), but it still sounds as though people are talking in a tin can. My new iPhone 4S shoots videos of surprisingly good quality. If you want to record a fun video of your friend who stops by the booth to post on your own personal Facebook page, then the quality of the video will not matter very much. But if you are using this video to represent your brand, you have to decide whether your smartphone is sufficient or if you need to bring in better equipment.

I'm not saying you have to hire NFL Films to shoot your video interviews and do the voiceovers (although that would be very cool!), but no one is going to watch a video that is too dark to tell what is going on with sound so bad you can't understand what people are saying. Some people will argue that when a video is overproduced, it does not seem "authentic" or "real." Luckily, your only choices are not poor quality and overproduced. You want to strive for a watchable video that does not distract the viewer with poor sound quality or inadequate or poor lighting. If your budget allows, you can always move toward a more professional production.

If you are launching a start-up business, are bootstrapping your way into a 10×10 booth at CES, and you cannot afford to even rent a good HD camera, using your smartphone as your video camera might be the right choice. Maybe you want that hot-new-startup-out-of-the-garage-devil-may-care image. The only bad advice would be telling you not to do it because you can't afford a better camera. That's like telling new parents not to take video of their baby's first steps because they don't have a decent HD video camera and proper lighting.

If yours is a smaller company that wants customers to see you as having the same resources as your larger competitor, you definitely need to use a high-quality video camera. You only have one chance to make a good first impression, so whatever you decide, it must reflect well on your company image. If you don't have the resources to get adequate equipment for the image you want to project, you are better off not shooting the video.

If you have the budget to hire a professional video crew, then by all means do it. It will save you a lot of time in the editing room and hassle of learning to properly use the equipment. If you need to go the DIY route, there are some excellent choices available that won't break the bank. A good quality pocket video recorder will set you back around $200. There are digital cameras that have video capability as well, and these run from around $120 up to $250 for what you need. The latest generation iPod touch will give you great video, and you can listen to some tunes or watch a movie while your booth is being set-up. Manufacturers are getting much better at creating phones that shoot high-quality video, and they run anywhere from $200 with a contract, up to $600 without a contract. Rest assured, there are some cost-effective options out there.

Going Professional

If you have the budget, I highly recommend you look into hiring a professional video team to shoot your interviews. This team might include a producer, crew, host, and editor. You can do the man-on-the-street videos you want to post right away yourself, but leave the ones you want to use for marketing to the pros.

When you are looking for the right company to work with, you want to make sure they understand the image you are trying to project, will work within your budget, and will work with your strategy and vision in mind. This isn't their project—it's yours—and they must be willing to give you what you want, when you want it, and how you want it. You could also hire a professional video journalist and get both the camera and the interview skills in one person.

You'll get more than just the professional-quality video if you take this approach. Having someone in your booth with a big camera, microphone, and lights will draw a lot of attention. Naturally, people will want see what is going on. You might even be able to get a few more interviews out of the deal.

Proper Lighting and Sound

Lighting can be even more important than your camera. Proper lighting can make cheap cameras look good, and poor lighting can make expensive cameras look bad. Poor lighting also makes your subject look bad, and he will not appreciate that. People will not share the video with others if they look bad in it. There are many resources available online that will show you the exact placement and angles to best illuminate your interviewees. Just understand that a setup with two or three lights is going to require a fairly large space. If space is not an option and you have to work with the show's overhead lighting, having something that will reflect light just might do the trick. A reflector positioned at an angle that will bounce light onto your subject can eliminate many of those nasty shadows that appear under the eyes and around the nose and mouth.

If you are roaming around and doing your interviews while on the move, try to find the best nearby light source. Natural light is always preferable, so take your subject outside or find a window to place your subject near (but do not shoot directly at the window). You could also have your subject angled to the window if you would like to provide some shadowing or contour to his face. Keep in mind that the light can be used to create a mood or a feeling as well. For example, more shadowing on the subject's face can be used for a more serious topic, and bright light on his face can be used for a more enlightening topic. The best times to shoot outside are before 11 a.m. and after 1 p.m. when the sun is not directly overhead. You can always have your subject stand in a shady area, provided that the background light is not blown out. Another option for the roaming interview is a camera light, a floor stand light, or a reflector.

Before you start shooting, do some testing of the camera and different light sources around the hall. A quick Google search on lighting tips for video will give you detailed advice on setting things like white balance and color temperature of your light source. Knowing how to set the white balance will help you eliminate those weird hues of blue, green, or orange you sometimes see in photographs and video.

To get the best sound for your videos, you should use an external microphone. These come in both wired and wireless versions. A wired microphone is cheaper but limits the distance between your camera and the subject, which is determined by the length of the cord. The wired microphone connects directly to your camera, while the wireless comes with a transmitter and receiver. The transmitter connects to the microphone and the receiver to your camera.

The microphone you buy will be dictated by the camera you are using. Be sure to check what kind of input jack your camera has and choose a microphone that will fit. You can also purchase a camera microphone adapter that will allow you to connect almost any external microphone to the input jack on your camera. Test as many microphones as you can get your hands on and buy the best one your budget allows.

Background

If you are doing your interviews in one spot, you might want to have a specific backdrop that has your company branding on it. Be sure to let anyone who will be standing in front of that backdrop know what color it is so they can dress appropriately. If your background is blue, your interviewee won't want to get lost in it by also wearing blue. You can prepare them and encourage them to dress in a way that will be a positive complement rather than a negative contrast. You never want anything to distract the viewer from the message or the person who is delivering that message.

If you are roaming around, don't forget to consider what might be in the background. Often if you take just a quick look, the area seems fine—it just looks like an exhibit hall. But when you get back to the office, you might realize that two rows over in the background is your competitor with its logo prominently appearing above your subject's head. That is something people miss quite often when setting up a shot—things sticking out of people's heads. Remember, you lose quite a bit of depth of field in photos and videos, so that sign 50 feet away will appear to be floating above someone's head in the video. Take a quick test video, and then watch the replay on the camera's screen. This will help you catch those awkward backdrops.

Also take note of what is in the background if you are shooting in other public areas. A great shot outside the convention center in the perfect natural light might seem ideal until you notice a billboard in the background for a gentlemen's club. This might not be something your customer wants to be standing directly in front of in a public video. In essence, don't just take a quick glance around. Really look at what is in the frame before you start shooting. What you see three dimensionally with your eye will look very different in a flat two-dimensional video.

Do You Need a Waiver?

Yes, you're going to need a waiver signed by the person you interview if you intend to post the video online. An oral agreement is not going to work, even if it is recorded. Some states do not recognize oral agreements. It's best to get things in writing, so there's no misunderstanding. A release should contain 1) how you intend to use the video; 2) full editing rights; and 3) permission to create stills from the video. Both parties should sign the release. If you are taking video of a minor, her parent or guardian must sign the release. You can find release forms online, but it's best to have your attorney create one specific to your circumstances.

Tips for Interviewing

You'll get much better footage if you make your interviewee feel comfortable. No matter what the purpose of your video, putting your subject at ease will help ensure his success. It is always painful to watch when someone is staring at the camera like a deer in the headlights and giving one-word answers, and this consequently reflects poorly on your company and your company's image. You can create better interviews from quick man-on-the-street interviews to longer, more serious interviews with customers or industry leaders by following these simple tips:

- Many people freeze up as soon as they see the red light flashing on a camera. People who love to talk are rendered speechless when the camera starts rolling. Usually after the interview starts moving along, they forget the camera and relax. Knowing that, start with a few warm-up questions. This way, you can gather more mundane information and your interviewee can get comfortable with the camera.

- When having a conversation with someone, you show your interest in what he is saying by interjecting comments here and there like "um hum," "of course," and "I agree." When shooting video, you might not want your voice in the interview, so you need to convey interest nonverbally. Be sure to nod and smile to let your subject know he is doing well.

- Put your interviewee at ease by explaining everything before you begin. Let him know how long the interview will take, how you are going to use the video, and where it will be posted. Offer him a mirror so he can check his appearance, comb his hair, and straighten his clothes if need be.

- Anecdotes make better stories. If you seem to have trouble getting your subject to express himself, ask him to tell you a story. If he says your product is easy to use, ask him to describe a situation that shows its ease of use.

- If you are having trouble getting your subject to answer questions with more than a word or two, ask two questions at once. This will force him to give answers in full sentences.

- By the end of the interview, your subject should be more relaxed. I like to end all my interviews with a final catch-all question that allows the interviewee to express any final thoughts. A great end question is "What is the one thing you want viewers to know?" or "Do you have any final thoughts you want to leave with the viewer?"

Have the interviewee practice on his friends and co-workers if he is not experienced at talking on camera. Also, practice using the camera so you don't end up with footage of your feet and nothing of the actual interviews. Finally, sit back, relax, and enjoy the chat!

Whom Should You Interview?

This is going to depend on what your show goals are and what strategy you lay out before the show. If part of your strategy is to showcase customers talking about your product, then that is who you want to focus on. But if you see a great opportunity to talk to an industry thought leader about the future of the industry, then by all means go for it.

The Man on the Street

Man-on-the-street interviews are fun, short little snippets that don't need a high production value. You can use these to ask people general show-related questions. Ask about sessions they've been to, new products they've seen, and parties or receptions they've attended. These are just fun little videos that you can use to generate buzz around your booth. While your subject is signing your release form, you can start a conversation around what your company does. Don't forget to let her know where she can find the videos, so she can share them with her friends and colleagues.

Customers

Customer interviews can provide a wealth of information. You can find out which features of your product or service customers find most useful. You can also find out which features they don't use and why. This could uncover features you could eliminate or instructions that are confusing. You can also ask whether there is anything new that customers would like to see your company offer.

You don't need to ask questions that are specific to your company to get valuable information. Ask your customers what one problem they would want to solve over the next year or ask what the biggest challenges are they face in their day-to-day operations. This will give you some insight into ways your company can help eliminate their biggest problems.

Ask questions about the show. Ask what their favorite sessions or keynote speakers were and something they learned if they attended the educational component. Ask whether they've seen any new products or services on the show floor they think are pretty cool. Ask if they've done anything really fun while at the show (use discretion on what you post). Videos like this are fun to post during the show. It's the kind of information other attendees will enjoy. Remember, social media is *social*— you don't want to just be promoting yourself constantly.

Don't be afraid to let the conversation go where your customers want to take it. Often, they will provide you with information no question could ever elicit. This is a great way to collect customer testimonials for use on your website and in your marketing materials to share via social media. Not all the videos or all the pieces of each video need to be posted online. Some customers might not make a compelling interview, but the information can still be valuable to various departments in your company.

Speakers and Presenters

The great thing about everyone walking around the show with a badge around their neck is that you know who everyone is and what their roles are at the show. Speakers are easy to pick out just by checking badges. You can either go find them or grab them as they are walking the aisles. Everyone loves getting in some self-promotion, so ask them when they are presenting and what topics they're presenting. Ask what the key takeaway is that they want attendees to go home with. If a presenter has already spoken, he'll likely still be happy to share his key points. This again is great information to post during the show because it provides both in-person and virtual attendees with a wealth of information on a variety of topics.

Industry Thought Leaders

If you want to interview industry thought leaders, you might have to do a bit of prep work. These people are highly sought after, and their schedule is usually booked solid during the show. You should schedule these interviews in advance and set them up as conversations with your key executives who are attending show. A situaion like this can make these industry stars more willing to have the conversation, and you might get more information than you would just grabbing them in passing.

These interviews don't have to be scripted, but talking points should be agreed upon in the weeks leading up to the show. They will have a pulse on what is happening in the industry and what is most important to your audience, so listen to their suggestions. Because thought leaders have name recognition within the industry, these video interviews will have a wider appeal than some of the others you are conducting. They might draw a crowd at the show, but it is also very likely they will be widely shared via social media as well. This content can be reused in many ways throughout the year.

Bloggers and the Media

Why not interview those who do all the interviewing? After all, bloggers and journalists are likely to have a lot of information stored in their heads from many sources and many points of view. Ask them about industry trends and where they see your industry going over the next two or three years. Ask them about the innovations they've seen at the show that they think will transform the industry.

Like the industry thought leaders, these people also bring name recognition with them, so you'll again attract a wider audience. They also bring with them a loyal following that is likely to spread your video via social media. Be sure to include their name and publication in the title of your video when you post it on YouTube to increase the chance of people stumbling on it when doing a search for the blogger or journalist online.

What to Do with the Video

Man-on-the-street interviews should be posted immediately. You should use these to generate buzz around your booth and get more attention online. Get those videos posted on YouTube or Vimeo, and start sharing the links through whatever social media platforms you are using. I prefer posting them on sharable public platforms, like YouTube or Vimeo, so they are easily shared and embedded on other people's web pages. Also, if you post them on your company's YouTube channel, people will be exposed to other videos you have posted there when they visit to view their own interviews. You never know what might catch someone's interest.

I recommend against posting customer interviews immediately unless you have someone who is editing your videos at the show. You don't want to just throw these up on social media channels without carefully reviewing and editing them. This is content you'll need to clean up and include in other marketing channels. You can use it for video case studies and customer testimonials on your website. You also can incorporate it into commercials and include it with proposals. Remember to pass along any pertinent information that is in these interviews to other departments.

Interviews with speakers, bloggers, and other media should be posted online to sites like YouTube or Vimeo, so you can share them via the social media tools you are using or other sites or communities the show is using. You won't need to clean these up because they are not showcasing your company or your products. For these types of videos, getting them posted quickly is key; otherwise, they are no longer relevant. People attending the show will find videos like these interesting, and the virtual audience will also like them. It's another way you'll help keep those who can't attend informed about what is taking place at the show. You'll continue to keep this audience connected. After the show, you can take these videos off your company's channel if you want.

You'll need to spend some time editing interviews with industry thought leaders. Posting them immediately is not critical to get the benefit they can provide. Posting these videos after the show is a great way to keep the conversation on social media alive after the show. You're also positioning the executives in your company as heavy hitters by appearing side-by-side with these industry leaders and showing that your company is on top of what is happening in the industry.

I'm sure by now you're thinking that creating videos is an awful lot of work. It can be, but it's worth it if you plan strategically for it. With a well-defined plan in place, you will go to the show knowing exactly who you want to interview and what you want to get out of those interviews. It will keep you focused on the content you are gathering, so you are sure to come home with valuable information for multiple departments within your company. If you just pack up and ship a bunch of equipment to a show with no defined plan for how to use it, you'll be running all over the place wasting your time and the time of the people you are interviewing.

Even if you have a bunch of grainy videos with sound quality that is not so great in the end, you probably still have a decent amount of usable content you wouldn't have if you didn't have the video. It might contain valuable information that can be transcribed and passed on to other departments. It might be full of compliments you can transcribe into customer testimonials. It might give you ideas for blog posts, industry articles, and white papers. So, as you can see, it's never a waste of time; it's sometimes the best way to gather all that information and more and have it in one place.

Summary

When incorporating video into your booth strategy, always keep your eye on your goals and objectives. Ask yourself if what you are planning helps you accomplish your show goal. If one of your goals is to position your company executives or other employees as industry thought leaders, don't focus on man-on-the-street interviews. Put your efforts into a more formal discussion between those employees and industry big wigs. If your goal is to introduce the industry to a new product you are launching, those informal man-on-the-street interviews will give you great feedback on what people think about your new product.

Use the best quality equipment that your budget will allow, and remember that good lighting can make up for a mediocre camera. Make your interviewees feel at ease by explaining what the video will be used for and asking some easy warm-up questions. Collect as many interviews as you can with a wide variety of people. Attendees and people who were unable to attend the show will appreciate the extra information. All those minutes of video add up to great marketing content you can use over the next year.

13

Live Stream
Your Message

I am a huge advocate of expanding your trade show presence beyond your booth to the Internet. I can see absolutely no reason why you should not allow people not present at the show to view your in-booth presentations and activities. You put so much effort into planning the event and creating great presentations, why limit who is able to participate? Your biggest potential customers might be sitting back in the office wishing they were at the show. Well, invite them in and turn your presentation into a hybrid event.

Exhibitors have been doing in-booth presentations, product launches, and demos for as long as trade shows have been around. Good pre-show promotion and crowd gatherers would almost guarantee a crowd for these presentations. But the exhibitor could only draw an audience from those who were physically at the show. Today, with social media and the ability to live stream your message all over the world, your audience expands across the globe. Where once each presentation might have attracted 30 people, now you can broadcast your message to hundreds. You can expand that audience even more by recording the presentation and making it available on-demand. No one needs to miss your presentation just because they needed to be somewhere else when you were presenting it live.

Two Different Audiences

If you decide to live stream your event, and I encourage you to do so, it's not enough to just stick a camera in the back of the room and hit record. A camera in the back of the room is not a hybrid event—that's C-SPAN. You want to deliver an experience to your audience watching from home or their office that keeps them engaged. Emilie Barta, hybrid event consultant and virtual emcee, defines a hybrid event as "A hybrid event occurs when a face-to-face event and a virtual event happen simultaneously to enable two audiences to participate as one. In this instance, you need to think of your in-booth presentation and your live stream as one event with two separate audiences."

What makes it a hybrid event is the integration of those two audiences. Attendees in your booth and those online can interact with one another. Also, both audiences can interact with the presenters. This is what makes the presentation come alive to your online audience, taking it beyond just a one-way webcast.

You have two distinct audiences with different needs. You need to provide your in-booth audience with a comfortable place to view your presentation. If the presentation is longer than a minute or two, you need to provide seating. You also need to design your environment so that everyone can see what is taking place. Even people in the back row need to hear the presentation.

Your virtual audience is no different. Of course, you can't choose their seating for them, but you can make them comfortable. You can give them an easy-to-use platform for viewing your presentation that gives them a way to interact with the presenter and other attendees. Be sure your camera is not sitting stationary on a tripod projecting only one view. Mix it up by zooming in on the presenter and then going out for a wider shot. You also want the camera to follow the action. Focus on whomever is speaking. If an audience member asks a question, have the camera focus on him while he's speaking, and then go back to the presenter. In other words, don't make it boring and static for the online viewer. Imagine what it would be like to watch a movie that used only one camera angle throughout.

It's also important to add here that any audience questions or comments should be made on microphone. I've often been frustrated when someone asks a question and I cannot hear it, and then the speaker goes straight into the answer. Having anyone who speaks do so into the microphone is good for both your in-person attendees and your remote audience.

It's easier to hold the attention of a live audience with a good presentation. It's much harder to do so with a virtual audience. Your virtual audience is surrounded by distractions. If you are not actively connecting with them, they will start checking email, get up to refill their coffee cups, or answer the phone. But do not fear! Actively engaging your virtual audience and creating an environment that supports this is indeed possible. I'm going to show you how.

Technical Requirements for a Live Stream

You need to choose a streaming provider, a viewing platform provider, and an A/V or production provider. Some companies do all three, while some companies just do one. As with just about anything when it comes to social media, free products and services are available as are those you pay for. This is truly a case of you get what you pay for. Here's what you need:

- **Streaming provider**—These are the folks who capture your video feed, compress it, and stream it over the Internet to the viewing platform.

- **Viewing platform provider**—A viewing platform is basically the website that your audience goes to view your presentation and interact with your presenters and other live and virtual attendees.

- **A/V or production provider**—These are the people who are behind the camera and those directing the production.

Free services include Ustream, which also offers a premium version that eliminates the ads that pop up inside your video for just a few dollars a month. (Something to keep in mind because you can't choose your ads.) In less than 10 minutes, you can set up an account on Ustream and create your very own channel. You can download the recorder app to your smartphone and begin webcasting, or you can connect an external camera for better-quality video. Another free service is Justin. tv, with which you can also create your own channel within minutes. Livestream is another option that, although not free, is low priced with plans that start at under $300 per month.

While I wrote this, I viewed a Ustream webcast of the Governors Conference on Extreme Climate. I have to say that the quality was quite good. (I'm guessing they used multiple external cameras of a high quality and not their smartphones.) This is not a dinky little event either. Presenters on the panel included California Governor Edmund G. Brown, Jr.; Former California Governor

Arnold Schwarzenegger; Dr. Rajendra Pachauri, chair of the United Nations' Intergovernmental Panel on Climate Change; Sir Richard Branson, founder of the Virgin Group; and Nancy Sutley, chair of the White House Council on Environmental Quality. I observed that Governor Brown did a great job looking into the camera lens, but the moderator, Dr. Pachauri, and Richard Branson did not—more on the importance of eye contact later.

Although this is a technical section, I'm not going to go into detailed instructions for using each service. Many excellent resources are available on the Internet with detailed instructions on how to run your own webcast using Ustream.tv or similar services. It is a do-it-yourself solution that will cost you the price of a camera and a good microphone. You might also need an inexpensive software program that will help you with switching among multiple cameras and incorporating graphics. Or, if DIY is not your thing, you can still use the free service but hire a production crew who has experience with live broadcasts and sit back and enjoy the show.

On the other end of the spectrum are the solution providers that can handle either the live stream or the viewing platform or both. The streaming provider's primary responsibility is to provide the compression of the video feed and the output to the virtual platform via the Internet. The platform provider will supply the website that will allow your virtual audience to view the presentation live (and in some cases on-demand, if you are also recording it). Sometimes either the streaming provider or the platform provider can supply or refer a production crew, including cameras, a director, lighting, and sound.

If you have buckets of in-house resources in the form of top-notch program-mers, you could even create your own viewing platform and embed it right into your company's website. What you need to ask yourself is if it's worth the time and money to build it from scratch if you are only going to do one or two virtual events. You'll also need the technical support staff on hand during the live presen-tation to field technical help questions from the audience. If virtual events are new to your company, I suggest you start by working with a platform provider and see-ing how things go before you jump into creating your own.

What to Look for in a Streaming Provider

Your streaming provider is the key to your success. After all, if they can't get the presentation onto the Internet properly, you'll lose what is potentially your largest audience. You need your streaming provider to deliver the following:

- A solid stream
- Redundancy
- Good customer service
- Good technical support

It sounds pretty straightforward, and it is. These folks are your delivery service. Think of it this way. All they are doing is sending your information from your booth to the platform. You want it to work, you want them to have some sort of backup in place if things go wrong, you want someone you can call if things go wrong, and you want that person to care that something has gone wrong and fix it quickly.

Although I'm always in favor of checking references and talking to a provider's past customers, nothing shows how good a provider is like the true audience experience. Ask to attend a presentation it's streaming as a virtual attendee. You'll mainly be looking at the quality of the visual delivery of the presentation. If the presentation stops and starts or appears pixelated, that's not good. Things tend to go wrong when technology is involved, and it's not always entirely preventable. If you are watching and the stream goes down, you'll want to note how long it takes to come back up. If it's minutes, that's not too bad. It it's closer to an hour, that's not good.

What to Look for in a Production Company or AV Company

There is a difference between an event AV and production crew and a crew who works on broadcasts. Simply using the crew the show organizer may have hired for the educational sessions and keynotes could be a big mistake. You want a crew that has experience following the action, employs creativity, and is quick on its feet—not someone who is only experienced locking down a camera and panning left and right.

Is your event going to be a high-energy fast-paced event needing many camera angles and switching from camera to camera, or is it much more static? If you have a fast-paced event, you need to make sure your provider has experience doing this type of event. Ask to see recorded examples of events similar to yours to see how fluid the camera action is.

You also need a crew that works well together. If the producer and the cameraperson do not get along, it will be obvious to your audience. Ask your provider if it has its own crew or if it subcontracts the job in each city. I've heard stories of camera operators the provider found on Craigslist falling asleep in the middle of a webcast.

What to Look for in a Viewing Platform Provider

Your viewing platform is just as important as your actual live stream. Just as you have provided for the comfort of your live audience, you must provide for the comfort of your virtual audience. You should take the following requirements into consideration when choosing a viewing platform. Is the platform intuitive and easy to use? Your audience should not need a degree in software engineering to watch the live stream of your presentation. Before you get a demo of the platform from the provider, ask to sit in as a virtual participant in a live stream event they are hosting. This will give you the same experience as your audience will have. Check whether the platform is easy to log on to, find and operate the viewer, ask questions of the presenter, interact with other audience members, and get help if you are having technical difficulty. If any of these things are not intuitive or help is not available, your viewers will get frustrated and leave.

Can you brand the page? You should be able to change the colors of the platform to match your brand and even incorporate your logo into the page. These days this is simple to do, and you should not be charged a premium to customize the page.

Will the platform provider supply technical support before and during the presentation for your viewers? Even the easiest-to-use platforms require technical support. Some of your viewers are just not going to be web savvy. I will never forget a live webinar I participated in where all the attendees were on the phone. One of the attendees kept saying he was having trouble viewing the slides. All he could see on his screen were photos of different animals. Finally another attendee told him that his screen saver was on and he should jiggle his mouse. Thank goodness other audience members were paying attention because tech support wasn't. Your provider should have technical support available to answer questions and assist viewers immediately.

The platform provider should also have a FAQs page with common support issues and solutions. Some people will not want to ask a question for fear of looking stupid. Or, they might just be do-it-yourselfers. The platform provider should be able to accommodate these members of your audience with an easily searched online support/help database.

Does the platform provider supply a way for your virtual audience to ask questions and interact with each other? Most platforms have a chat function or a Q&A button (or both) next to the video viewing window. This is how your virtual audience can engage with one another and the speaker. It is best to have someone on your staff or a trained virtual moderator monitoring these areas, passing the questions along to the speaker, and interacting with the viewers.

Keep in mind that the chat function is different from the Q&A button. The chat function allows your virtual audience to chat amongst themselves and with the event organizers. These chat windows/rooms/functions become the equivalent of the open spaces in your booth or the convention center where your face-to-face attendees can chat among themselves.

The Q&A button is traditionally used to provide a dedicated way for your virtual audience to ask a question of the speaker. These questions need to be asked of the speaker by a moderator or a virtual emcee; otherwise, the speaker must have a confidence monitor, laptop, or mobile device on which to see the questions that are being asked of her.

Do you have the option to view slides and the speaker at the same time, or does the platform provider orchestrate switching between the two? Many platforms have two viewing windows if you have a speaker working off of presentation slides. Viewers have the option to enlarge whichever window they want. They might want to have a large view of the slides and just a small window running next to it with the speaker view. Some providers switch back and forth between the slides and the speaker for you at appropriate intervals thus requiring only one viewing window. If you have viewed TED presentations, you will recognize this. The camera focuses primarily on the speaker. When the speaker refers to the slide, the view switches off the speaker and onto the slide.

Does the platform and/or streaming provider support only PowerPoint, or can it also support Apple's Keynote software or presentation software such as Prezi? This is very important. Prezi is becoming more and more popular with presenters, and many providers cannot support it. If your provider supports only PowerPoint, be sure to let your speaker know. If you find a majority of your presenters are using tools such as Prezi, you should probably make that a requirement of potential platform providers. You never want technology to take priority over a presenter's optimal delivery.

Can your audience view the presentation with a wireless connection? "Wait a minute, you keep saying wireless connections are too unreliable to use." This is true for you but not for your viewers. Many people access the Internet via wireless these days. The live stream should require a low bandwidth appropriate for Wi-Fi viewing so that online viewers can have a good experience even when using a wireless connection.

Can your live stream be viewed on a mobile device? Again, you may have an audience who is accessing your live stream via a smartphone or tablet. Be sure your viewing platform works on these devices if that's where you think your audience will be. If it's viewable only on a PC, be sure to include that information in all your promotional materials and instructions.

If you decide to create your own platform in-house, your programmers should take all these items into account. You might be thinking to yourself, "Why on earth would I want to use a platform provider when I can use Ustream for free? The platform sounds expensive, and if it's only a website, really, what's the difference?" There are many differences, but here are two key differences you need to take into consideration: branding and support.

You can apply some branding to your Ustream channel, including a custom background, logo, and branding on the bottom of your video. If you choose the premium service, you'll stop the ads that appear on your video. However, across the top of the screen is a menu bar of all the channels available on Ustream. At the bottom of the screen are links and screen shots of recent videos, and rotating on the right of the screen are featured videos. You cannot turn these off, and you cannot choose which videos will be featured. The Friends of Felines Rescue Center 24/7 Kitty Channel could pop up—and you know how people cannot resist videos of kittens when they are online. How can you compete with a room full of them? Or you might be presenting to a conservative audience and have a "Girls Gone Wild" channel pop up.

With a free service, support is pretty much nonexistent. If your audience is having an issue using the chat window, no one is on hand to help them. They must dig through the online support files to find the answer to their questions. By the time they figure out what they are doing wrong, the presentation could be over. When you use a good platform provider, they will provide this service for your audience—and you.

Unless you sign up for the premium versions of the free services, you're going to be on your own as well. Trying to figure out how to change the background image? You're going to have to dig through those support documents, too. I don't know a lot of exhibitors who have extra time on their hands when they are getting ready for a show.

So which should you choose? I suggest getting the best service you can on your budget and that is most appropriate for your audience. Activities that could generate sales are never the first place to cut costs. Areas to reduce spending in your exhibit program do not include activities that involve your customers. You could save money by taking your top clients out for fast food for dinner at your next show, but you would never do that. Why would you deliver an inferior experience if you don't have to?

You should use free services when you have *NO* budget. If your only options are to use a free service like Ustream or do nothing, then use Ustream. I have a friend who has a small start-up company, and he is taking everything his start-up has and investing it in a 10"×10" booth at a large national industry trade show. He loves the idea of live streaming his product demo, but he definitely does not have any money to invest in a streaming provider and a viewing platform. Instead, his company will find a friend who has a camera and who can figure out how to stream the video to Ustream and broadcast the demo. He has my blessing to do this. I would never tell him to miss the opportunity of reaching a larger audience. It's too important to him and the success of his business.

He's trying to get the biggest return on his investment, so he's looking to get the most possible exposure at the show but sees the opportunity to also reach a wider audience of people across the globe who will not be at the event. By live streaming his product demo and promoting it through different social media channels, he can get much more marketing bang for his exhibition buck. He's also able to not only live stream the demo but also record it and post it on YouTube and Vimeo as on-demand content. He's also increasing his rankings in a Google search by optimizing his videos with key words because Google loves rich media content.

On the other hand, if yours is a Fortune 500 company, you should at the very least pony up for the professional streaming service. Save your money by having your executives fly coach to the show.

Internet Connection

Plain and simple, you need a dedicated T1 line in your booth if you want to create a professional, clear broadcast. If you are using a streaming provider and a viewing platform, you must have a T1 line. You cannot depend on the show's wireless connection to get you through a broadcast.

Even if you are using a free streaming service, you're going to need a reliable Internet connection. I recently used Ustream to broadcast my #expochat live from the show floor at the International Association of Exhibitions and Events' Expo!Expo!. I tried using the convention center's wireless connection, but it was constantly dropping out. I then connected using a cellular Internet service. I had a good strong connection that didn't drop, but the connection speed was a bit slow and caused the video to jump here and there. It was fine for what I was doing, which was having a little bit of fun; but I would not have wanted that for an important presentation or product showcase.

I do not recommend anyone try to live stream over the show's free wireless connection. Chances are good that it's not going to work. The bandwidth is not intended for uploading video and your live stream could drop in and out. It's also possible the available connections will be maxed out and you will not be able to connect to the wireless network when it's time to do your demo or presentation. You'll have defeated your entire purpose and can even come out looking bad or unprofessional. If you are like my friends with no budget, I will let you slide with a good cellular service provider—but I won't be thrilled about it.

Virtual Emcee

A master of ceremonies is a person who presides over a formal event or entertainment and who introduces guests, presenters, or entertainers. The role of virtual emcee is similar to your traditional event's master of ceremonies, but with added responsibilities. It is a more personable role rather than a formal one. A virtual emcee not only introduces the guests and presenters, but also represents your virtual audience as a whole. Your presenters can see what's going on in the audience right in front of them, but they have no idea what is happening with the online viewers. The virtual emcee becomes the voice of your virtual audience as well as your virtual audience's eyes and ears in the room.

Because many of the events that really engaged me as a virtual participant were emceed by Emilie Barta, I asked her why this is such an important role. "The virtual emcee is similar to a traditional emcee, but there are specific skills required to connect with an audience that cannot be seen, that is spread all across the globe, that is participating throughout many time zones, who might not speak the same language, and who has many demands on their attention. It is much easier for a virtual audience member than a face-to-face audience member to be distracted, so it is a very distinct personality that can hold their attention and keep them engaged in the event."

So a virtual emcee is the bridge that connects your virtual audience to the face-to-face event. She must have the ability to engage easily distracted virtual attendees. She must be able to multitask, fielding questions and comments coming at her all at one time and communicating through different channels all at once. Although she is there to inform the audience and guide them through what is taking place, she is not the expert—she is the representative of your virtual audience.

Your virtual extension of your in-booth event should begin a few minutes before the face-to-face event. This gives your virtual emcee time to brief the online audience on the format of the event. She will cover logistics such as these:

- What time the presentation will start and end
- A quick platform how-to explanation
- How your virtual audience can get technical assistance
- How your virtual audience can submit questions or comments
- How your virtual audience can communicate with the face-to-face audience (that is, via a Twitter hashtag such as #gizmolaunch or through the chat function)
- Ways your virtual audience can get more information (download links, email contacts, phone numbers, and so on)

And those are the basic, easy parts of the role. A good virtual emcee must also be able to improvise. Let's say you are live streaming a product demonstration that is taking place in your booth. Someone walks past the camera, gets caught on a cable, and takes the camera down. All your virtual audience knows is that in the middle of a demo the screen went black. Without a virtual emcee on hand, your audience will simply give it a few seconds and if nothing comes on the screen again, they will shut down and begin doing something else.

A virtual emcee, given this circumstance, could immediately let the audience know what happened and let them know how long it should be until things get up and running. A virtual emcee could quickly do an impromptu interview with one of your staff members just for your virtual audience while they wait for the camera to get back up and running. If things cannot be repaired to get back online, the virtual emcee can let her audience know what the next steps are. Perhaps it is collecting contact information to send an announcement of a new demo time or announcing that a special online demo will take place just for them after the exhibit hall closes for the day.

It's very helpful but not entirely necessary for quick in-booth presentations to have your virtual emcee on camera. Just understand that if she is not on camera, you will lose a lot of your ability to engage your virtual audience. If you had your virtual emcee on a separate camera during the previously mentioned snafu, you would have a much more engaging exchange and would be able to retain more of your audience.

The other benefit to having the virtual emcee on camera is eye contact. Every presenter knows how important it is to maintain eye contact with her audience. Your virtual audience is no different. A virtual emcee will draw the audience in through direct eye-contact while she is on camera and, as a result engage the audience in your presentation. Your virtual emcee will be on camera to introduce the presentation, which helps make a connection with your virtual audience. She can go on camera again when she directs the audience's questions and comments to the presenters. Finally, at the end of the presentation, she can go on camera to wrap up the presentation.

Another great idea is to have dedicated content for your virtual audience. This shows them your appreciation and enables them to feel even more a part of the experience. For example, you could have a special Q&A session with the presenters following their presentations. This is the virtual equivalent of rushing the stage after a presentation for a little one-on-one time with the presenter. It also shows your virtual audience that they are just as important to you as your face-to-face audience.

Tips for a Professional Virtual Event Experience

Your virtual audience is just as important as your face-to-face audience, so prepare your stage and your presenters for their on-camera experience.

Background

The cleaner the backdrop behind your presenters, the better for your virtual audience. Remember, they are seeing the presentation as a flat two-dimensional image. So that logo positioned behind the presenter becomes a growth coming out of the side of the presenter's head. The seam that is barely noticeable to the face-to-face audience becomes a distracting line projecting from the top of the presenter's head.

Give your presenters a heads-up on the background color so they can plan their wardrobe accordingly. If they wear a blue suit almost identical to your background, they might appear as floating heads. That is going to be incredibly distracting to your virtual audience, perhaps even a bit frightening.

Wardrobe and Makeup

The camera sees light differently than the human eye does. White is the biggest offender. A white dress becomes washed out on camera and is hard to look at. Black and navy blue lose all their detail and become big dark blobs. Clothing with fine patterns such as herringbone and small checks produce a very distracting wavy effect. The best wardrobes are of solid and/or pastel colors. Also, ditch the sparkly jewelry. This can catch the light and cause a glare.

Most video these days is shot in high-definition (HD) video. HD video has the menacing ability to enhance even the tiniest blemish. Warn your presenters of this, too, so they can go a little heavier on the cover-up. Makeup also reduces the shine you get from the natural oils in your skin. The camera will emphasize that shine and turn you into an oil slick. Ladies should avoid bright red lipsticks and lip gloss. You should stick to a more neutral tone and dab on a bit of powder.

Eye Contact

Let your presenters know that they will also be speaking to a virtual audience, and remind them that the camera is the window or the portal to these individuals. It is just as important to make eye contact with your virtual audience through the camera as it is with the members of the face-to-face audience. Your presenters should occasionally look directly into the camera lens throughout the presentation, but never is it more important than when fielding a question from your virtual audience. When the virtual emcee presents your presenters with a question from this audience, they should not address their answers to the virtual emcee, but directly into the camera.

Information Front and Center

Two key pieces of information should always be available to your virtual audience
and placed front and center of your platform:

- **The hashtag and communication platform**—If you are using a
  Twitter hashtag during your presentation, it should be shown prominently throughout your presentation. Make sure both the face-to-face
  and your virtual audiences can see it. The same is true if you are using
  another means of communication. If you are fielding questions via a
  LinkedIn group or Facebook page, then the name of the group or page
  and an easily remembered link should be visible at all times.

- **Presenter names and contact info**—You cannot possibly overdo this.
  Displaying headshots of your presenters and their names underneath
  will help your virtual audience follow along much more easily. Or you
  can create a graphic called a *lower third* that runs at the bottom of the
  viewing window and tells the audience who is speaking at any given
  time. You see this a lot in documentaries on TV. Don't just flash it at
  the beginning of the presentation. Include it throughout intermittently.
  That way, those who joined late will still know who is speaking.

  You should include the presenters' preferred method of being contacted for more information as well. If you are using a Twitter hashtag
  for your event, include presenters' Twitter profiles so those tweeting
  can attribute quotes to the appropriate presenter. I cannot tell you
  how many times I've heard someone say something brilliant and have
  wanted to credit him in a tweet but had no idea if he had a Twitter
  profile. It goes without saying that your company contact info and profile information should also be prominent.

In-Booth Presentations That Can Go Virtual

Many of the activities you will be doing in your booth will appeal to a wider audience who are not at the show. Most of your investment has already been made to
do these presentations in your booth. You can maximize that investment by adding
on a virtual component, therefore creating a hybrid event. Instead of just several
hundred people at the show watching your presentation, you can now open that
audience up to several thousands tuning in from their home, office, or coffee shop.
Expand it even more by archiving those presentations for on-demand viewing.

What makes for great online viewing? Product launches appeal to both your potential customer base and members of the media (both traditional and web based).
But don't stop there. Product demos will appeal to a wider audience, as will education sessions and interviews with industry thought leaders. Why not live stream

Q&A sessions with internal experts covering topics such as installation require-ments, upgrade tips, feasibility studies, how-tos, and more. Let's take a look at each of those scenarios to give you some ideas for your own booth activities.

Product Launches

Trade shows have been the site of many a product launch. Many companies build their delivery schedules around their trade show calendars. They want the cap-tive audience of both potential customers and the industry press that a trade show provides. By adding a virtual component to your product launch you are creating a hybrid product launch. You've extended your reach because your audience no lon-ger needs to be physically present to participate in the event.

Don't think about your virtual event as the only component in the online world, but as one key piece. Encourage your virtual audience not just to sit and watch the event on the platform you provide, but to also engage their own communities in the ways they prefer.

What do I mean by this? Why not give your virtual audience a tip sheet for cre-ating their very own product launch party? Give them all the instructions we've already talked about for optimal viewing of your launch on the platform you pro-vide. But also give them tips to set up a tweet chat, Google Hangout, Facebook event, POD (a group of people who get together in person to view a virtual presen-tation), and so on. You are providing ways for your entire audience to interact as well as encouraging them to find ways to interact with their own communities. If their communities are big enough, you might even want to have a company repre-sentative participate with them to answer any questions that come up.

Example: Product Launch of New Digital Hard Disk Recorder for the Music Industry

You've already covered the bloggers and industry press who will be at the trade show, and you've put together a virtual event and gotten word out to industry bloggers and press that will not be at the show. One of those bloggers who will attend the virtual event writes for a an active community of 275 recording studios whose niche is the folk music industry. This group has a weekly online chat forum where they talk about issues related to their day-to-day jobs.

You should reach out to this blogger and encourage him to invite his community to view the product launch along with him. They could have their own private chat about the launch via their regular weekly chat platform that everyone is already familiar with. This way, they could block the noise of a larger audience who might have different needs and focus on their own specific applications. For a large audience like that, you could provide a company representative to participate in this chat and be available to answer the community's questions.

Product Demos

Product demos are great candidates for hybrid events. I've viewed some online demos that were better than the face-to-face versions. Sometimes when you are in a face-to-face audience and at the back of the room, you have difficulty seeing each component. By having a camera operator who can get in close on the action, your virtual audience will have closer than front row seats to your demo.

Just be sure the person who is doing the product demo remembers that she has an online audience following along. She must beware of the camera and not stand in a way that blocks the view. She must also remember to look into the lens occasionally and speak directly to your virtual audience. The camera operator needs to be experienced at tight shots and focusing on the feature that is being discussed.

Industry Education and Interviews with Thought Leaders

One way to draw a crowd is to provide your attendees with up-to-date information and education delivered by industry thought leaders they respect—the key being *up-to-date* and *cutting-edge* information and education. If your audience can Google it and read about it in five minutes, it's not cutting edge. If it's self-promotional and irrelevant to your audience, they are not going to stick around for long.

Let's say your company has a software program that compiles online medical record data. Data security and HIPAA (Health Insurance Portability and Accountability Act) compliance is a very hot topic that appeals to a wider audience than just your current customers. Bring in a panel of industry thought leaders to discuss the latest regulations and compliance issues. Your face-to-face audience and your virtual audience can ask the panelists questions that relate to their day-to-day job issues and concerns. To tie in your product, you can have a white paper specifically outlining how your product addresses these issues. This type of download will draw people to your website and your product.

Q&A Sessions

I recently sat in on a few virtual presentations that the American Public Works Association did as part of its "Continuing the Conversation" series live from a trade show floor. They had interviews with the outgoing and incoming presidents of the association. They also had a few interviews with some of the keynote speakers talking about their presentations and interviews with industry experts on hot topics for the public works community.

The most popular interview was with a company that has a product that uses infrared technology for pothole repair. With the other interviews, there was some online chatter and a few questions coming from the audience, but you could feel the audience come alive with the pothole interview. The interviewer who was also playing the role of virtual emcee was peppered with question after question coming in from the online viewers—very specific questions on costs, temperature, and pot hole size. She actively listened to both the audience and the pothole expert so that she could ask even more questions and get the most information possible.

I became so engaged that I almost found myself asking questions before I remembered I have nothing to do with pothole repair. Hands down this was a clear winner. It was a winner because it was delivering specific and pertinent information the audience needed in their day-to-day jobs, it was cutting-edge technology, and it involved an industry expert who openly and honestly answered the audience's questions and addressed their concerns.

Why not do this in your own booth? You could crowd-source some questions or issues your customers have via social media in advance of the show. During the show you could have a hybrid clinic where your customer service people walk attendees through the solutions to their problems. You could use your crowd-sourced questions to get the ball rolling and then invite the audience to present their issues or questions about the product.

Many companies are afraid to do this. "What? Let our customers tell us what they find difficult about our product in front of people?" I assure you that pretending customers do not have problems using your product or service is not going to help you. You might discover that your customers just don't know how to use your product correctly. Maybe there is a whole bunch of people out there using it incorrectly. Now you have an opportunity to show customers the correct application; then you can fix the manual or add a special help category online.

As you can see, there is much going on in your booth already that you can open up to a wider audience. If you only make these presentations accessible to those who are attending the show, you are missing out on a huge potential audience. By investing just a bit more, you can increase your return exponentially.

You need to figure out, based on your show strategy, whether a hybrid event is right for your exhibit and what kind of event you should be using to accomplish your show goals. If one of your show objectives is to show your customers you are accessible, a clinic can be the perfect solution. Or, if your objective is to position your company executives as thought leaders in the industry, in-booth interviews with other respected thought leaders might just be the right step in that direction.

Summary

An excellent way to get more bang out of your trade show budget is to expand what you are already doing for your face-to-face audience by including virtual audience. Just be sure your planning addresses the fact that these two audiences have very different needs based on their locations. Planning for your virtual audience is not something you tack on at the end; this audience must be considered throughout the entire planning process.

Presenters need to be prepped, and the environment needs to be designed for an online viewer as well as a face-to-face audience. The production team is just as important as the technology needed to create the online experience. Make sure they have the right skill set for your type of event.

Although careful planning is essential, there is no need to go overboard on the type of event you will be live streaming to your virtual audience. You don't need to create the business equivalent of a three-ring circus. Product demos, Q&A sessions, and interviews with internal experts as well as industry thought leaders all make for excellent hybrid events.

14

Tune In and Listen

Listening to what people are telling you at trade shows is one of the most important things you can do. Yes, you are there to sell, but spending three days of doing nothing but broadcasting your message limits your overall success at a show. Trade shows should be viewed as a research Mecca for savvy marketing and business people. Yet, I can rarely find more than a handful of exhibitors who bother to ask visitors what they need or what problems they are trying to solve.

The conversations taking place in your booth are just the tip of the iceberg. Think about it—your booth is just 100–1,000 square feet of an event encompassing as much as 40,000 square feet for smaller shows and 1,000,000 square feet or more at larger shows. That doesn't even take into consideration the hallways, communal areas, and classrooms. Thinking you need to pay attention only to conversations taking place inside your booth is like thinking you're getting a good picture of the world's business news if you read only the business section of the Akron Hometowner. There's nothing wrong with reading the Akron Hometowner, especially if you live in Akron; it's just not representative of what's taking place the world over.

Some of the best conversations take place outside of your booth. They happen in the bar when the show floor closes, they happen in the hallways at the break stations, they happen in sessions during Q&A, they happen in the men's and ladies' rooms, they happen on the hotel shuttles, and they even happen on the planes going to and from the show. If you just hang out in your booth, you will miss a wealth of information.

These conversations have always been taking place but you had to be present to hear them. But now, with social media becoming more and more widely used, it's even easier to eavesdrop. You can see what people are posting to the show's Facebook page, LinkedIn group, Twitter hashtag, or online community to find little nuggets of information. The best conversations you want to listen in on start with "I wish..." or "What I really need..." or "I hate when...".

During a recent show I attended, a conversation started on Twitter when someone tweeted, "I hate these clunky apps that use up my cell phone battery." That was followed by several people saying they too hated that and that they wished there were more charging stations and outlets. Others lamented leaving their chargers in their hotel room and asked if someone had a spare. Someone else added that he wished that there was a place where he could check his phone and charge it so he didn't have to stay tethered to it. That conversation was about a total of eight to ten posts. Let's break it down for two groups that might have been listening. How might they respond when they see these tweets?

- **Show management**—Next year look into charging stations where attendees could check their phones to charge for an hour, much like a coat check. You also might want to provide additional self-service charging stations throughout the show floor complete with power cables. Or create networking areas on the show floor with seating areas, charging stations, and anything else that would be of benefit to the attendees and encourage them to stay longer on the trade show floor.

- **Exhibitors**—If you have a few extra outlets open in your booth, reach out to show attendees who are tweeting and invite them to drop by to get a quick charge. Next year set up a seating area with charging stations so booth visitors could charge their devices while having a conversation with the company booth reps. You could even have a "phone check" service that brings booth visitors back more than once. You might want to reach out to show management and suggest sponsoring a charging station or phone check.

Now imagine that this conversation took place at the Consumer Electronics Show (and I guarantee you it does—it happens at every show I've been to):

> **Exhibitor:** You make battery boosters for smartphones. Think about partnering with the show to sell those battery boosters onsite or per-haps in convention business centers.

> **Exhibitor:** Does *your* app drain a battery pretty fast? Based on the tweets you're seeing, you realize this battery thing really annoys people but it has never come up as an issue in your focus groups. Maybe you're not asking the right questions. Check in with customer service to see whether they are hearing this as well. Talk to research and devel-opment (R&D) about what can be done to make the app more smart-phone battery friendly.

Important information that is valuable to you can be gleaned before the show as well. I read a post on an association LinkedIn group before a show that said, "I'm being flooded with pre-show booth marketing but not one message contains what the exhibitor does. All I know is what they are giving away. I'm not coming to the show for free stuff; I'm coming to find new products." If you were listening to that conversation, you could quickly check your pre-show marketing and make sure it's clear what your company does and that it mentions any new products or services you are announcing at the show.

Research company Gartner thinks listening is so important that it has built listen-ing in to its annual IT Symposium in Orlando. Gartner gives attendees rides from one building to another in golf carts, which are driven by Gartner event staff and even sometimes members of its executive team. While ferrying attendees back and forth, Gartner employees have an opportunity to talk to them about their Symposium experience and either correct a misperception or use the information to improve the experience.

When you are really listening to the conversations taking place, you have the abil-ity to react immediately. You can fix a misperception on the spot, which might improve a potential customer's opinion of your company. Complaints and compli-ments should be forwarded on to the department in your company that would find the information valuable.

At a show I attended recently, I made a comment on Twitter about how disap-pointed I was that I wasn't seeing anything new in event apps. I got two quick responses. One vendor in that category gave its booth number and invited me to stop by to see two new components launching at the event. The other invited me to its booth to see an app the vendor felt was very different and less expensive than other event apps.

I went to see the second exhibitor immediately (I am highly motivated by price as most of the products I'd seen are out of my budget). I was very impressed. That vendor was in fact different from many of the other vendors in terms of the quality and usability of its product (excellent), and their pricing was within my budget.

Next, I went to see the first exhibitor who responded. I knew what their pricing was and that it was beyond my budget, but who knows? Maybe the new feature would actually be a revenue generator and my budget could be juggled. I was keeping an open mind. As it turned out, one of the new components this vendor was launching was something no one else was doing and it was indeed a revenue generator.

Had those two exhibitors not been listening, I may never have stopped by their booths. And if I did, I would have gone there with a preconceived notion that I was not going to see anything different. They set the stage by opening my mind to a new possibility, and I found myself much more receptive to their demos. I also started telling my colleagues to visit those booths.

What about the other exhibitors? Let's assume they saw the tweet and decided not to respond because they knew they had nothing new or innovative going on with their products. Let's hope they sent an email to management telling them what they were hearing. Perhaps those exhibitors' R&D departments were focusing on things that didn't matter to customers like me. Maybe they were focused on speed and platform when what we really wanted was an easier way for people to log in or ways to generate revenue to justify the budget.

Where to Listen

I keep my eye on many shows in different industries and watch the chatter taking place on social media leading up to a show. I have noticed that most pre- and post-show conversations of substance take place on industry blogs, some micro blogs, LinkedIn groups, and sometimes Facebook. Twitter is used more often during the show, likely because it is accessible via smartphones. Yes, other platforms like LinkedIn and Facebook have smartphone apps, but they are still a bit clunky. Twitter is very easy to use on-the-fly. Most pre-show Twitter conversation falls into three categories: show organizer promotions, exhibitors' "come see us in booth xxx" tweets, and attendees announcing they are attending and looking for others who will be there. Personally, I think there is a lot of room for improvement. See Chapter 10, "Be THE Source for Content," for ideas.

Why Is It So Quiet?

If no one is talking about your company, there is a reason. There might not be a lot to talk about. Innovation is taking place in every industry, so are you doing something innovative? People do not talk about what they've already seen a million times. They talk about what is new and exciting. They talk about what is going to transform their industry and their jobs—whether it is positive or negative.

No one was talking about the sound quality of some new portable disk player at the Consumer Electronics Show in 1997 when Audio Highway announced Listen Up, the first portable MP3 player. Sound quality is not innovative, and it's not changing the world. But a portable MP3 player, the first on the market, is innovative and that's what everyone was talking about.

In a presentation I gave on exhibiting at a Sales and Marketing Executive International meeting, I emphasized the need to promote what you are doing that is innovative and new. A member of the audience asked me, "What do you do if your company isn't doing anything innovative and new?" I was rendered speechless for a few seconds and then answered, "If my company was not doing anything innovative and new, I'd be updating my resume."

If you are trotting out the same old horse year after year, your listening time is going to be even more important. Your company needs to know what is going on in the industry and what your customers are talking about. You need to know what makes people so excited that they want to share it with friends.

What to Listen For

One thing social media is not short of is content. The problem is that much of it is irrelevant to you. Some of it is incredibly interesting, yet still irrelevant to you. There is no limit to the amount of time that can be wasted. That is why you need to have a plan of action and need to stick to an agenda when you use social media. Otherwise, you'll get sucked right in and before you know it, the sun will have gone down and you'll have accomplished nothing of any importance. Learn to listen to only what is important and filter out the noise.

Listen for Talk About Your Company and Its Products and Services

Listen to conversations before, during, and after the show that involve your company and your products and services. For an even better overall picture of conversations that apply to your company, listen in on conversations by and about your competition. Also, listen to conversations about your product or service category in general. This will give you a big-picture view of what is going on at the show that relates to your company.

Conversations you might overhear might start with "I missed this morning's session by [Your Company] about packaging safety trends. Did anyone catch it?" Your response can be, "Sorry you missed the session—come by booth #892. The session presenter is in the booth now and can answer any questions you might have." Then let your booth staff know to be on the lookout for this visitor.

Listen for Industry Hot Topics

Keep your ears open for breaking industry news and trending topics during the show. You might see a particular subject coming up often in your Google Alerts, RSS feeds, and Twitter searches. If a particular topic keeps coming up, it's likely to also be on top of your customers' minds. Alert your booth staff to these trending topics because they create a great conversation opener with booth visitors.

If you do any in-booth presentations or lead session topics at the event, your presenters can quickly incorporate those hot topics into their presentations. This will show your customers that you are in tune with what is going on in the industry; it can also give you a much wanted edge over your competition.

Listen for Your Customers

Be sure to include alerts and feeds for your key customers and potential customers in your monitoring. Your booth staff is going to want to know about any major business announcements or breaking news that affects their customers' businesses. Imagine that a key customer at the show announces that his company has just merged with another business. This could directly affect that customer's purchase of your product or service, negatively or positively. It's likely your booth staff has not heard the news. After all, they are busy working the booth. That customer's account rep might not even be at the show. You can quickly make sure your key executives are aware of the new information so they can reach out directly to the customer, or even just have the information for when that customer comes to your booth.

And this brings us to the biggest point of all when it comes to listening: You must pass along the information you are hearing to everyone staffing your booth. Include the information in morning, mid-day, and afternoon briefing sessions with the booth staff. Be sure to give everyone a heads-up about key news updates as the shifts change. Post any new information in the booth and be sure all the staffers know where to look for it and why it's important to check when they start their shift.

I am reminded of a scene in the movie *Devil Wears Prada* where Meryl Streep's character is attending a function with her assistants at her side. The assistants would whisper pertinent information about each guest into her ear as he approached her. You can essentially play that valuable role of knowing everything about everyone when it's most needed. Here's an example:

> **You to your key executive:** That's Jane Smith, VP of purchasing for Giant Customer. They just announced this morning that they are purchasing our competitor's biggest customer for $5 billion and moving manufacturing from Texas to a new plant in Ohio.

Tools for Listening

Listening can be as simple as following along an event hashtag on Twitter, a Facebook page, or a LinkedIn group and culling nuggets of information. Automate it a bit by setting up Google Alerts for keywords. At the top end of the listening spectrum are companies that provide social media monitoring tools. As an exhibit or a brand manager, you're going to be way too busy to do this yourself so I suggest you assign a social media monitor. The good news is that this person doesn't even need to be at the show. This is definitely a task that can be done back in the office. Just make sure they are keeping those at the show informed about what they are hearing. Social media allows you to listen in on some of those conversations taking place in the hallways, around break stations, and even on the plane without ever leaving the office.

Google Alerts

If you can do a simple search on Google, you can create your own Google Alerts. Google Alerts are email updates based on keyword searches that you create. They let you search everything found on Google or narrow down your searches to news, blogs, books, videos, or discussions. For your show, you can create searches on your company, your specific products or services, your competition, hot industry topics, the show organizer, the name of the show, and your current and potential customers. You can choose to have these alerts sent as they happen or daily or weekly.

RSS Feeds

Whereas Google Alerts are great at finding information you don't know is out there, Real Simple Syndication (RSS) feeds will keep you up-to-date on sites you know you want to track. When you come across sites that report regularly on your industry, sign up for their RSS feeds. Each time the site is updated with new posts or entries, that information is sent to your reader. You can choose from many readers, but two popular, easy-to-use web-based readers are FeedDemon and Google Reader. Signing up to receive these feed updates makes your life much easier. You can use RSS feeds to stay up-to-date on trade association announcements and any updates your competition makes around show time.

Twitter Advanced Search

If you want to search topics, people, or company mentions on Twitter, then Twitter's advanced search tool is perfect. You can narrow down your search to specific words, hashtags, who was mentioned, who tweeted, and even geographical regions. You can also narrow results to positive or negative comments and tweets that were questions. This is a handy tool to use during the show to ensure you don't miss anything being said that is important to you. Don't rely on following only the show hashtag if one is being used. There can be a lot of chatter on Twitter from people not using the official hashtag.

Social Media Monitoring Tools

So many social media monitoring tools are available today, and many more coming on the scene every week. These tools help you keep track of what is being said about your company and your brand. They also help you see what's giving you the best return on your investment, as well as where you could stand to improve. They run the gamut from free to low-cost to expensive. When choosing one of these tools, you need to decide which features are right for you based on your social media strategy. If your company is active on social media already, check with your marketing department or PR department; they might already be using such a tool and can set up special monitoring around your trade show program for you. I will warn you, though; the more features the program has, the more complicated it is to use and the longer it will take to learn to use effectively. I suggest you start with a free or low-cost tool that provides the basics you need to get started. Only you can decide whether the time it takes to get up to speed is worth the time you save by using feature rich system.

Here's what these tools will generally deliver to you after they have been set up:

- Complete and detailed coverage of your company activity on all social media platforms
- Detailed analytics or statistical data on your social media activity
- Reports that show who your influencers (people who spread your message) are
- Reports that show sentiment analysis (were the tweets negative, positive, or neutral)

- Lists of what specific content about you, your industry, and/or your competition is going viral
- Lists of customers looking to purchase
- Information broken down by geographical regions

Just be very careful you're not getting yourself into a situation of information overload. Start out by keeping things simple with Google Alerts, RSS feeds, and Twitter searches. This can be done without spending more than 30 minutes a day on it. Break it up by spending 10 minutes first thing in the day, 10 minutes mid-day, and 10 minutes in the evening. This way, there is not much time lag if you find something you feel you need to respond to. If you find that there is too much data to sift through by hand, try social media monitoring tools. And I suggest waiting until things slow down to begin playing with them and learning how to use them effectively. The last thing you need is a situation in which technology prevents you from managing your booth.

Collect and Save the Conversations

While you are listening, it's important that you hang onto the pertinent information you've found. You're going to be able to use it when you are doing your post-event reporting. But for now, don't worry about how you are going to use it—just make sure you are saving it. It will save you hours of digging after the show, and you won't have to worry about not being able to find an important piece of information.

Many tools for saving and collecting information are available. My favorite is Evernote, a free web-based collection bin where you can store all that information and then access it from anywhere you have Internet access. The tagline is "Remember Everything," and it is so true. You can use it to store notes, web pages, images, screen shots, and copied screen text including tweets. You can create a tag for the show and then use that tag on everything you are saving for easy access later.

I would err on the side of too much information. If in doubt, clip it and save; you can decide later whether it's important. I use Evernote for everything to make my life simple, but I find it's extremely helpful in keeping track of important tweets. Because of the sheer volume of tweets being sent, Twitter searches are limited to about a two-week window of time or less. If you don't clip them and save them somewhere, you might never be able to access them again.

Evernote is not just a tool you'll find useful for your social media strategy. Give it a spin for a couple weeks for any information you want to hang on to. I think you'll find that you come to love it as much as many others who use it.

Conversations have always been taking place everywhere at a show. Social media gives us the capability to listen in on those conversations even when we are not present for them. It's up to you to take advantage of the opportunity and use the tools that are available to make that job easier.

Through these conversations, attendees are actually telling you what is important to them. They are telling you what they struggle with, what bothers them, what they wished existed, and what they are looking for on the show floor. The exhibitor who has a listening strategy in place can react immediately if needed and drive more traffic to her booth.

Taking your role beyond just booth logistics and adding value to your company through activities such as listening and reacting are what you want to be remembered for. You can execute a flawless trade show presence and barely capture the attention of upper management. But when you start providing valuable information, such as what your potential customers are saying and what's hot in the industry, suddenly people will start to sit up and take notice.

Summary

You should be listening to conversations before, during, and after the show. Listen by reading industry blogs, watching LinkedIn group discussions, and using the show's community platform, if there is one.

Listen for mentions of your company, your products and services, your competition, industry hot topics, and customer news. If you're not hearing anything about your company, take a step back and seriously ask yourself whether there truly is anything worth talking about. It's better to be alerted before the show so you can fix it, rather than not at all.

Make your job easier by using the available social media listening tools, such as Google Alerts, RSS feeds, Twitter advanced searches, and social media monitoring tools. Make sure these conversations don't go in one ear and out the other by having a system in place to save all these nuggets and to pass them along to the people who need to know about them.

15

Unleash the Power of Mobile

You can incorporate mobile marketing into your trade show program in two ways: the right way and the wrong way. You can use a well thought-out plan that supplements your overall show goals, or you can fall prey to the shiny object syndrome. Unfortunately, most of the exhibitors I've seen using mobile have a bad case of shiny object syndrome. They've heard about some hot new game or app and immediately want to incorporate it into their booth strategy—or, perhaps I should say, wedge it into their booth strategy no matter what.

Just like the social media tools you use, the giveaways you hand out, and the activities taking place in your booth, your use of mobile technology must support your overall show objectives and business goals. You can't have everything you are doing in your booth carefully aligned with your show goals and overall company goals and then suddenly throw in some new app because it's cool. Doing so creates a disconnect and a distraction for your audience.

About a year ago quick response (QR) codes were the hot new thing that everyone was talking about. People were sticking QR codes on everything with little thought as to what they were really trying to accomplish. They were hot, everyone was doing it, and no one wanted to be left behind. They were put on business cards, print advertisements, websites (I'll never understand that one), and even signs and billboards (try scanning a QR code on a billboard while driving 65 mph...no, please don't). Many of the codes I scanned took me to a company's home page. I could have typed in the URL in less time than it took me to scan the image. Some marketers were in such a rush to get their QR codes out there that they never bothered testing to see whether they worked. I came across a full-page color ad in a national magazine once with nothing on the page but a QR code and the brand logo. I scanned the code and was sent to a page that didn't exist. That is a very expensive mistake.

I've also seen some great implementations of QR codes that fit very well into the company's marketing strategy. It is clear they had a plan and saw where QR codes would be the perfect tool to use to implement the strategy. One example I liked was an exhibitor who had a great mobile app that helped their customers estimate the costs of different areas of their operations. Instead of making customers go to the app store and search for the app and then download it, the QR code did all that for them.

If you find yourself getting excited about the next must-have mobile app, take a deep breath and step back. Is it something that makes sense to your overall booth strategy? Is it a tool that will help you achieve your exhibit goals? Do you have the budget and manpower in place to do it right? Or are you just doing it because it's cool?

Sometimes it is hard to resist—especially if the app that is causing so much excitement or is something your CEO just loves. You will have to clearly explain why Angry Birds will not fit into your exhibit strategy and not get you closer to your show goals. As an exhibit manager, this is not a new problem; it's the same battle, just with a new opponent.

When mobile apps are used appropriately, they are a fantastic way to engage your audience and let them interact with your brand in a fun and even educational way. Or, they can be useful tools for your audience to get exactly the information they need quickly and in the way they want it delivered. Either way, the app serves a purpose that fits into your strategy and gets you closer to your goal.

Are Mobile Apps Right for Every Audience?

In late 2009, I was onboard with the argument that not everyone had a smartphone and you had to know your audience before investing money in a mobile app for your exhibit program. According to a comScore Mobile Lens study ending in December 2009, 17 percent of mobile phones in the United States were smartphones.

Today my feeling is that you get onboard or get left behind. In October 2011, Nielsen reported that 43 percent of U.S. mobile phone owners had a smartphone. comScore reports that "U.S. smartphone subscribers surpassed the 100-million mark in January 2012." In March 2012, Apple reported they sold three million iPads in under four days. We should know by now that technology is moving faster than ever, and we can no longer sit around on our hands waiting to see what will happen.

This notion I often hear that trade show attendees are older and don't use smartphones and tablets is just wrong. Today my fellow GenX'ers are the older folks. The oldest of us are in our mid- to late 50s, and the youngest are in their 30s. For those GenX'ers reading this, if you are like me, you are shocked to realize that the oldest of the Millennials, born in 1981, can not only legally drink but somehow have turned 30. That's right; people who might not even have been born the year we graduated high school are in positions of power. Affinity's American Magazine Study reports released in 2011 show that 54 percent—or more than 25 million Millennials—currently own a smartphone and 18 percent plan to purchase one within the next six months.

This is where our marketing focus needs to turn. To stay relevant, you must turn your eye to the future. Take a look at the next, as yet unnamed generation. You'll have to pry their phones out of their cold dead hands. According to Neilson, some 40 percent of those aged 12–17 now own smartphones. Even in households with an income of $30,000 a year or less, 59 percent of teens have cell phones. Fully 72 percent of all teens—or 88 percent of teen cell phone users—send text messages.

As far back as 2007 teens and tweens loved their phones, and loved them more than some very popular teen pastimes. The Disney Mobile Cell and Tell surveyed more than 1,500 kids aged 10–17. When asked "If you had to choose between your phone or something else," they got these results:

- One-third would give up listening to the radio, playing video games, or going to the mall.
- Nearly one-fourth would give up their MP3 players.
- One in five would give up TV.

I spent some time with my eight-year-old niece just the other day. I was taking photos of her with my iPhone, and she asked if I had any games on it. She's never used an iPhone, but in about 30 seconds she mastered an app called Cat Paint. She intuitively knew that she could "pinch" certain things to make them smaller or expand them. In just minutes she found features I did not even know existed after two years of using the app.

Long story short, there is going to be a learning curve for some of the technology you choose to use in your booth. The older folks are going to need some handholding, while the younger generations will just be able to figure it out on their own. Until today's teens and tweens start taking over our boardrooms, you'll have to dedicate some resources to instruction and explanation of what you are doing.

Also, don't expect everyone to play along. We all use our devices differently, and no one size fits all. Even six months ago, I saw no point in adopting a text messaging strategy for our events. To me, this seemed like an unwelcome invasion. Then I went to a conference where the organizer was using it to deliver information to the attendees. I got off the plane, turned on my phone, and there was a short text message telling me where my ride would meet me to take me to the hotel. Next I received a text telling me exactly where to go at the hotel for express check-in for our conference. I was relaxing in my room getting some work done when I got the third message, just a half an hour before our opening cocktail party. The text told me what time the party would start, where it was taking place, and how to get there. By this time, I was a huge fan of text messaging. No digging for confirmations and agendas—all the information was sent to me exactly when I needed it.

Some people will jump on board right away, others will have to be converted, and still others will simply have no interest. That's okay. Mobile marketing is just another tool in your toolbox. You can have different tools for each audience preference. Here are a few mobile tools you can try.

Event Apps

Many of the mobile apps that will have the highest adoption rates by attendees will be those that are sanctioned by the trade show organizer. A mobile event app is a customized mobile app that essentially replaces the big bulky printed show guide (see Figure 15.1). It allows attendees to access all that information and more on their smartphones and tablets. When a show moves from printed guides to a mobile app, the sky's the limit when it comes to the content that can now be shared. Instead of just listing their exhibitors with a short description, logo, and booth number, listings can now include links to video, product brochures, pictures, social media accounts, websites, and more. I am seeing more and more shows both large and small adopting these event apps and as the pricing for developing them continues to drop, this trend will only increase.

Common modules found in mobile event apps are

- Exhibitor list
- Networking tools
- Organizer messages
- Personalized attendee agendas
- Product showcases

- Registration
- Schedules
- Social media sharing tools
- Speaker bios
- Trade show floor map

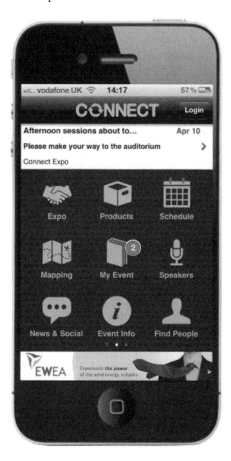

Figure 15.1   *Sample home screen of a mobile app.*

An event app is not something that is purchased or arranged for by you the exhibitor. It is simply another tool the show provides to you. Your responsibility is to participate to the fullest extent you are able by providing the content that will reside there just like you used to provide your company logo and description for the printed guide. Much of the information that populates the event app is pulled from the trade show website and other content the show organizer already has access to. Be sure you have provided all the information the show organizer needs about your booth in the correct format. Many of today's show websites and event apps offer exhibitors a plethora of marketing opportunities, yet many exhibitors don't take advantage of them.

Attendees now can click on an interactive show floor map to get detailed information about each exhibitor. And I'm not just talking about a description and contact information. Exhibitors can now upload white papers, brochures, videos, pictures, and press kits to the show's website, which becomes something of an "exhibitor portal." Much of this, if not all, is often made available through the event mobile app as well.

Keywords are very important to the way these new exhibitor portals work. Show organizers now request exhibitors to use keywords so attendees can search by their specific product and services needs. Some mobile event apps let attendees search the exhibitor list on a certain category and set appointments directly through the app or mark as favorite certain exhibitors they want to see. These exhibitors are then automatically highlighted on the trade show floor map. Some apps will even give the attendee walking directions from one booth to the next.

Consider a Mobile App Sponsorship

As with just about everything at a show, organizers are striving to monetize mobile event apps and offer branding opportunities to exhibitors to help them offset the cost of the app. Many shows are branding their apps with a sponsor's logo prominent on every screen, or they divide the sponsorships, selling off different categories. As an organizer, I've seen these event apps cost anywhere from $5,000 to over $100,000 to develop. The majority are usually well above $25,000, so this branding opportunity is not going to come cheap.

The good news is that as mobile event apps gain in popularity and competition increases amongst developers, the pricing will go down. That means if you do decide to buy into a sponsorship, you need to be strategic when it comes to the partnership/sponsorship contract. With most sponsorship or branding opportunities, it pays to get in on the ground floor and sign a multi-year contract to lock in pricing. But that might not be the case with event app sponsorships. These apps are still very new, so it's hard to place a value on the exposure they bring to a sponsor. Most organizers base their pricing of the sponsorship/branding opportunity on their cost instead of the marketing value.

Many organizers are pricing their sponsorships very high to cover their costs. Sponsorship pricing is all over the map depending on the show. I've seen some sell for $20,000 and some as high as $125,000. Next year that same app, either through the same vendor or a competing vendor, can cost half that or even less. Based on this "cover your cost" pricing structure, your sponsorship investment should go way down, no? But if you lock yourself into this year's prices for three years, you could be paying inflated prices.

Instead, work with your show organizer to create a contract that is a win/win for both parties. Your investment should be directly related to the adoption of the event app and therefore your exposure on it, not the cost to build it. The first year the app is launched might see only a 30 percent adoption rate by attendees. That could go up fairly significantly the second year as more people see its value; then it could really increase the third year. As a sponsor you might come to an agreement with the show organizer that you might pay an investment cost for the sponsorship of $5,000 and then $2,000 for each 10 percent of adoption of the app. If in the first year only 30 percent of attendees use the app, your sponsorship fee might be $11,000 (the $5,000 investment plus the $6,000 for the 30 percent adoption rate). In year three, when they have 70 percent of attendees using the app, your fee would increase to $19,000.

With a contract like this, you make an investment with the show at a time when you might not see a huge return. The show organizer needs to understand that. At the same time, if the app grows in popularity, you need to understand that its value increases, and it becomes a huge asset in the organizer's sponsorship toolkit. You need to agree to a contract based on adoption rates as well as investment values.

The other thing you need to consider before committing to a sponsorship is the usability of the app. Some app vendors do a much better job than others. Some apps are so clunky and hard to use that it's too difficult for attendees to find what they need; they just give up and close down the apps and never refer to them again. I've used some mobile event apps that were so intuitive that once I downloaded them, I never had to look at the printed program again. Keyword searches tied into educational sessions, showed presenter bios and linked right to exhibitors and even downloads that they made available. That is the kind of app you want your name associated with. Not the clunky one that everyone is complaining about throughout the show.

Because you don't want your name on a lousy app your going to want to see and experience what you're investing in. Simply ask the show organizer whom they have contracted with to build the app; then contact the vendor and ask to see what other mobile event apps they have developed with modules and content similar to the show you are sponsoring. You should download them to your smartphone or tablet and start playing with them as a show attendee. Do not have the vendor walk you through a demo. You should not need any instructions on how to use the apps. The app should be intuitive and should let you easily find what you are looking for. If an app is complicated and requires a demo, attendees are not going to use it.

If you decide to sponsor a mobile event app, work with the show organizer to market it to show attendees. Make sure it is being marketed early and often to ensure higher usage. I would even go so far as to suggest having a branded (your branding of course) help kiosk on the show floor to help attendees download the app and navigate it. Yes, it should be intuitive, but us old farts might still have some trouble.

Location-Based Social Networks

With location-based social networks, users check in to places they visit with their mobile device using an app, such as Foursquare, Yelp, and Facebook Places. They can then push those check-ins to their LinkedIn, Twitter, and/or Facebook accounts. Users who check in might win special prizes or get discounts provided by the businesses they are visiting.

Show managers and exhibitors are using these types of location-based networks to drive traffic to booths much like how the low-tech passports were used in the past. The idea of the passport was that visitors had to go to certain booths to get a stamp. Once they filled their books, they could be registered to win a prize. This is now being done by checking in to certain booths and gathering points.

I am not a fan of this gimmick and never have been. Back in the day of passports, visitors would race from booth to booth to get their books stamped. The exhibitors had to pay a premium to be included in the passport book. What did it get the exhibitor? A crowd of people who stayed in the booth only long enough to get a stamp and then were on their way. They didn't even know whose booth they were in half the time. They could care less what the exhibitor was displaying—all that mattered was the end prize.

I see the same thing happening with these location-based social networks. Attendees are running around from booth to booth, checking in to gather points but never once talking to the exhibitor. Some apps build some type of scavenger hunt into the game and require that players actually get answers to questions, which is somewhat better, but it is still distracting to an exhibitor's real goals. I have never met one exhibitor who felt his company's participation paid off in sales. Time will tell if someone comes up with a legitimate use of these types of apps in a trade show situation. Right now all I'm seeing is a distraction from your exhibit's true purpose.

Augmented Reality

I am getting more and more excited about augmented reality apps the more I see them used wisely by marketers. Augmented reality occurs when technology adds to reality. You may be familiar with the use of augmented reality without even realizing it. If you watched hockey on television back in 1997, you might remember the introduction of the blue halo around the puck to allow viewers to track the puck better. Well, that was not much of a success, but it did start the company Sportvision. That company went on to create that yellow first down line shown on screen during football games. That is augmented reality. It's technology adding to reality.

Imagine visitors in your booth using their smartphones' cameras to point to a product on display and up pops a customer testimonial video on their screen. You could tag signs and products in your booth using GPS and a digital compass, and then direct visitors to point their cameras in that direction for more information. Keep in mind that this technology is very new to people so there will be a learning curve. You're going to need to figure in the cost of having resources available to show people how to download the app and use their smartphones to point and view. But this is one gimmick that could have big payoffs by providing education in an engaging memorable way. Instead of just looking at your product in your booth, the visitor could be transported to another customer's location via video, and see your product in action. Augmented reality applications could easily tie into your trade show strategy.

Another idea would be to create a tour of your product or service using this technology. Let's say you have a product, such as LED lighting, that is used in several places throughout the city the show is located in. You could give booth visitors a tour map (and thorough instructions for how your augmented reality app works) and send them off to view how your lighting products can enhance their everyday surroundings. It just might give them ideas for how to use your product in their own businesses. Perhaps your audience at the show are hoteliers. Why not take them on a tour of the venue, highlighting spots where your LED lighting could create a better experience for their guests and telling them how much money could be saved yearly by using LED lighting in those areas.

Sounds great, but what's to stop a competitor from tagging your booth and showing her own promotions? That's where Geofencing comes in. Geofencing creates a virtual boundary around your physical space. It's quite a lot to think about, but your app developer can help you through all the technology.

If you are curious about augmented reality and want to see some examples, download the Layar app available for both iPhone and Android devices. Layar was used by events like the Canne Boat Show and Eureka's Arts Alive! Monthly art tour. Another fun app you can try right now is Pocket Universe available for the iPhone, iPad, and iPod Touch. It will set you back $2.99, but it will give you a fun tour of the night sky. It might get your creative juices flowing for possible applications in your booth.

Mobile Polling

The first year of our consumer show we had a lot of difficulty getting attendees to participate in our surveys. We had a team armed with clipboards, paper, and pens asking attendees a few questions while they wandered the show floor or as they were leaving. Attendees just didn't seem to have the time to answer even two or three short questions. The next year we decided to ditch the paper and pens and used an online polling service for our surveys. We picked up a few iPads and sent the crew out onto the floor again. This time everyone wanted to participate. There was something about the fascination of the technology that lured everyone in.

But fascination aside, this tactic saved us bundles of time analyzing the data. It was also much faster to implement the survey using this online tool, which might have helped with our participation rate. You could put this type of tool to use in your booth to find out what product features your customers like the most or what features they'd most like to see added. You could collect customer satisfaction feedback or even find out how your company is perceived in the industry. Just make sure if you are using a web-based survey tool you have a reliable Internet connection in your booth.

If your audience likes to text, you could use SMS mobile polling. You might be familiar with this via American Idol, which lets the audience vote for their favorite performer by texting a code to a certain phone number. You could do this in your booth to get customer opinions on features they would like to see you add to your product or service. Most mobile polling systems allow you to display the results on a monitor in real time. This way, your booth visitors can see what their peers are interested in as well.

Whereas SMS polling is good for getting opinions of your customers through simple poll questions, a more involved survey could be used as an icebreaker or even to better qualify your booth visitor. Low-cost or free apps are available for download to smartphones and tablets. You can set up your survey online and download the survey to each booth staffer's mobile device. No Internet access is needed to complete the survey after the app is loaded. All the data will be automatically uploaded once an Internet connection is available. You could even use something like this to collect leads with customized qualifying information and requests for specific follow-up.

Lead Retrieval

Speaking of lead retrieval, most shows partner with a registration company to manage attendee and exhibitor registrations. Part of that deal is that the registration company also provides lead retrieval equipment to exhibitors for a rental fee. The lead retrieval equipment reads the attendees' data stored on their badges and then holds that data for each exhibitor in a format that is easy to upload into the exhibitor's customer management software. However, many exhibitors have had frustrating experiences with the equipment used to scan badges. Sometimes they work and sometimes they don't. As your booth staff fumbles with the equipment, the booth visitor, in a hurry, will often give up and leave before you can collect her contact information and qualify her.

More registration/lead retrieval suppliers are coming out with applications that exhibitors can download right to their own smartphones. No swiping is required; you just enter a visitor's badge number into your smartphone and presto! All the visitor's information is downloaded into the app for easy retrieval later. These apps can even be customized with qualifying questions or demographic information.

The best part about these new lead retrieval systems is that they are native apps. Once downloaded, you do not need Internet access to use them to enter badge numbers. The other thing I love about these mobile apps is that you can use the app anywhere, not just in your booth. If your booth staff is in the hallway, at a luncheon, in the bar, or on the elevator, he can easily enter an attendee's badge number and collect the data.

You can also go low-tech with your mobile lead retrieval. Many inexpensive business card scanner apps are available for the iPhone and Android and Blackberry devices. You simply use your phone to capture the card data, and the program automatically loads it into your contact database. The downside to this method is that you get only the data on the card. You'll have to fill in your own notes to indicate the level of qualification. Also, you'll need some sort of tagging system to know which contacts were collected at the show.

Whatever you decide to use, the most important factor is that you are able to follow up with booth visitors in the way they requested with the specific information they were looking for. If your system does not accommodate this type of specific information, it is useless.

QR Codes

I have a love/hate relationship with QR codes. When done right, I think they are very useful. However, many applications of QR codes are nothing more than a silly gimmick and deliver nothing of value to the booth visitor. They also require the user to download a QR code reader to her smartphone or tablet device to scan the code. This means you need to have staff on hand to teach those not familiar with QR codes how they work. While QR codes have caught on in other countries, we're still not completely on board with them in the United States. That can be partly because we still don't know what they are. And that poor implementation in the past has left those who know what they are very disappointed, so let's not blame the tool when it's been used improperly.

The Gartner Symposium/ITxpo did a fantastic job incorporating QR codes into its event. Codes were included in presentations and signage throughout the venue that clearly stated what would be delivered via the scan. Attendees used the codes to get access to specific Gartner research, video, and webinars. Gartner also alerted attendees prior to the event how the QR codes would be used and that they would need to download a scanner available via the attendee's smartphone or tablet app store. Granted, this is a tech savvy group, so they did not need a lot of instruction.

On the flip side, I talked to one exhibitor who used QR codes in his company's booth to eliminate much of the paper passed out in his booth. A scan of QR codes in the booth would launch a specific product video. This company's audience was not as tech savvy as Gartner's, so very few people actually scanned the QR codes (notice they had a way to measure whether they were being used). This company felt the real estate they gave up on their graphics was not worth the effort.

Another problem was the fact that Internet access was spotty in the venue. Although booth visitors could scan the QR code, the videos required too much bandwidth to load. As I've said earlier, if anything you do requires Internet access, you need to make sure you've taken steps to have a solid connection in your booth.

More and more show attendees will be walking around with smartphones in their pockets or tablets in their hands in the very near future. The right mobile app can be a key tool in your trade show strategy. We're going to start seeing these apps used more and more, and attendees will come to expect them. As smartphones grow in popularity, tools such as QR codes and augmented reality will require less hand-holding and instruction on use. Your booth staff will spend very little time showing attendees how to use the technology and will be able to focus more on a conversation about the attendees' need for your product or service.

I've named just a few types of mobile applications I think could work well with your booth strategy. But remember, they are just tools and should have a larger purpose than just a wow factor. Sure, that will help you draw in visitors, but then you need to deliver something to the visitor that helps connect them to your company. There was a time when the telephone was new and exciting—now it's just a faster, easier way to communicate. The same could be true of augmented reality in a few years' time. Technology moves at a much quicker pace these days. Six months from now I'm sure there will be many more cool new tools on the market.

If you have a large budget and the human resources to commit to it, you might want to think about trying something that is very cutting-edge. If you don't have a large budget for this, tag along with what the show organizers are doing and take advantage of their marketing. But one way or another, you need to start going mobile, or you'll be left behind.

Summary

With more than 100 million people using smartphones, it's time to think seriously about incorporating mobile technology into your trade show strategy—*strategy* being the key word here. Use mobile technology strategically and only if it brings you closer to achieving your goal. Don't get caught up in following trends just because they are the hot topic of the month.

Many show organizers are realizing their attendees are smartphone-wielding, mobile-savvy buyers, and are developing event apps. Make sure as an exhibitor that you are taking full advantage of the opportunities the show organizer gives you by submitting any and all content your buyers will be looking for on the event app.

Consider incorporating mobile technology such as location-based apps, augmented reality, mobile polling, texting, lead retreival, and QR codes into your booth strategy. However, whenever you consider using any type of mobile tool, ask yourself whether it will help you achieve your goal, or whether it's just a gimmick. Until your audience gets up to speed on new technology, you'll have to plan for the on-hand staff to do some hand-holding.

IV

You're Not Finished Yet

The show might be over, but there is still a lot of work to do. Often what you do—or don't do—post-show has the biggest impact on your trade show program. Imagine if you collected 50 A+ quality leads and no one followed up on them. I'm talking about buyers who are ready to buy; all your sales department needs to do is pick up the phone. That one mistake can turn your most successful show into your biggest failure. It is the same with your social media efforts. You've done all that work before and during the show, so the last thing you want to do is let it all go to waste.

Adding virtual and social media components to your show strategy doesn't fundamentally change your post-show strategy. But it does add a few to-dos to the list of tasks. It adds a few components to your post-show return on investment (ROI) reporting that just might help boost your show's return.

In this post-show part, we focus on the new tasks your social media program adds to your post-show to-do list. I'll say this now to get it out of the way: Nothing is more important than your lead follow-up system. That should always be priority number one on your post-show to-do list. After those leads go into the sales and marketing funnel, you can start on your other post-show tasks.

If you've done some of the things I discussed in earlier chapters, you will come back from the show with buckets and buckets of information, ideas, and content: information you collected when you were in listening mode; ideas that came out of sessions, interviews, and surveys; and content in the form of video, session summaries, pictures, and audio podcasts. Just like great leads, none of that is worth anything until you do something with it. But doing something with it is exactly what you will do. In the end, you will have enough quality content to open a publishing house.

Content is the art of your post-show strategy, and metrics and measurement are the science. You can only properly measure your event's success or failure by having a measurement system in place. How do you know whether you collected enough leads to qualify the show as a success if you didn't have measurable objectives attached to that goal? How do you know whether your social media strategy was a success if you cannot properly measure its contribution? Proper measurement gives you the information you need to decide whether something was a success and should be invested in for future shows or if something was a failure and needs to be scrapped.

You also have to keep your social media connections alive. You can't just suddenly stop communicating and figure you'll start where you left off when next year's show rolls around. If you do this, you are missing one of the key benefits of adding social media to your trade show program—the 365-day-a-year communication plan. By keeping the conversations going with customers, prospects, bloggers, media, and industry thought leaders, each year your social media communication plan gets easier and easier. It will also grow stronger and stronger.

It sounds like a lot of work, and it is indeed. But you won't do it all in a day, or a week, or even a month. You'll spread it out over the course of an entire year. You will be smart about it and put plans in place to manage your time and work flow. Rome wasn't bulid in a day...and it wasn't built by one person, either. You will create a team that crosses all silos of your organization and taps into many different departments. Social media is about your customers, and customers should be the responsibility of your entire company. So now that your leads are already being processed and sales is following up on them, we can start looking at all that fabulous content and turn your role into one the company cannot live without.

16

Repurpose Your Content

If your team has done as much listening as they could during the show and you've done even just one or two content creation show activities, you've likely got a treasure trove of information just waiting to be repurposed and incorporated into your overall marketing and communication plan. You'll also have information and feedback that will be valuable to other departments in your company. I love this process because it satisfies both your creative and analytical sides. You have to make sure you have a plan in place and that you divvy up the actual content creation work to the appropriate people. Otherwise, you will soon be overwhelmed and completely consumed by the task at hand.

Most event managers and trade show managers are incredible project managers. The nature of your job requires you to be a great planner and scheduler. It also requires you to delegate tasks and stay on top of those people who've been assigned different tasks. So I don't need to tell you how to be a project manager, just what you'll need to manage. You'll soon be turning your marketing department into a content publishing house.

Why Should You Even Care About Content?

Let's first take a look at what content can do for your company in general. Customers are no longer satisfied with your company's "About Us" web page for information they need to make a purchasing decision. They want you to have an "About Them" website. They expect you to not just push your products and services, but also to provide them with information they need to do their jobs better. Only after you've gained their trust will they consider hiring your company as a vendor.

Michael Brenner, senior director of integrated marketing for SAP, put it well when he wrote on his blog (*B2B Marketing Insider*, http://www.b2bmarketinginsider.com), "No matter what business you are in, buyers are constantly seeking information to either grow their revenue, reduce their costs, or eliminate risks. They are not waiting for just the right campaign to come along and solve all their problems with an offer they can't refuse."

Good content is written to provide buyers with the information they are seeking. Good content is there when they need it at every step in the buying process. Good content gets your company on their radar early in the buying process and keeps you there throughout. Good content creates thought leaders who customers turn to when they're making buying decisions. And it is important to remember that thought leaders can be found everywhere, not just in your c-suite. They could be product managers, designers, and salespeople. A thought leader isn't born; he's appointed by his audience.

And what about your trade show? Content is what keeps your presence at the show alive long after it is over. It's what keeps your company on top of people's minds. It', what makes them seek out your company at the next event. It's what makes your job easier during your pre-show preparations next year.

By staying on top of attendees' minds throughout the year, they won't forget who you are. They are more inclined to pay attention to your pre-show marketing because they know you provide them with valuable information. They are more likely to stop by your booth next year because they know your in-booth presentation will be worth sitting through. They have been trained to *not* tune you out because they have seen a lot of relevant information coming out of your company.

They are more likely to attend a session your executive is speaking at because they find your information useful to them in their day-to-day jobs.

You will also likely find yourself on the show organizer's radar. He may have seen all the information you've published and want to tap into your company to deliver key sessions or sit on panel discussions about where the industry is headed. When he asks attendees who they want to see speak, your company's executives' and employees' names might start to come up more and more.

Having members of your company participate in key industry sessions or be featured in the show daily is one of the best ways to drive traffic to your booth. That drives attendees to come to your booth for more information. You're no longer a company selling widgets but are the company that really understands the industry and the needs of its customers. That's why you should care about content.

So Exactly What Is the Content You Will Be Repurposing?

All that stuff I had you running around collecting during the show is what is going to make up your content. All those video interviews you did, all those pictures you took in your booth and at events, and all those tweets I insisted you collect—that's what is going to supply you with months' worth of great content that you can repurpose. I asked you to send employees to sessions to take notes and observe. If they did a thorough job, you could have five or six articles or even a white paper as a result. So let's take a look at everything you collected.

Tweets

Hopefully while you were in listening mode, you archived any tweets you thought would be useful into Evernote or similar information collection application. If you tagged them with keywords as you collected them, your job is going to be very easy. If you didn't, well buckle in because this is going to be a bit more time-consuming. However, you must do it because it is worth it. The tedious exercise will certainly stick with you and ensure you collect as you go next time.

First, search Twitter on the event hashtag. Do it soon after the show ends because a search returns tweets for only about the past two weeks. You are looking for five main things. If you did archive your tweets during the show, you won't have to search the hashtag; you can just start sorting them as follows:

- Any mentions of your company. Tweets posted during the show can be used in your post-show brand reach reports.
- Any mentions of your customers' companies and what your customers

were talking about. This information is going to show you what is important to them.

- Any mentions of your competition and what they were talking about. This could be a treasure trove of competitive intelligence.

- Important industry issues that were discussed, including hot topics, innovative concepts, and of course tweets that start with "I wish..." and "I hate..." This information is going to show you what is important to the entire industry.

- Who is doing all the talking and who is retweeted the most. These people could be industry thought leaders and respected key opinion leaders, and possibly people you want to align your company with or tap into as a resource for future content.

You can use the information you get out of these tweets to start a topic list for future blog posts, industry articles, white papers, marketing messages, sales materials, and so on. This information comes straight from the horse's mouth, and it makes for the best content. Your customers and potential customers are telling you what their pain points are, and you can either show you have a solution or start creating one. I walked away from the last show I attended with about three months's worth of content. You also might find among a tweet's 140 characters bits of information, new ideas for product or service lines or product or service improvements.

Any significant mentions of your company can be used as anecdotal evidence of your show's success and included in your post-event reports. But don't hang onto only the positive mentions. Negative reviews about products or what you are doing can be even more valuable. It can stop you from going down the wrong path and stop an investment in failure.

Audio Interviews

Listen again to the audio interviews you did and separate out the wheat from the chaff. But before you go deleting any of the chaff, again, make sure there is nothing in there that might be great information for your marketing department or other departments within the company—even if it might not be great for public consumption. A piece of audio that has too much background noise might not make it to a public space, but it could still be information useful to customer service, R&D, technical support, billing, and so on. Don't always think of these interviews as an end product, but cultivate the information you find within them.

Now on to the recordings you can publish as podcasts, customer testimonials, or transcribed into text. Clean them up as needed by editing out clumsy starts or finishes. It's okay to also edit out any bits in the middle that are just not working for you. You should keep the best sound bites. If someone gives a great answer on question one but drones on and on in question two, it's perfectly fine to use only the first question. You can also add a nice intro piece to the recording to give context to the interview.

What is the optimal length of time for a podcast? There are a lot of theories about this. Some say no longer than 5–10 minutes; others say less than 15 minutes; still others say podcasts can go on for 30 minutes. My opinion is that your podcast should be just long enough to get your message across and not a minute longer. I have an entire collection of podcasts on my iPod that are 30–60 minutes long. If they are interesting, I will listen to them all the way through. If they have not captured my attention, they get deleted after the first 5 minutes.

Customer interviews are probably going to be fairly short. An interview with an industry expert on a topical matter relevant to your audience might go 10–15 minutes. If your podcast is communicating a more complicated topic and position and you are using it to motivate or persuade, it could be 30 minutes or more. Again, my mantra is long enough to get your message across and not a minute longer.

You can also strip the audio portion out of a video and create a separate audio podcast from that. The advantage to doing this is that people can listen to the audio when their eyes are engaged in another activity like driving or working out at the gym. The disadvantage is that if the content relies on the video portion, it makes for a less-than-ideal audio podcast.

As far as the technical how-to aspect of creating MP3s, hosting them, and then creating RSS feeds for distribution, there are plenty of detailed instructions on the Internet. Just Google "how to podcast" and you'll get to choose from about 120 million results. You can also search that phrase on YouTube and get step-by-step instructional videos. I can assure you it is a do-it-yourself process. There are many steps, but they are all pretty simple. Of course, if you have more money than time at your disposal, hiring someone to do it for you is a smart choice. After you've created the podcast, you can go to iTunes for instructions on how to submit them there (http://bit.ly/ituneinstructions).

Pictures

I find it's best to do a quick sweep through all the photos you took at the show and delete any that you quickly decide are not usable. Then, do a closer sort into different categories. Get rid of blurry photos, unflattering photos, and ones that provide no context. It's entirely up to you how you sort them for further use depending on what you've captured and what you want to use them for.

One quick visual way to further sort through the photos is to separate out event shots and wide group shots from close-ups of individuals or small groups. You could also sort them by booth photos, event photos, and candid shots of individuals or small groups. It all depends on where you were taking photos. Keep the following in mind:

- Booth shots can be used in future show marketing.

- Candid shots of customers can be shared with your sales staff to pass along thereby providing another contact point with this customer.

- Event photos can be posted online and shared via social media, possibly via Flickr, Facebook, Animoto, or your own website.

- Photos of individuals in the booth or with staff members can be used in marketing materials (be sure you have permission).

- Product or demo photos taken in the booth can also be used in marketing materials (if they feature a booth visitor just be sure you have permission).

- Appropriate photos can be used as a highlight or visual element in blog posts.

Videos

Start sorting through videos the same way you sorted through pictures. A good amount of the videos might actually be unusable, because of bad lighting, bad sound, or boring segments. That's okay, though, because the more video you took, the better chance you'll have of finding something really valuable.

Before you delete video because it's boring or has bad lighting, see if it contains any important information that you can capture. Look for clips such as feedback from customers on your products or services and industry trends. You might be able to use the audio portion for soundbites or podcasts, even if the lighting is not so good.

If you have good videos of product demonstrations, you can post them on YouTube and then use them as instructional videos or pass them along to customer service. Remember that some people process information better via reading and others via video. Listen closely to what people are saying as well in these videos. Candid comments like "this is so easy to use" or "I had no idea it could do such-and-such" are marketing gold.

If you have videos of in-booth presentations, these can be cleaned up and used to create a video blog or be embedded into a post with a transcript. Why both? Again, some people like to view and others will prefer to read.

Videos of presentations by industry thought leaders are valuable. These are not just something to be posted online as is or promoted via social media, traditional marketing, and email. These videos are filled with concepts and ideas that can be further expanded on and used as thought leadership articles.

Video testimonials are fairly obvious. These can be used in their entirety, or you can pull out quotes to use all over your sales and marketing materials. If you have collected customer testimonials, you'll need to make sure you have permission to use them before making them public.

Customer interviews may have been videotaped for internal use only. A video interview is quicker and often produces more candid results when done well. You can either document everything useful to the company and pass it along to the appropriate departments or just pull off the information you need and pass along the video to other departments to pull from it what they need.

You can send these videos out for cleanup or do it yourself with easy-to-use tools available for Windows or Apple computers. YouTube has its own user-friendly video editing tool that you can download (available at http://www.youtube.com/editor). You can smooth out the intro and the endings and even add a bit of graphics and title page.

Get these videos posted on YouTube, iTunes, and Vimeo, and then embed them into your website. YouTube, at the time of this writing, is the second-largest search engine behind Google. Be sure to tag your videos with the appropriate keywords. Do this and you could see an increase in your rankings on other search engines.

But don't stop at YouTube and other video hosting sites. You can submit your best videos that appeal to a niche audience to industry publications, blogs, vlogs, and podcasts. Editors and hosts of these sites are looking for media rich content as well. This will extend your reach to a wider audience than your company can reach through your website and random searches.

Session Notes

If you've sent staff to industry relevant sessions and they were taking notes, you can turn that information into content for blog posts, white papers, industry articles, product or service improvements, or even new product or service offerings.

Even though you might have had someone live blog during these sessions, you can still use those notes to create meatier, lengthier content. When I am taking notes during sessions, I scribble down each and every question that is asked by the audience. If one person has a question, then I have to assume more people out there need the answer as well. Answering these questions makes for valuable content.

You'll have the expertise in your company to answer some of those questions if they relate to the solutions your company provides. Others might not be in your company's area of expertise but can still be great fodder for content. Remember, it isn't always all about you; it's about your customers and what they need.

Let's say one of the questions asked during a session was, "What's the best way for someone with my educational background to break into this particular field of focus?" This can be an indication that it's getting tougher for your customers in a particular role to find work in their present field. Maybe they are being phased out because of new regulations, automation, or changes in the marketplace. I bet if that's the case, the one person asking the question in the session can't be the only one with job security on her mind.

This is where you can really add value by writing an article or a blog post around this topic. Interview HR directors and hiring managers within your customers' companies and ask them exactly that question. How do people with different backgrounds break into this field? Even though an article like this may not result in immediate sales, it does position your company as one that is in tune with the needs of its customers.

If the expertise is not available in your company, go to where it is available. Someone's going to write about this topic eventually, so why not your company? You create the framework for the article and let the subject matter experts fill in the meat. Even if posted or printed in a trade publication or industry blog, it will tie back to your company through the byline. It will show up in a search online with a link to your company website. And remember that it doesn't just have to be formatted in the written word. It can be done as an audio interview or even video.

Track What You Pass On To Other Departments

Any information like new product ideas, customer complaints, common questions on how your product or service works, and so on needs to be passed along to the appropriate departments. But it only gets off your plate—for a while. If you want to use this information in your post-event reports and track results, you'll have to track the information's progress. It doesn't do you any good to gather valuable information and pass it along and not be able to tie its success or an opportunity to improve back to your show. You'll also need to know what didn't pan out so you can either fix it for the next show or ditch the effort in the future.

Keep notes on what information you are passing along to each department and track how it's used or even whether it has been used. Let's say you passed along several tips on what customers are looking for in your product to your research and development team. One year later a successful new product is launched as a result of the information you passed along. That is something you need to get credit for—and you can only get credit for it if you've been tracking it.

You might have passed along video footage that showed several customers strug-gling to figure out where the on/off switch was for your equipment. You find that by tracking that information through customer support and product development that the switch was moved in future models cutting down on a significant number of calls to customer support thereby saving the company money and improving product satisfaction. You'll be able to credit your participation in the show with that cost savings and improved satisfaction, which will in turn effect your show return on investment (ROI).

This type of information tracking is no different from the leads you collect at a show. Counting leads collected at a show doesn't give you the information you need to show ROI. You have to track each lead through the sales cycle to be able to show the results of your company's investment in the show. It's the same theory with these golden nuggets of information.

What to Do with What's Left

What you should have left is a bunch of great content to be repurposed and a list of topics for articles, white papers, blog posts, and audio and video podcasts. The first thing I like to do is create a file that lists all the bits of content I have accumu-lated that are ready to go as-is. This is the content you can post online immediately and share via social media while the event is still hot in people's minds. If you can get it posted within a week of the event closing, you'll get the best pass-along rates via social media as everyone will still be following the hashtag on Twitter and using the event social media platforms to keep in touch with the people they've met through the show.

I also create another file that lists all the content that still needs to be created based on the notes I've taken. I cross-reference that with any pictures I have that could go along with each topic or any audio or video I can include with it. Create draft headlines for each piece of content. These don't have to be the final headline, just something that will jog your memory weeks from now as to what the subject mat-ter is.

My ready-to-go list might look something like this:

- Product demo video taken in booth.
- Compilation video of customer interviews asking, "What is your favor-ite feature of Product X?"
- Compilation video of customer interviews asking, "How did implemen-tation of Product X save your company money?"
- Video of "State of the Industry" in-booth presentation.
- PowerPoint presentation from session titled "Cloud Computing Security."

My list of content still to be created might look something like this:

- "The feature you didn't know you could live without...until now" (customer interview bsmith.mpg, product demo video)
- "Five things you need to know before upgrading to version 5.0" (internal experts available in sales support)
- "How to increase revenue using Service XYZ" (internal experts available in sales)
- "Interview with the top three leaders in innovation" (panelists from conference: Jim Smith, Sally Thompson, and Randy Gold)
- "Predictions for the top five skills every CIO will need going into the new year" (notes from closing general session)

At a recent conference I attended (not even exhibited at), I walked away with a list of 43 potential blog posts and articles. That supplies me with almost a year's worth of content if I were to release one blog post every week. And that's just one conference. Much of those topics came from questions asked during sessions, things I overhead in the hallways, and viewpoints of speakers I disagreed with or topics I felt I could cover better than the speakers.

Create an Editorial Calendar

What happens to all those great bits of content and list of ideas after you close that folder? If you don't have a plan in place to publish them, it's likely not much at all will happen. You'll start planning for your next show or get busy with other work, and the list will gather dust. You'll keep saying, "I'll take care of that as soon as I'm finished with this project." Days will turn into week and weeks will turn into months, and before you know it, you'll have a list of great content that other people have beat you to publishing.

There is no feeling worse than opening your customers' industry publication six months from now and finding an article that was on your list written by or quoting your competition titled, "Predictions for the Top Five Skills Every CIO Will Need Going into the New Year." It gets even worse if it's popular and is spread all over the Internet and referred to in 20 other blogs.

An editorial calendar will not only ensure you actually get around to creating and posting that great content, but will also help to ensure you are not overwhelmed with doing it all at one time. It quickly shows you, at a glance, where the holes are that you need to fill. It also lets you know when you are falling behind. If you have a company blog, after you establish expectations with your readers, you'll need to keep up the pace. So decide what those expectations are going to be and be sure it is a schedule you'll be able to keep up with, even when your workload increases.

Your calendar might look something like this:

Month	Important Dates	Blog Post	Article	Audio/ Video	Podcast	White Paper	eBook
January							
February							
March							
April							
May							
June							

First, fill in any important industry dates that are relevant to your audience. If you supply products or services to the tech industry, CES in January is an important date. If you supply products or services to the collegiate industry, August (enrollment) and May (graduation) are important dates. This will help you position the right content at the right time. You're not going to post one of your best tech industry articles during the height of CES, as no one will be around to read it. This is a great time to fill the gap with show-related content—maybe a "Best Restaurants in Vegas for CES" post categorized by price points with a good descriptive headline that includes the show name you're likely to drive traffic to your website.

Decide how often you will publish certain types of content, and then fill in the calendar accordingly. If you decide you will publish white papers or e-books only once per quarter, then you can decide in which months those will be released. You'll be able to see at a glance when you posted your last video to YouTube and see that there has been a two-month gap; that means it's time to get another one posted. It can also help you plan and budget for outside professional writing help or help internal contributors budget their time.

Just Exactly Who Is Going to Do All This Work?

Unless you're sitting around your office each day with a couple extra hours to kill, it sure can't be only you. Not to mention, you can't be the expert on every topic you want to cover in your content. You're going to have to enlist the help of others within your company to do some of the heavy lifting. This is where all that digging around within your company for people who support your social media efforts comes in. Remember that guy in programming who has his own blog? Why not ask him to write a blog post that dovetails with his expertise?

Also tap into your executive team for some of these articles. It's important for them to gain visibility this way, and they'd probably be happy to work on some of the articles that you are targeting for industry publications or blogs. Use them for audio and video podcasts if they are great on camera but not such great writers. This is where you editorial calendar will come in handy. You can give them plenty of time to make sure those key articles are coming out at the most appropriate times.

I love interview articles because they do not require a lot of work on your end. You can simply come up with four or five questions that further expands on topics covered at the show and send them to industry leaders to answer. But be sure to let them know their answers will be published verbatim and only cleaned up for spelling and grammar if that is what you intend to do.

I recently heard a complaint from a speaker who was interviewed for this type of article on an event blog. English was not his first language, but the blog was written for an English-speaking audience. He assumed the text would be edited for proper English phrasing, but his answers to the interview questions were posted exactly as he wrote them. He was very upset that it made him sound less intelligent.

I was interviewed recently for an article and thought my comments would be used as part of a larger piece. It turned out to be a Q&A interview, and the author quoted my responses verbatim, including the very casual conversational tone and grammar. Had I known this, I would have requested to have the questions in advance and time to craft my answers for clarity. To avoid these types of misunderstandings, be very clear to your interviewee how you intend to include their responses. Will they be edited for clarity and grammar or just dropped into the post as is? I find it's good practice to send them a copy of the article for review before it's posted.

You can enlist the help of freelance writers or ghost writers to fill out the information you gathered at your show. A freelance writer will interview the necessary people to get accurate information to write the article or blog post. Many good freelance writers do not even need to know much about the industry or topic they are writing about. It's all in the questions they ask and in probing for more information. The advantage is that the piece will be written in a way that ensures it is easy to understand. It will not contain complicated industry jargon and will be broken down to the essential points. Your CEO might be the smartest person in the world but not a very good writer, so it's perfectly acceptable to bring in the freelance or ghost writer. Many memoirs of famous people are actually written by ghostwriters, but they are not just for the rich and famous. Everyday busy people use them all the time.

Your job is not to create all the content. Your job is to project manage the content. Some of you are lucky enough to be able to pass this on to someone else in the marketing department. If you are passing it off to another department to manage, make sure you keep tabs on it. If four articles get published in trade publications this year on content you brought back from the show, it should be noted on your show reports as part of your ROI reporting.

You might not have everything listed in this chapter, and that's fine. Quite frankly, it would probably be overwhelming if you were doing every single thing on here, especially for the first time. At least it would be without a team of about 10 people at the event focused on just collecting content. What is important is that you use what you have. Don't let it gather dust on a shelf. Squeeze every last bit of information you can out of whatever you have. Even if it's only five good tweets and thorough notes from two sessions. Create a list of content you can create from it; put it on your calendar; and assign people to create it, get it published, and track the results. Next show you can add some new tools to your bag of tricks.

Bringing all that show content back to the office to repurpose and build new content extends the life of the show and your audience reach. That in itself is wonderful but tracking the results of what happens to the information coming back from the show can improve your exhibit program's ROI and ensure funding in the future. You may even be able to grab a few extra dollars in future budgets.

Of course, you also want to distribute that great content across all the different social media channels you are using to provoke conversation in the industry. That way you can track what content is getting the most attention. This will help you plan your strategy and continually refine your tactics for future shows.

Summary

One way you can extend the length of your show is by extending the life of the content you've created and collected at the show and repurpose it. Tweets can turn into blog posts, session summaries can turn into industry articles, and questions asked during your in-booth presentations can turn into white papers. Create and repurpose content your customers and the industry are hungry for and will help build trust in your company. But don't just think of content in terms of text. You have pictures and videos that can be posted online and spread through various social media channels.

Planning ahead allows you to budget time and resources you need to implement your content project plan. By organizing all the information you bring back from the show and setting up a editorial calendar, you have a much better chance of that content seeing the light of day.

But don't just pass along information to other departments and publish great information and forget about it. Be sure to track how that information is used and what content resonates best with your audience. This way you can track your exhibit program's ROI and decide where to invest your money and efforts in the future.

17

A Case for Metrics and Measurement

I am one of those marketers who believes the purpose of marketing is to drive sales.

The American Marketing Association's (AMA's) definition of marketing is, "Marketing is the activity, set of institutions, and processes for creating, communicating, delivering, and exchanging offerings that have value for customers, clients, partners, and society at large."

Phooey! It even sounds like something a marketing department would write. Ask any CEO, CFO, or board of directors what marketing's purpose is and they will tell you it is to drive sales. Now in fairness, I'm sure (hoping) the AMA considered the words to drive sales at the end of that definition is assumed.

After all, a company cannot stay in business just because everyone knows what it is selling. A company stays in business because it sells stuff. Everything you do in marketing must have a purpose, and that purpose is to sell stuff.

Your social media plan for your trade show is no different. In the end, you do it because you want to sell stuff. This is why I'm not a huge fan of "fun" contests to drive traffic to your booth. I think they are gimmicky and often done with no plan to drive sales. "But it's for brand recognition," you say. But what is the point of brand recognition if not to sell more product or services?

If your company has so much money that you can invest in a trade show for the purpose of brand recognition, then your company probably has all the brand recognition it needs. If your company doesn't have much brand recognition, it's probably because you're not selling very much stuff. Save the brand recognition for when you are flush with cash because your sales are so high.

And, when it comes right down to it, brand recognition is not the end game. Which would you rather have—a million people who recognize your brand or a million people who buy your stuff? I guarantee the million people who bought your products recognize your brand.

Focus on Sales

I do believe marketing does all those things the AMA says it should. Everything you do might not directly lead to a sale, but everything you do should bring you one step closer to that end goal of making a sale. Paying attention to what people say on Twitter might not directly result in a sale, but it should bring you closer. You want to focus your participation and conversations on social media to those that bring you closer to a sale.

If you spent time and took up real estate at a show that encouraged Foursquare check-ins for a prize, you need to show what the return on investment (ROI) was for this effort. If it didn't fit into your strategy and was there only as a gimmick to "drive booth traffic," here's how the conversation might go:

CFO: How did the show go?

Brand Manager: It was great; we had 30 percent more traffic this year than last year.

CFO: That's great? What do you owe the jump in traffic to?

Brand Manager: We participated in a Foursquare check-in contest.

CFO: What is that?

Brand Manager: All attendees who checked in using Foursquare at certain booths were registered to win a grand prize.

CFO: So what happened in our booth when they checked in?

Brand Manager: The person checking in got access to our show specials.

CFO: So when they checked in, they talked to a sales rep?

Brand Manager: Well, no, not exactly, but if they are interested in the show special, they'll contact a sales rep.

CFO: So, you are able to qualify those leads you got from Foursquare?

Brand Manager: Well, no, not exactly because it was all done through Foursquare, and it was so busy we didn't have time to really qualify them.

CFO: How much did this game cost?

Brand Manager: It was a $5,000 sponsorship to be included in the contest.

CFO (*blank stare*): I have to go to a meeting now.

This is not an extreme example. I have this conversation with way too many brand managers and trade show managers who are focused on driving traffic to their booth. They get caught up in the numbers game. They put a high value on quantity of visitors and almost no value or focus on quality of visitors. You'll get much more respect and be taken seriously in your company when you focus first on quality instead of on quantity.

Determine exactly who is a qualified lead and then focus your marketing efforts on those visitors. Try to get as many of those people into your booth as possible with promotions that would appeal to them and also move them closer to a purchase. Sure, a qualified visitor might flock to your booth for a chance to win a car. But only a qualified visitor seriously interested in buying your product will come to your booth for a chance to win free service for a year after he has made a purchase. Those are your real potential customers.

Now imagine a conversation that goes something like this:

CFO: How did the show go?

Brand Manager: We saw a significant increase this year in qualified buyers in our booth.

CFO: That's great. What do you owe the jump in traffic to?

Brand Manager: We did several things to attract decision-makers to our booth to win a year's free service contract if they purchase our software before year's end. One of those was our use of a social media tool called Twitter.

CFO: Twitter? Isn't that just a bunch of people talking about what they ate for lunch?

Brand Manager: Funny you say that because we did end up giving several purchasing agents tips on where to eat when at the show, but no, it's much more than just that. We were able to reach a broad audience we didn't even know existed just by tweeting about this special offer. We tracked it by asking them to show us the tweet to be registered for the free service contract.

CFO: How much did all this cost?

Brand Manager: There was no cost associated with using the tool; however, we did have one person dedicated to monitoring the account and tweeting. That investment over the four days was about $900 in salary and another $1,500 in travel, hotels, and meals. However, we can tie 15 qualified buyers directly to that effort. If one of them results in a sale, our investment will be worth $20,000.

CFO: That sounds like a sound investment. I'm looking forward to seeing your full report.

Brand Manager: We also forwarded some information to R&D about which features our customers are saying they need to do their jobs better. It's just very vague information right now, but it's something they can follow up on and do more research on. It's at least a start for them, though.

CFO (*smiling and shaking your hand*): I have to go to a meeting now, but we'll talk more when we go over your full report. Sounds like a very successful event.

That's a fantastic conversation to have in the hallway back at the office. You have just conveyed to the c-suite that you understand business and you know that business is sales and profit.

So, How Do You Put Together That Show Report?

Proof of a show's success or failure does not come from a feeling inside. Proof can be found only in cold hard facts and numbers. Your staffers might feel the show was a huge failure because they barely had any traffic. Yet six months later, two people who stopped by your booth could end up each making a $250 million purchase. Was it a success or a failure? Wait, before you can answer that question you need to know how much that show cost. You also need to know how much it normally costs the company to make a sale like that. If it costs $50,000 to make each sale made from the show and the average cost of a sale in your company is $25,000, then the show was not such a success.

But then factor in the fact that you met with 25 key purchasing managers at that same show. They are not sold yet, but what dollar value does your company place on a meeting like that? It's important to have these numbers; otherwise, your calculations are meaningless. This is exactly why I suggested you have lunch with your CFO because she will be able to help you fill in the blanks.

Before we get started on how to put together your report, it's important to stress that not every tactic will show up as a success. You're going to have some failures, and some of those failures will be whoppers. That is what marketing is all about. Some things you try will be small successes and some things will be huge successes. Some strategies or implementations of those strategies will fail. What is unforgivable is not knowing what succeeded and what failed. How will you know what to do next year and what not to do if you're not measuring for success? Henry Ford put it well when he said, "Failure is only the opportunity to begin again, only this time more wisely."

You don't need to make a separate post-show report for your social media efforts. Just include them in your regular reporting like you would expected leads and product demos. This all ties back to your exhibit goals, objectives, and strategy. Let's look back at our sample objectives in Part I, "The Social Strategy." We talked about doing 500 demos and collecting 200 qualified A leads. The strategy was to allow visitors to test-drive new products in the booth and give test-drivers a way to share that experience with their colleagues and friends who are either at the show or at home. After the test-drive, you planned to evaluate their interest, buying power, and timeline for a new product. The tactic was to set up seven kiosks for live demos or test-drives. Upon completion, each visitor was able to send a tweet, Facebook message, text, or email to a colleague telling him about the demo or giving him a link to an online demo of the product.

In your report, you need to show what you set out to do and what you accomplished. You also need to document which parts of your plan succeeded and what failed and pinpoint the reasons why. Table 17.1 shows an example of goals and objectives calculations.

Table 17.1   Goals and Objectives Calculations

Goal	Estimated Value	Actual	Total Value
500 product demos	$500,000	400*	$400,000
200 qualified A leads	$400,000	220	$440,000

Goal	Estimated Value	Actual	Total Value
125 shares after demo experience	$12,500	250 (shares)*	$25,000
Twitter		172 (shares)	
Facebook		64 (shares)	
SMS (text)		1 (share)	
Email		13 (shares)	
Unexpected results		Five new ideas for product features based on audience tweets	$10,000
		Half-page ad in the show daily about our product demos and use of social media	$6,000
Show Total	**$912,500**		**$881,000**

* We found that the amount of people who, after taking a demo, wanted to share the information with their friends was twice what we anticipated. Because the sharing feature was on the kiosks that contained the product demos, 250 of the demos took significantly longer. We attribute this factor to our drop in actual demos performed. The kiosks were simply in use. While the $25,000 value obtained through social sharing is significant, it does not make up for the value loss of $100,000 in demos. For our next show, we will adjust accordingly and either add more demo stations or separate the demo from the sharing.

As you can see here, your demo numbers are way down. But you know exactly what happened based on observations in the booth during the show and the numbers when you totaled everything. During the planning phase, you figured you'd be lucky to get 125 people to share their demo experiences with a friend. Really you had no idea what to expect because you'd never done anything like this before. Without a number there, though, you would not have been able to measure it.

Lo and behold, more than half the people who took the demo shared it with their friends. This clogged up the kiosks, giving fewer people an opportunity to take a demo. You know exactly how to fix this next year if you decide the $25,000 worth of exposure you received from it is worthwhile.

Notice how I also broke down the sharing feature by the tools people used to share with their friends. Twitter was the most popular, Facebook was second, texting could have just been a mistake, and email was hardly even worthwhile. It gives you an idea what your audience's favorite social media tool is—or does it? As this is marketing, we know that many factors come into play. Maybe people chose Twitter because it was the first option. Next time with the same audience, you might want to swap the Facebook and Twitter options to see whether it makes a difference.

In the end, you are only off on your objective's total value by $31,500. That is not too bad; it's less than a 4 percent difference. You can also add in to your calculation the value of new Twitter followers or Facebook likes. Figure out how much each mention of your company in blog posts and tweets or in Facebook status updates is worth. Are these potential customers your company has never done business with? Are they purchasing agents who were not even in your sales database? That's worth something. Exactly what it is worth is different for every company.

You're also going to need to look at how you spent your money and just how much money you spent to determine whether your efforts were worth it. If you were able to program the kiosks for social media sharing for at a cost of $5,000, you're ahead of the game, with a total value of $25,000. If, on the other hand, those kiosks cost $10,000, it would have been a gamble as you estimated their value at $12,500. Hindsight shows us they were a payoff, but it was taking a chance nonetheless. Creating a cost calculations will allow you to see what efforts were worth the money spent on them. Table 17.2 shows what a cost breakdown might look like.

Table 17.2   The Cost Calculations

Cost Breakdown	Estimated	Actual
Kiosks	$15,000	$15,000
Programming to include social media sharing	$5,000	$5,000
Total booth costs including, rental, labor, Internet, hotel, travel, etc.	$400,000	$395,000
Pre-show e-mails	$10,000	$10,000
Direct mail	$60,000	$60,000
Social media	$5000	$5,000
Total marketing	$75,000	$75,000
Customer appreciation party	$25,000	$25,000
Sales reps dinners	$5,000	$3,950
Customer entertainment	$30,000	$28,950
Total costs	$505,000	$498,950

There, you have all your costs broken down. I made this a very simple chart, but you'll need to report to a greater detail using your particular line items and costs associated. The more detailed you get is always a good thing. This way, you can see what each piece cost and where you got the most bang for your buck. Is it better to throw an elaborate party for customers, or do you get more results when your sales reps and executives have smaller dinner parties?

ROI Calculation

Until you know how much revenue you've generated as a result of your efforts, you cannot calculate ROI. For now, you can only estimate what it might be if everything goes according to the law of averages. To get the true ROI from your show, you will have to track each lead through the entire sales cycle. Also keep in mind that these examples are very basic. Your formulas might have different weights assigned to each marketing activity. That means that if a show lead closes, your trade show presence might only get credit for 25 percent of the entire marketing efforts. Trade publication advertisements, webinars, user-group events, and direct mail may make up the other 75 percent. Again, this is where having conversations with your CFO will come in handy if you are not already familiar with metrics and measurement.

The ROI of attending a show is calculated by subtracting your expenses from the revenue generated by the show and then dividing by the total expense. The resulting number is a percentage, which is your ROI. If you're above zero, you're making money. If you are in the negative numbers, you're losing money.

$$ROI = (\text{gain from investment} - \text{cost of investment}) \div \text{cost of investment}$$

Expense to Revenue Ratio

This is the number you'll have to be satisfied with for now. You will be working with values you've assigned to each effort instead of actual sales. Your expense to revenue ratio is very similar to ROI. You take your total value and divide that by your total expenses. Move the decimal over two places to the right, and you have your expense to revenue ratio percentage. In this case, it is 176 percent. Not bad for a few days' work!

$$\text{Expense to Revenue} = (\text{total value/total expenses}) \times 100$$

You can do this same calculation with each tactic you implemented at the show to find out which ones are giving you the best return. Using this calculation, you find that your social media kiosk was valued at $25,000. The programming needed for each kiosk cost about $20,000. So you made about 25 cents on each dollar you spent there.

Breaking down each and every piece of your social media efforts will help you figure out what is worth investing in as you move forward. As time goes on and you are able to assign ROI to what you are doing, you'll be able to have the cold hard facts of what is worthwhile.

What About the Results That Don't Have an Obvious Value?

How do you assign a value to ideas for R&D that came from a tweet or to 20 ideas for blog posts you found when going through session notes and customer interviews? In the case of the ideas for R&D, that's as simple as figuring out what you would have spent on a focus group. Personally, I would assign an even higher value to the tweets because focus groups are often an inaccurate depiction of what customers really think. If your last focus group cost you $20,000, you could see those tweets as a $20,000 saving. Or, let's follow along in the life cycle. What if one of those ideas came to pass and it meant a new product release? You could calculate the revenue earned through upgrades and give some percentage of credit on those sales to the fact that adding that particular feature came from the survey you conducted on Twitter.

As far as figuring the value for those 20 ideas for new content., you need to follow them through their life cycles, too. Blog posts can have a call to action that you can track to see how many people responded. A white paper might lead to landing a large client. An article in a trade magazine could result in a speaking engagement for your CEO that nets your company 20 leads, which might turn into five sales.

No one said calculating ROI would be easy or cut and dry. If you are doing this kind of in-depth measurement, the good news is that it's likely you'll be around a long time to do it. When budgets are getting cut, the person who can prove the value of what he does is not the person companies get rid of. Companies keep people who drive revenue, and you'll be able to prove that you do that with cold hard numbers.

Your Report Tells a Story

When I deliver post-show reports to clients, I make sure I have all the numbers front and center, but I also like to weave a little story in there. I create an executive summary with all the data and numbers. That's what everyone is going to focus on. But I also add a bit of narrative to that report. Don't assume that the only things people want to read about are the numbers. Everyone loves a good story. If you have specific anecdotes you think would convey the success of your show or show that you understand the failures, add that in there. If one of your sales rep is on his way to closing a big deal because someone on your team was listening and caught the news about that customer taking over another company, take credit for that. Tell the story about seeing a prospect you've been trying to land tweet that she was dying for sushi and how you got word to her sales rep, and he got on the phone immediately and set up a dinner. This kind of thing happens all the time at shows I attend.

Every year at the EXHIBITOR show, I hear the same thing from at least 90 percent of the exhibit and marketing managers in our advanced strategy class. They say their role in the company is not respected. They feel they have no authority or decision-making power. They are all very smart people who know what they are doing, but they have something else in common. They're not measuring ROI. They can't show how their exhibit program has a positive impact on their company's bottom line.

If you want respect and authority, you must start measuring ROI—not just the revenue to expense ratio.

Summary

Measurement is a key component in your trade show program. Without measurement, you can't show what you are doing successfully and where you should continue spending money. Without being able to prove that what you are currently doing is working, you'll never get a bigger budget. Without being able to see what isn't working, you'll never know what needs to be fixed.

To really measure the results of your efforts, you have to follow those efforts along their entire life cycles. If you are in business-to-business (B2B), it's likely your sales cycle is a year or more. Assign what value you can that makes sense after the show, but keep following up to measure the actual ROI that your executive team will be looking for. It doesn't have to be all dry numbers; spice it up with a good story here and there.

18

Keep the Community Alive

Your company's social media strategy for trade shows should not have a beginning and an end. Well, it had a beginning when you first started it, but from here on in, it should be one continuous strategy weaving through every show you attend. You will tweak it here and there as you go. And it should evolve as your marketing plan evolves and as social media tools change, but it should not start and stop with each show.

Your social media strategy takes time to build, but build it will. Most people getting into social media go through three stages. The first stage is Enchantment. You are enthralled with each new follower or friend you get. Each comment on your blog posts is an epic moment to be celebrated. You experience a rush every time someone retweets something you share. You track your RSS feed subscribers like a diabetic tracks his blood sugar levels. And this is great! Enjoy it because, without this enchantment, we would all quit using social media after the first week.

Then at some point those numbers no longer matter. You're now in stage two: Quality Versus Quantity. It's hard to pinpoint when this stage occurs. You just realize one day that you can't remember the last time you checked how many people friended you on Facebook or who's following you on Twitter. Working the numbers is no longer your sole focus. You now care more about the quality of your efforts. You are focused on what you're doing and the relationships you are building. You're in the flow, and it's all moving along naturally.

After you've reached that point, it's time for stage three: Working It. This is where you start taking your social media efforts much more seriously with a specific purpose and defined objectives. Connections become more important—but only the right connections. You start developing and nurturing connections with industry thought leaders, customers, and potential customers. You are more selective about the information you share. You now consider social media as just phase one in the relationship, believing that it's not really a relationship until you start getting people in the social media world to engage with your company in other ways.

What you should end up with is a continuous series of loops. You are constantly making connections with new people, nurturing those connections into social media relationships, turning those social media relationships into valuable connections with your company at many levels, and then finally using social media to stay in touch and check in here and there. Today you might be hitting on all these phases with different people at one time. It seems like having too many balls in the air at once, but by the time you are in the Working It stage juggling those balls will be second nature.

Many people get stuck in stage one. All they focus on are the numbers. All they care about is quantity without giving a second thought to quality. They jump on the bandwagon of every social media platform that comes out without any thought of whether it's right for them. They never take the time to really develop their presence on that platform. One month they are focused on Twitter, the next month it's Google+, and before they've established a plan there, they are off to Tumblr.

These people are incredibly busy and probably call themselves "social media experts" or "social media ninjas." But they've completely forgotten their goal. They've forgotten that the goal was selling more products and services, not having more followers than Justin Bieber. Don't be that person. Keep your eye on the prize, and as soon as you realize you are in stage two, quickly push yourself to the Working It stage.

Platforms Are Not Strategies

Developing a strong presence on a platform like Google+ or Twitter is not a strategy, any more than giving away jump drives in your booth is a strategy. Your social media strategy can combine the use of several tools to help you develop relationships. The purpose of developing those relationships is to position your company as a trusted source of information. Gaining that position will help your sales team get in front of more clients and close more sales.

I was recently on a tweet chat where the topic was "Social Media Strategies for Events." The first question posed by the moderator was, "What is your social media strategy to market your event?" Participants started replying with answers like, "I use LinkedIn Events," "I participate in Twitter chats like this," "Google+ is getting more and more popular so that could be a good strategy," and "I love Pinterest."

What's wrong with this picture? Let's look first at the question: "What is your social media strategy to market your event?" You should have a marketing strategy for your event that *includes* social media. It should also include traditional tools like direct mail, email marketing, invitations, and press releases. The tools they mentioned are just that. They are tools you decide to use or not use based on your strategy.

It's the same as you saying, "I need to find a place to live," and me telling you to get a hammer and nails and some drywall tape. Building a house is not the answer to everyone's question about finding a new place to live. You might just need a place for a month or two while you're waiting to close on your new home. You certainly don't want to build a temporary house. You might just want to move back home with Mom and Dad for this period, or you might want to rent. This is why figuring out your strategy first is so important. I've got you building a house when all you needed was your old bedroom for a few months.

Don't get caught up in the fascination of tools. Have a strategy that includes how you'll manage your social media efforts not just before and during the show, but in the time between your shows as well. If you stick to your strategy, you'll stay focused and not get caught up in shiny object syndrome. If you stick to your strategy, you'll have much better success in the long run.

You Participate in Social Media to Build Trust

In her book *Fascinate,* Sally Hogshead talks about trust as a trigger to persuade and captivate your audience. Trust is a very important trigger in the business-to-business (B2B) world. Three of the five pillars of trust Hogshead talks about that you can use effectively in social media are

- Become familiar.
- Repeat and retell.
- Be authentic.

Showing up on social media for a month or two around a big show and then disappearing does not build trust. Being there day in and day out with a consistent message builds trust. Being authentic on social media is easy because people expect you to have a personality. Your interactions on social media shouldn't sound like they passed through your legal department before being posted.

Jeff Hurt is one particular person I follow on Twitter and whose blog I subscribe to. He talks consistently about one thing—adult education and effective learning models. For the two and half years I've been following him, this is all he has talked about. Some people (mostly his competitors and people who are not in the position to hire him) complain that that is all he talks about. They say, "He just keeps saying the same thing over and over again but in slightly different ways." I guarantee you, if you were to do a word association exercise with those in the conference world and ask for the first name that comes to their minds when you say "education," Jeff's name would come up first every time.

That's what you want to achieve—company name recognition as a leader in your area of focus. Who cares what your competition and critics think about your strategy? If your company is the first company that pops in to your customers' or potential customers' minds when anyone mentions your area of focus, then you've done an excellent job building trust. You've stayed on message, and you are clearly familiar.

I can hear you asking, "But is all this work worth it really? I can see how it helps the company, but what about my shows? How will it all get done?"

Keeping Up

You can't just "do" social media in the months leading up to your show and during the show itself and then forget about it the rest of the year. Well, you could, but that would mean you'd have to restart your efforts practically from scratch each show—and that's a lot more work. By keeping up with your efforts all year long, you'll keep building on your relationships and making them stronger. Next year you won't be inviting strangers into your booth. You'll be meeting there with friends and colleagues.

I talked to one marketing director who has been working social media hard for the past three years. His areas of focus are Twitter, blogs, and videos on YouTube. He uses Twitter to build relationships and find out what his customers are talking about. He also uses it to drive traffic to his blog and YouTube videos. He tells me he has seen a huge impact on his company's trade shows due to his activity on Twitter. Ninety percent of his followers who attend industry events that his company exhibits at come to his booth.

He doesn't use contests or give aways to get them there. They show up because they've gotten to know him, and they want to stop in to say hello. But not just hello. They are more interested in talking to a booth rep about the products his company offers. He reports that this traffic, which he can directly link back to relationships started on Twitter, keeps growing every year. Relationships like this don't happen overnight. They take time to develop and nurture. Just make sure the time you spend has balance.

Time Management

Be warned: If you don't practice disciplined time management, social media can be a vortex that sucks you in and takes up all your time. You'll log in to your accounts first thing in the morning to quickly check what's new. But before you know it, it will be lunchtime, and you will have gotten nothing done.

It's like going out with friends after work. You intend to be there for just an hour or so, but conversation is so good that you lose all track of time, and before you know it, it's 9 p.m., and you've completely missed dinner. Social media can be just like that. It's not a waste of time, but you can waste a lot of time doing it.

The best way to keep up with your efforts without getting sucked into the vortex of lost time is to stick to a strict schedule. The best advice I can give is to buy a timer and set it for 15 or 20 minutes when you open Twitter, Facebook, Google+, or whatever it is you are working on. My most productive days on social media are when I limit myself to just 45 minutes a day: 15 minutes in the morning, 15 minutes at lunch, and another 15 minutes at the end of the day. But for me, that alarm ringing after my allotted time is key. Otherwise, I'll be link-clicking through the entire Internet for two hours or more.

Here is a peek at my 15 minutes on social media each morning:

8:00 a.m.—Pour coffee and rub sleep from my eyes.

8:01 a.m.—Quickly scan through RSS feed updates. Because there are so many updates, I scan titles and open any that look appealing to me or that might be appealing to my audience. Most of these posts are quite short and take only 30 seconds or so to speed-read through them. My feed reader has options built in for me to share a post via Twitter and Google+. If a post is worth sharing, I do so immediately with a few words about why I'm sharing it. If anything requires more concentration and reflection, I tag it to read later or possibly comment on. (I use Google Reader on my desktop and laptop and MobileRSS on my iPad.)

8:07 a.m.—Switch over to Twitter to see whether anyone has mentioned me or sent a direct message that requires a response. I scan my list and hashtag columns for anything interesting I might want to comment on or retweet. (I use TweetDeck as my Twitter browser, though others swear by HootSuite.)

8:10 a.m.—Switch over to Google+ and quickly scan updates for anything interesting that I can add a comment to.

8:15 a.m.—Disconnect from social media and concentrate on my day.

I repeat this process at lunchtime and at the end of my day. During one of those times, I skip the RSS feeds and opt to look through LinkedIn activity instead. These are the social media tools I focus on and use daily. I save blog posts and podcast creations for special project days. I also have a few days that I participate in tweet chats that are relevant to my business. It's not that I don't think other tools can be used effectively. These are just the tools that work best for me. These are the tools I am most comfortable using, so I can therefore maximize my efforts in a short amount of time.

On days that I don't set my timer and keep to this strict schedule, it's 11 a.m. before I know it, and my mind has turned to mush. It is amazing how important reminiscing over callaloo soup recipes with a Twitter friend from Trinidad can seem when your mind has tricked you into thinking you have all the time in the world. So now the question is, "How and what should you be doing with that concentrated time?"

A Few How-tos for Keeping Up with Your Connections

The following are a few ideas to continue the conversations you started on some of the more popular social media tools especially for B2B marketing. It is by no means an extensive list, but you can adapt the strategies to other programs. No one strategy is right for every company. You should experiment and come up with strategies that work best for your marketing efforts.

Twitter

If you were using Twitter during the event, it's important that you stay in touch with all those new connections you made. You want to listen to what they are saying and observe what is important to them through the links they share. This will give you a better idea of what content you should be sharing with your followers who have similar roles. If something they share seems relevant to your wider audience, retweet it with a note as to why you think others would be interested or offer your opinion on the information. Listen also to the questions they are asking; you might have the answer or be able to connect them to someone who does.

I advanced my relationship with a potential customer I was following when he asked for sushi restaurant recommendations in Amsterdam. He was exhibiting at a show there, but was unfamiliar with the city. I happened to know a few people who lived there and quickly put out a call for help. Within an hour, he had five different recommendations from locals. This very small gesture meant something to him, and he decided to follow me back. We now chat with one another regularly on Twitter and continue to build a relationship.

Twitter is a marketing tool like any other. It is rare that one touchpoint on Twitter will turn someone into a customer, just as it is rare that one advertisement or direct mail piece will do the same. Twitter gives you the opportunity to make a connection; it is up to you to build on each connection you make and turn it into a business relationship. You have to be an astute observer, listening to what people are saying and then take note of what they are sharing. However, you will need some method to this madness if you are to be successful.

Once you have more than 25–50 accounts you follow on Twitter, it's hard to keep up with the speed of the Twitter stream, especially if those people are active and frequent tweeters. Twitter's list feature helps you segment your followers into distinct categories. Programs like HootSuite and TweetDeck allow you to create separate columns to view each list and hashtag separately.

There is no one right way to set up lists in Twitter. You have to do what makes sense for you and your company. Create lists that make the most sense to you. You can always change them as new areas of interest emerge and as your strategy changes and adapts. To give you an idea, I'll share the structure I use. This is not so you can replicate it, but just so you can get an idea of how lists will streamline your time on Twitter.

I have one list for event professionals I follow on Twitter. These could be suppliers to the event industry, other conference organizers, industry thought leaders, and industry associations. Because trade shows are a sub-category of events I am interested in, I break down my event professional list even further with a list for people involved specifically in trade shows. With a quick glance at the columns I've created on TweetDeck for these two groups, I can see what's happening in the event industry in general as well as what is going on specific to the trade show industry.

I also like to stay in touch with people on Twitter who tweet with a focus on marketing. I have created a special list for marketing in general. Again, this includes suppliers, marketers, agencies, thought leaders, and associations. I have two more lists broken down by job title and business focus. One list is where I keep all my senior-level marketers because I want to keep abreast of what topics are important to these high-level decision-makers. My other list is marketers who work in B2B. Again, one quick glance tells me what is going on in the marketing industry.

Two other key lists that I keep up with daily are my "favorites" and "get to know." My "favorites" list changes over time. Some people get dropped off and others get added. These are the people who always have interesting things to say and people I want to put more effort into establishing a relationship with. Not everyone on my "favorite" list is business focused. I have a few people on that list who strictly entertain me, like Andy Borowitz (@BorowitzReport), Mo Rocca (@MoRocca), and Ellen Barkin (@EllenBarkin)—I like to mix my business with pleasure.

My "get to know" list is for people whom I've just started to follow and look like they'd be worth the effort to pay a bit more attention to. The jury is still out on these people. Will they end up on my favorite list or just be segmented into another more appropriate list? They might even get dumped altogether. Having a separate column for them ensures they get a little bit extra attention as my Twitter stream flies by.

Having these separate columns benefits me in two ways. I can really streamline my focus when it comes to Twitter and accomplish much more in a shorter amount of time. A few quick glances let me know what the events industry is talking about and sharing and what's on top of the minds of Chief Marketing Officers. I can also find the people I want to target with my messages much more quickly. If I want to reach out to other trade show organizers, I can run through my list and start connecting with them individually.

After a show, you could create a list for people you met at the show and others who might not have been to the show but were still connecting to it remotely via Twitter. This will help you to stay in touch with those individuals without them getting lost in the shuffle. It will also give you a place to start when you do your pre-show promotions next time around.

LinkedIn Groups

If you participated in LinkedIn groups before the show, you'll want to keep that activity up. Other group participants have gotten to know you, and if you did things right and didn't only promote your company, they trust you now. They look to you for good information and count on your opinions and viewpoints in discussions.

Keep making those connections and participating in the discussions. When the next show comes around, you won't be coming at people from out of nowhere. If you've started your own group on LinkedIn, it's even more important to keep it up. This doesn't have to take up a lot of time or resources. You can give it a quick check a few times a week to approve and welcome new members to the group. Sweep through to make sure there is value being added to the group through real discussions and not just individuals promoting their own businesses. If you came across a few articles you think your group would enjoy while going through your RSS feed reader, you can post those as well and create a discussion around the post.

You'll also be able to send messages directly to individuals you've gotten to know through those discussion groups. Instead of being viewed as spam, your messages will be seen as normal correspondence sent from one colleague to another.

Facebook

By now, it has probably been established that I am not a big fan of Facebook in the B2B marketing world. I'm not saying it can't work; I'm just saying I've not seen one single good sustainable example of its use in B2B. (I do think you should grab your company's identity on Facebook before someone else does, though.) It might build up a bit of steam when you are really pushing it for some kind of contest. But is that really sustainable?

So, let's say you used Facebook in your booth strategy this year, you gained some traction, and you want to keep it up. By all means, keep the page active. Try different things within Facebook's application arsenal to see what engages your fans the most. You could use a polling app to get an idea of where your customer fan base or "friends" stand on certain issues or what features they like the best or least about your product or service. Whatever you decide to do, it's important that people coming to your page don't see a three-month lag in your activity timeline. You have to keep social media fresh for it to be effective.

But what if no one is going to your page or interacting with what is going on there? No matter what you post or what applications you add, no one seems interested. Don't simply let your page die by suddenly stopping updates and activities. Use it as a directional sign. Create a final status update that points interested parties to the social media platforms you are engaging in. Include this information in your profile as well. This way, it doesn't look like you simply lost interest or, worse, are not paying any attention to people. It's similar to a change of address notice. Let people know that you do want to have a conversation with them and invite them to join you on the social media tools you are focused on, the ones that make sense for you and your community.

This goes for any social media tool. It's good to claim your space before someone else does. If you want to make sure you have ownership of your company's name on Twitter, be sure to create an account there. If you don't intend on using it that often, include an invitation on your profile to invite your audience to join you where you are active. Just check to see what the rules are for inactive accounts. Some tools will delete accounts that are inactive after a certain period of time.

Note: If Facebook is really working for you in your B2B marketing efforts, please let me know. There are hundreds of B2B marketers who haven't figured out a good fit for Facebook in their strategy, and they'd love to hear about your success.

Google+

If you are using Google+, be sure to add all the contacts you made at the trade show to your circles. *Circles* are what Google+ gives you to organize your connections. Like Twitter, you can reach out directly to these people (if they have an account and are using it) through Google+, but now you have the luxury of communicating in more than 140 characters.

I like to create a circle for each event so I can remember where I ran into each person. I meet so many people at all the events I attend, and I've got a lousy memory. I hate being introduced at an event to a familiar name and not being able to remember that we actually met the year before or that we've never actually met, but it feels like it because we talk online. I can use circles to group people into events we've been to, areas of interest, or both.

The ability to search for people based on their areas of interest is what makes Google+ such a useful social media tool. You can use your customer demographics to search for like-minded people on Google+. You can also search for people and companies based on specific interests or business categories. Unlike Facebook, you don't need permission to connect with people on Google+. It is similar to Twitter in this way.

As you build these different circles and connect with people throughout the year, you'll be at a distinct advantage moving forward with your next show. You will be able to customize your message for each particular circle. When it comes time to announce that you will be at the show, one message can be customized and sent to those people you met last year saying you look forward to seeing them again. If you get free passes to give to attendees, you can send a customized message with an invite to people you've discovered who might want to attend but have never heard of the show. You could send another customized message to individuals you know are going and whom you want to make sure your executives and sales reps get some face time with.

Google+ offers a lot of flexibility in how you follow people, who sees your messages, and what you can include in your posts. Because Google favors this platform in its search engines, it also gives you the added bonus of potentially higher search rankings.

Taking It Beyond Simple Chatter

Once you get more comfortable using social media in your marketing program and you've entered into the Working It phase, you're going to be able to really begin to maximize your efforts and see those relationships grow. Participating in weekly tweet chats targeted to your audience is a great way to connect with new people, establish professional relationships, and learn what your customers are talking about.

A *tweet chat* is an online gathering of people using Twitter. Participants use a hashtag to promote an area of common interest and to identify the tweets as belonging to that particular chat. Tweet chats are a great place to meet potential customers and industry thought leaders. They are also a place to mine valuable information.

This is even more evident if you start your own weekly or monthly chat that's focused on your area of expertise and relevant to your customer demographic. You are in control of the chat and the topics discussed. Basically, you're inviting a bunch of people to an hour-long weekly (or monthly) market research event. Want to know what's on the minds of your customers? Set the topic for the chat and ask four or five specific questions to drive the discussion. By the end of the chat, you'll have sneaked a peek inside the minds of your customers.

I started a weekly tweet chat using the hashtag #ExpoChat; it takes place every Wednesday at 3 p.m. EST. I partnered with two other trade show industry leaders, so I didn't have to go it alone. When I'm struggling with a problem, I can simply make it the topic of my next tweet chat and get tons of helpful advice from my peers, exhibitors, and vendors. We've also reached out to chat participants for topic ideas that are relevant to them through polling applications and survey tools.

A company that does a fantastic job using its tweet chat to connect with customers, potential customers, and others in the industry is a2z, Inc. a2z is a developer of online, event, and conference management and marketing software as well as mobile applications. The company's monthly chat uses the hashtag #a2zusergroup, and topics focus on technology as well as issues and ideas that are specifically relevant to its customers.

a2z even takes it a step further by engaging an industry thought leader to moderate the chats each month. This is smart for two reasons. One, it exposes the chat to all the moderator's followers. Two, it shows that a2z puts the needs of its customers over just promoting the company. While adding value to its customers, a2z is strengthening its position as a leading company in that space. These chats help to put the company name in the front of potential customers' minds.

You could use Google Hangouts (a video chat feature of Google+) to have smaller online chats via a video connection. To participate in a Google Hangout, you need to have a Google+ account and a webcam. You are limited in that you can have only nine other people join you in the video chat, but that creates scarcity and you might find it works to your advantage. The video adds to the experience because you can really put faces to the names you know.

You could create a sort of "book club" using Google Hangouts; instead of people discussing favorite books, you could invite your target customers to talk about their favorite industry events. This could give you great ideas for where your company should be exhibiting in the future.

You could have a different topic each week or month just like in a tweet chat. You could have different employees, selected based on topic expertise, host the video chat each week. Or, you could have a Q&A session with different product managers or developers. The more time you spend with people face-to-face like this, the more trust you build in your industry. The more trust people have in you, the more likely they will be to share your message with their friends and colleagues and introduce them to you at the next show.

Social media isn't like direct mail. You can't shelve it after the show is over and start it up again next year. When you make a commitment to use social media, you need to keep at it. That's why I encourage people to start small in the beginning. If you don't, you'll soon find yourself in the weeds with no hope of catching up and getting out.

Just like you have a plan for lead follow-up, have a plan for your social media follow-through. Just as lead follow-up has a better chance of success when the plan's in place before your show, so does social media. You need to get back to your office after the show is over and hit the ground running. But don't let social media become a time suck. Buy a timer and work quickly and efficiently. One thing that will put a halt to your social media program is talk like, "All she does all day is talk to her friends on [insert social media tool here]."

Summary

Don't let all those efforts incorporating social media into your trade show program go to waste after the show. Keep the conversations going so that your pre-show work next year is not only a bit easier but shows more results by way of booth traffic. Stay focused on your strategy and remember why you are using the tools in the first place. A good social media strategy will help build trust with your customers and, as a result, drive sales.

It takes time before you really see the fruits of your labor, but it's well worth the effort. Just make sure the time you spend working it is time well spent. Choose the platform that works best with your strategy and one your customers want to interact with you and concentrate your efforts there and build those relationships.

Don't worry about what is new and trendy—just stay focused. As you become more and more familiar with the platform, push yourself to get more and more out of it. You don't need to only participate in someone else's conversation, you can create your own.

V

Problem-Solving Sponsorships

Now is my chance to get up on my sponsorship soapbox. I find myself up here quite a bit. Sponsorships are an incredibly valuable piece of your trade show marketing strategy, but only if they are done correctly. If you haven't taken full advantage of all the opportunities given to you as an exhibitor, then don't even go here. Real sponsorships don't just require you to write a check. When done the right way, they are an investment of employee time across your entire company, so make sure you are ready for that responsibility—a responsibility well worth the effort.

The days of slapping a company logo on a banner or lanyard and calling it a sponsorship have passed. Unfortunately, many show organizers are stuck in the 1990s, so that is all they are offering. When you ask about sponsorship opportunities, they give you a list of one-off opportunities such as badge branding, hotel key card branding, lanyard branding, banners (wrapped columns, outdoor, floor, lobby, and so on), registration banners, show bag branding, speaker intros, and web banners or ads. Things that are forgotten as soon as the show is over or they land in the garbage.

They probably also offer the completely useless platinum, gold, silver, and bronze packages. Sometimes they get creative and call them diamond, ruby, and emerald or president, ambassador, and diplomat. These sponsorships are created so the organizer gets what they need (money) with little thought about what the sponsor needs (return on investment). But they provide almost zero real value to the attendee. These sponsorships are also easy for the organizer to fulfill. All they have to do is check off items on the list of things promised. Logo? Check. Banner ad? Check. Speaker intro? Check. These are not sponsorships. They are branding opportunities.

A true sponsorship is one that is customized to meet the marketing needs of the company that is sponsoring. It should benefit both the organizer (sponsee) and the sponsor, but first and foremost, it should add value to the attendees.

The attendees who even notice your logo and advertising will find them infringing on their space, and what's more, they will view them as annoying. They will do their best to tune them out, but it's just so hard when your huge banner takes up half the stage and takes their attention away from the speaker they paid to see. If you're lucky, they won't remember you five minutes after they leave the event. If you're unlucky, they'll have a negative impression of your company.

Attendees understand that sponsorships help pay for their event, so at best they simply tolerate this assault on their enjoyment of the trade show. But let me tell you, they all hate sitting through your commercials before the speaker they are there to hear comes on stage.

At a recent conference, I was looking forward to hearing a particular keynote speaker. I arrived a few minutes early and settled in for what I hoped would be a fascinating talk. Much to my dismay, the first 20 minutes were taken up with association announcements and news. Next came the first sponsor, who was given commercial time on stage in exchange for a big check. He spoke for his allotted 10 minutes, but apparently what he had to say was more important than the keynote because he went over his time by about 5 minutes. The next sponsor who came up to give her commercial—not to be outdone by the previous sponsor—also took about 15 minutes.

By this time, those who were on Twitter were fired up and tweeting over and over again, "get off the stage," "we came to see [keynoter], not listen to a commercial," and some other tweets that were, shall we say, less than complimentary. A murmur was going through the audience that was full of complaints. People were getting up and walking out.

Then the third sponsor came up on stage. He also had commercial time and apparently wrote a huge check because he had the honor of introducing the keynote. He walked up to the podium and said, "You have all been incredibly patient, and I know you are not here to listen to me talk so I will not keep you any longer. Ladies and gentlemen, I would like to introduce today's keynote speaker, [keynote speaker name]." There were hoots and hollers and a standing ovation. It was not for the keynote—it was for the guy who "got it." He was on stage for all of 30 seconds, but the positive impact he made on the audience was astounding.

This sponsor understood that the audience's needs were what were important. He created a positive impression of his company on about 2,500 people in that auditorium in a matter of seconds by placing the audience—his potential customers—first. A year later I asked a bunch of people who had attended this keynote speech whether they remembered that day. Every person knew exactly what I was talking about and they remembered who that third person was and which company he represented. He left a very positive impression on them. When I asked who the other two sponsors were, no one remembered. Lucky for them, I guess.

If you are working with a savvy show organizer, she will customize sponsorships to meet your company's marketing needs. If you're working with an organizer who thinks logos on banners are the be all and end all, not to worry. You can build your own custom offering and present it in a way the show organizer can't refuse—and in a way that will get the attendees' attention!

19

How to Create
a Winning Sponsorship

A well-crafted sponsorship has the attendees' needs front and center. If it adds value to the attendees' experience, it naturally will add value to the event, making it appealing to the show organizer. If it adds value to the attendees' experience, it creates a lasting and positive reaction to your brand. But that is just the start. The sponsorship also needs to align with your company's overall objectives as well as your marketing objectives.

If you run off and create something that is completely out of the ordinary for your company, you cannot integrate it into your other marketing and communication efforts. By creating a sponsorship that adds to what you already do, you can save money and resources. It won't need its own campaign, and you could potentially tie the sponsorship into other things you are promoting.

So how do you go about creating a win-win-win situation? You first need to get your priorities straight and create some sponsorship guidelines. Many companies post their sponsorship guidelines on their website to weed out sponsorship seekers who are not a fit for their organizations. But I find the exercise of creating them to be of even more value to your company.

A good set of guidelines will be a roadmap to what sponsorships work best for your organization and will help ensure you are not wasting valuable resources on opportunities that sound great but really do not enhance your brand.

Things to Consider When Creating Your Guidelines

Remember, you are not creating a guide for branding opportunities. These sponsorships allow you to engage with your target demographic in a meaningful way. These guidelines are not just for social media sponsorships, but for all your marketing sponsorships. They will be your base for all your event sponsorships whether they are trade shows, national conferences, or smaller regional events. The following sections discuss areas you should address in your guidelines.

Brand Personality

When you are considering a sponsorship, you must first decide whether the opportunity fits your company's personality. To do that, you need to first define what that personality is. What do you want to be known for? Is your personality irreverent and edgy, or is it formal and buttoned up? Do you position yourself as innovative? Or do people see your company as a trusted partner who's consistent and never changing?

A sponsorship must fit your company's personality. If it is at odds with the impression you want to create, you'll be sending your customers a mixed message. I believe the partnership between the Susan G. Komen Foundation and Kentucky Fried Chicken created in 2010 sent a huge mixed message. Many felt an organization focused on saving women's lives should not have been partnering with a fast food giant, and there was a significant outcry among Komen's supporters and breast cancer education and awareness advocacy groups. So be sure you carefully consider how the sponsorship fits with your company's mission.

Desired Demographic

Notice I didn't say your *target* demographic. You might want to use your sponsorship to connect with a very specific demographic, not just a general audience. Ask yourself, "Who are we willing to pay to get to meet?" Your exhibit gets you in front of a general audience, but a sponsorship could get you in front of CEOs who are going through or about to go through the process of being acquired by another company. You have the ability to really drill down to a very specific demographic.

Goals and Objectives

What do you want to get out of your sponsorship? Are you looking for a market research opportunity? Do you want to make new connections with people the organizer has access to? Are you looking to position your CEO as an industry thought leader? Do you want to position your company as a brand leader? If you are looking to make connections with your industry's up-and-coming leaders, a tweet-up that brings that audience together in an informal setting may be just the fit for you. Whereas a tweet-up is not going to position your CEO as an industry thought leader, but a VIP dinner with other CEOs just might. Knowing what you want to accomplish will help you craft the right sponsorship.

Time

How much lead time do you need prior to the event to ensure you get the most out of your sponsorship investment? Again, these are sponsorships, not branding opportunities. You can't just write a check and expect the show organizers to do everything else. Your company is going to have to invest money, time, and personnel into the sponsorship. If you are doing social media sponsorships, it's very likely your IT department will need to be involved. How much lead time do they require? You'll need to integrate the sponsorship promotion into your other marketing. What are the lead times required to do that? Include all departments your sponsorship will effect so you can plan accordingly.

Exclusivity

How important is exclusivity, and are you willing to pay for it? If the show organizer is looking for several sponsors for the show's Wi-Fi lounge but you want exclusive rights to the sponsorship, you're going to have to pay for that right. You can't expect the organizer to lose money just to make you happy. If you are sponsoring a tweet-up, you cannot expect to demand your competitor not be allowed to sponsor a keynote speaker—something completely unrelated to your tweet-up. However, asking for exclusivity as the sponsor for just the tweet-up is perfectly reasonable. There is nothing wrong with asking for exclusivity, just be sure it is a reasonable request for the amount of money you are willing to invest.

Sponsee Investment

How much do you expect the organizer to invest back into your sponsorship? I'm sure you understand that there is a value associated with your sponsorship, and that is what you are paying for. You are not just covering the hard costs of your sponsorship. You might require that the show organizer invest 20 percent of your sponsorship fee back into the sponsorship. This could be to pay for equipment needed, signage, and marketing.

This helps to keep you out of a bidding war and avoid spending money that will not give you the return you are looking for. Another company might be willing to do the sponsorship for more money and with less investment on the show organizer's side. That's fine because you know what you need and when it's time to walk away.

Control

How much control do you need over the decision-making process of your sponsorship? Do you need to have final approval on the vendors used to make your sponsorship happen? Is it important that you approve the invitation designs or the marketing? I have a friend who speaks on meeting design and how it affects the brain. She requires control over the room layout, seating, and food that is served; otherwise, she and the event are sending a mixed message. For example, if you are sponsoring the show's live stream of the conference, you should approve which vendors are used. The wrong vendors could make you look bad, as your name will be associated with the remote attendee experience.

Customer Access

Do you require that your selected customers have VIP access to certain events? You can negotiate special event pricing for your customers, access to front row seats for a keynote, special parking, access to speakers, and so on. Maybe your customers have a special VIP one-click registration and a special line to check in at the show. Maybe there is a special virtual pass for your customers who are unable to attend physically. This sweetens the pot for you, so to speak. It also benefits the show organizers because it means you will be actively promoting their show to your customers.

Product Placement

Do you require the show to use your product or service throughout the event? If Coca-Cola is sponsoring the closing night party, then the beverage company is going to want only Coca-Cola products served. If you're a manufacturer of HD monitors, do you want the show to use your monitors throughout the show floor as digital signage, or is it okay to use someone else's—possibly a competitor? Decide how important this is to you and whether it's a deal-breaker up front.

I went to an event recently that was sponsored by a full-service registration company. The event organizers were using a free online registration system instead of the sponsor's system. This was a huge mistake for two reasons. The sponsor missed out on a huge opportunity to show its target market just how easy its system is to use by having them experience it as attendees. Also, it gave the impression to the audience that yes, you could pay the sponsor to do your registration, but why do that when this free online tool does just as good a job?

Pre- and Post-Show Opportunities

Is it important that your sponsorship include special pre-show activities? It might include branding on pre-show marketing materials or pre-show webinars. What about post show? Will the show organizers give you access to their audience via the website by allowing you to do monthly blog posts or articles for their monthly newsletter? What about a banner ad on their website promoting the event or add-on you are sponsoring? Let's say you are sponsoring the show's mobile app. Maybe your company could put together a short video showing the attendees how to use the app to get more out of their show experience.

Access to Premium Content

Many shows sell their conference content online or by DVD. Like other customer perks, you could negotiate access to that exclusive content for your customers—or at least a certain number of sessions and for a specified time. Maybe you could get your customers free access to online content for one or two months after the show. This is a perk your customers will find extremely valuable, especially if they were unable to attend the event.

Visibility for Key Employees

Your position in the industry might be one of having the best customer service. What better way to showcase that at the show than by sponsoring a social media help desk or a roaming genius bar? Members of your customer service department could staff it. You already know they are great with people; now let the trade show audience get a chance to experience that firsthand.

I can just picture the wording on the back of the staff shirts. *Need Help? Find out why we rank #1 in customer service.* Okay, maybe that's too long for a t-shirt, but it would make for great signage.

What Can You Offer?

Obviously, you could offer money, but you can also offer a show organizer other things that are just as valuable. These added extras can often make your sponsorship offer more appealing than a competitor's that is focused only on a cash contribution.

Space on Your Website or Company Blog

Just as the show offers advertising in the way of banners on the show website, you can offer the show banner space on your website or blog. You can work with the show's marketing department to create a design that is appropriate to your site's branding. Many shows offer predesigned banners or badges for speakers, attendees, and exhibitors to promote their presence or attendance at a show (see Figure 19.1).

Figure 19.1   *Blogworld speaker website badge.*

If you have negotiated special access for your customers, you can include that in the design of your banner with a link to special VIP registration. You could also promise a number of informational blog posts promoting the event to your readers. Just make sure they are not just advertisements but contain information the show attendees would find valuable.

Social Media Promotion

If you already have a very active social media presence with many dedicated followers, you could commit to using those tools to help promote the event and your presence at the event. Show organizers constantly struggle to bring in new attendees, and your social media audience could be just the boost they are looking for.

Promotion to Your Database

You could work with the show's marketing department to design specialty invitations to send to your marketing database. Include both digital invites and print for direct mail. The invitations could include a special discount or registration link that gives your customers the special access you negotiated.

Content

It's difficult for organizations to come up with original content week after week and month after month. You could offer to do a year-long series of articles for use on their website, blog, and newsletter. This is a great way to gain exposure, position key executives as thought leaders, and hang onto your industry ranking. It goes without saying that you are offering good original content, not overblown press releases.

Brainstorm with others on your communications, PR, and marketing teams. Ask other departments if they have something they think would be valuable, not just to the show, but to the organizing association or company. These ideas will stretch out your sponsorship beyond just 3 or 4 days to 365 days of the year. You just might come up with something that is a huge benefit to you, the show, and the attendees.

As you can see, there is actually quite a bit you might have to offer beyond just money. All these opportunities do not just benefit the sponsee, but you, the sponsor, as well. You are providing the assets, but it's yet another way to get your message in front of your target audience. That message is not just another marketing message, but one that says, "Hey, we thought of you and your needs, and we want to make this a better event for you." A message like that helps build trust.

What Is the Show's Sponsorship Marketing Plan?

You're going to be putting a lot of time, human resources, and money into your sponsorship. You should expect the show organizer to do the same for you. At the annual Professional Convention Management Association meeting, I listened to a panel of show organizers talking about education on the show floor. I was astounded to hear one organizer say he does nothing to promote the education theater or its sponsor. He felt that building it and putting up a banner was enough. Someone asked if it was successful for the event and the sponsor. Did he measure its success? I almost fell off my chair when he said, "Who has time to do that?" The follow-up question was did his sponsor return the next year. He said, "No, we have to get a new sponsor every year." No one in the audience was surprised by that answer.

If your show organizer has a "build it and they will come" mentality, you might want to rethink your investment. Steer clear of working with an organization that values its sponsors so little that it doesn't put the time and effort into promoting the sponsorships. It's clear the organization doesn't put a very high value on its attendees if it is not willing to promote something that would make the attendee experience better.

Ask the show for a marketing plan showing how the organization is going to promote your sponsorship. If there isn't a plan in place, work with the show organizer to create one. Remember, some show organizers are not used to this type of sponsorship. They are only familiar with selling logos on lanyards and show bags. This is why you need a lot of lead time to craft your sponsorship. A month before the show is not when you or the organizer want to be worrying about this.

What Makes a Great Sponsorship?

A great sponsorship adds to the attendees' experience. It makes the event better for attendees, thus putting your company in a positive light. It can't start with the idea of "how will we get the best exposure to the show's attendees?" It has to be framed like "what can we provide the show's attendees that will reflect well on our company?" Kim Skildum-Reid, author of *What Every CMO Needs to Know About Sponsorship* says, "Your job as a sponsor is not to involve people in your brand story; it's to involve your brand in their stories."

To come up with good ideas, start by making a list of everything the attendees hate about the event, including things you've heard a lot of people complaining about in the previous years. Social media makes it easier to know exactly what attendees' issues are because they are broadcasting it to everyone who is listening. Issues that come up at just about every show include

- First-timers find it hard to fit in.
- People find it difficult to network.
- People have trouble finding their peers among the thousands of attendees.
- There's not enough coffee.
- The rooms are too cold.
- Attendees' feet hurt.
- Attendees' phone/tablet/laptop batteries have died.
- There are no outlets in the classrooms for their laptops.
- People think there is too much paper waste.
- There is no access to Wi-Fi.
- People wish they could attend, but their bosses won't let them leave the office.
- People wish they could attend, but they just lost their jobs.

Now, all you have to do is figure out ways to solve those problems that fit within the sponsorship guidelines you've established.

In the following chapters, we talk about some general sponsorships and include social media and virtual solutions or tie-ins to some of these problems. At first glance, there doesn't seem to be a social media solution to cold rooms, sore feet, and lack of coffee, but think creatively. This could be a great opportunity if you are a supplier to the HVAC industry. You could create a Twitter hotline or text message system for attendees to contact if rooms are too cold or too hot. If you're a company that manufactures memory chips (which speed up attendees' computers), you could have a hotline to tell attendees where break stations are set up and when the coffee (which speeds up attendees' bodies) is refilled.

Sore feet could be comforted with a massage station. These sponsorships are popular at shows, but you could up the ante by creating a social media appointment system. Maybe you ping the attendees through social media to let them know what the wait time is currently at the massage station.

A really great sponsorship, like an exhibit program, uses social media as a tool. In the previous example, your sponsorship might be the massage station, and you could use social media as one of the tools to leverage that sponsorship. You should use as many communication channels at your disposal as you can to expand your audience.

Creatively think of ways to connect your company with attendees by providing them with something they are looking for. Fix a problem they are having at the show, make it a better experience for them, and they'll remember you. They'll remember you a lot longer than the company who bought the column wraps.

Note: Reid's website is a fantastic resource for sponsors http://www.powersponsorship.com. Another great resource for smart sponsorships is Gail Bower at http://www.gailbower.com. The more you read by these two experts, the more you'll get out of your sponsorship dollars.

Your Sponsorship Team

Your sponsorship cannot be created and leveraged by your marketing department alone. You're going to need to get a lot of other departments involved if it's to be successful. Don't just include them *after* your plan is in place. Get input from them to create the best sponsorship and a winning communication plan.

Your PR department will be able to leverage your sponsorship by getting news out to the appropriate media outlets, industry magazines, and bloggers. Your IT department will be a key player in any kind of social media sponsorship you are doing. They'll be able to advise you on bandwidth or the equipment needed for any tech sponsorships. Your sales department will need to be kept in the loop so they can communicate with their customers and prospects about any special show offers they can pass along. Your HR department might even need to be involved if they are responsible for employee communications.

If you are using the sponsorship to get exposure for members of other departments in your company, like customer service or research and development, they'll want input on the creation and planning of the sponsorship packages. The more people you have on your team, the more successful the sponsorship.

How Will You Measure Success?

Measuring the return on investment (ROI) of your sponsorship can be done, but only after you've actually closed business. In the business-to-business (B2B) world, it's likely that might not happen for months or even years depending on your sales cycle. I'm not saying it's not important to do this, just that you will not have the information you need immediately to calculate it. But you can measure success immediately by measuring return on objectives (ROO). Measuring ROO is just what it sounds like: Did you accomplish what you set out to do?

Just like your exhibit strategy, you must first start with goals and objectives for your sponsorship program. It could be as simple as having an objective of getting 50 people to attend a tweet-up. Maybe add to that an objective of 20 attendees who are not yet in your marketing or sales database. That's 20 new people exposed to your company or that your company is exposed to. They might already know all about you, but you just didn't know about them.

If part of the sponsorship package includes market research or you want to know how people's perception of your company changed as a result of the sponsorship, it's best to carry out that research the same way you currently do with the same questions you are using already. That way, you can compare the results you get from the show against other marketing or PR you do as well as other sponsorships in your marketing portfolio.

What you can't do is expect the show organizers to value the success of your sponsorship. All they can do is provide you with show data to assist you in your evaluation. They can't tell you how attendees' opinions of your company might have changed because you sponsored a Wi-Fi lounge, but the organizers can tell you how many attendees used the lounge. If that number is important to you, be sure to include it in your sponsorship contract. You can't expect the show organizers to be monitoring that if you never told them it was important to you.

Give Sponsorship a Chance

Don't get discouraged if your show does not proactively solicit creative customized sponsorships. I've not yet met a show organizer (outside of that one guy speaking at the PCMA event) who isn't looking for ways to make her attendee experience better. If you have an idea you think would be a good fit for your company and enhance the attendees' experience, pick up the phone and ask to talk to the sponsorship director (or whoever makes decisions about sponsorship). She will probably welcome the ideas. If she doesn't, you're not talking to the right person. Go higher on the event food chain until you get to a strategic thinker.

If the sponsorship director seems stuck on selling branding opportunities, consider bundling that with a sponsorship to help her understand. The sponsorship director's ears will hear you offering to buy into a branding opportunity, but for even more money. But only do that if it works for you and if the branding opportunity is really valuable. Spending $30,000 on lanyards in order to sponsor an expensive social media helpdesk is going to diminish your ROI.

Personally, I think I'd cry tears of joy if one of my exhibitors called me with an incredible idea that made my event better for everyone. These types of sponsorships are catching on, but very slowly. Get in on the ground floor, and you could have that coveted spot for years to come. Which reminds me—be sure to negotiate first right of refusal and pricing for that sponsorship the next year. You don't want someone coming in and stealing your great idea for a few dollars more.

Summary

Successful sponsorships don't focus only on how you can get exposure to the show's attendees. That's a branding opportunity. At the heart of every great sponsorship is creating a positive attendee experience and giving attendees something they want or need. As a result, the sponsorship creates a positive interaction with your company.

Create a set of guidelines for all sponsorships and stick to them. Be sure your sponsorship fits in with your overall company goals and objectives, not just those of the show. Work closely with show management and other key departments in your company to ensure your sponsorship's success. A good sponsorship takes time and effort to leverage properly.

20

People Connector

One of the top three reasons people attend conferences and trade shows is to network. People want to get together with their peers and exchange ideas, make connections, find help, and sometimes even find a new job. Organizers tend to see this networking need as fulfilled just because they bring thousands of people together in one place. They stick attendees in a convention center or hotel and say, "There you go; now network."

The problem is that a lot of people are overwhelmed in this situation. How do they meet the people they actually want to network with? It's especially daunting when thousands of people are wandering around the event. A sponsorship designed to connect attendees to one another based on areas of interest, job roles, and issues can solve this problem. Your company can be remembered as the company who helped attendees make meaningful connections. Let's first take a look at the situation without this help that's so badly needed.

Let's take a look at my friend Sam. Sam and his boss go to the annual meeting and trade show. They are there to find out what's going on in their industry and get educated. They are also there to see new products and talk to some potential vendors. Sam is looking to connect with other people who do what he does and is hoping to grow his professional network. This is his first trip to this show, but he's not really worried because he doesn't think of himself as shy.

He goes to the opening night party with his boss and walks into a room filled with strangers. His boss runs into some people he knows from years past and introduces Sam. Pretty soon his boss is deep in conversation, and Sam decides to start doing some networking on his own. But where does he start? He heads over to the bar to try sparking up conversation in the line. But even then, he is only meeting the person in front or behind him. They chat a bit, but after they have their drinks, they part ways.

Sam starts wandering around the room looking for someone to talk to. But everyone is gathered in groups and having their own conversations. It's really not that easy to just walk up to a bunch of strangers and introduce himself. He keeps moving, hoping an opportunity will present itself. By the second loop around the room, he has completely struck out. He can't even find his boss in the crowd.

Only a half an hour in to the event, Sam is on the elevator heading back to his room to check his email. After all, what's the point of hanging out if he's not going to get the chance to talk to anyone?

During the rest of the show, he meets a few random people in the educational sessions and at breaks and exchanges cards. The conversations are pretty brief, though, and he doesn't feel like he really has gotten to know anyone. He didn't connect with anyone who had a similar job as his at a similar company. Just about the only place he went where people did want to talk to him was the exhibit hall.

He leaves the conference with 10 business cards in his pocket but still feels like he doesn't really know anyone there. This was not a successful networking event for Sam. And trust me, he's not the only one who has felt this way. There are probably hundreds of Sams out there at every show who feel like they are missing out of a key component of the event.

Debunking the Mixing Myth

A study conducted by Paul Ingram and Michael W. Morris of Columbia University titled *Do People Mix at Mixers? Structure, Homophily, and the "Life of the Party"* shows us that while people have the best intentions of meeting strangers, the results don't quite match up with our desires.

In their study, 97 business people attended a cocktail mixer; their only instructions were to mingle freely. Each guest was outfitted with an electronic nametag that tracked who they interacted with and how long their conversations lasted. Ninety-five percent of the guests stated that their goal of attending the mixer was to build new ties rather than reinforce old ones. Sound familiar?

So what actually happened? Did 95 percent of the guests attain their goal?

Not at this party. "Mixer parties are supposed to free their guests from the constraints of preexisting social structure, so they can approach strangers and make new connections. Nevertheless, our results show that guests at a mixer tend to spend the time talking to the few other guests whom they already know well," asserts this study.

It's clear people need help meeting new people. They need to have the crutch of people they already know removed. They need to be encouraged to reach beyond their "safe" bets and walk right up to that stranger and start conversation.

How Does a Sponsorship Connect People?

There are many ways you can help people connect at a show. Think about popular online dating sites and offline dating services. What do they do? They find people who have similar interests and values and introduce them to one another. Some make the matches and leave how and when to meet up to the individuals. Some arrange lunch dates for people who want to connect casually. Some even arrange restaurant dinner parties to bring several compatible people together and let the participants sort out the pairings.

Just like these dating services, you can figure out ways to connect people with similar interests and provide a way for them to meet. You are helping by sorting through the thousands of attendees and finding for them the handful that would be an appropriate professional match for them.

As the sponsor, you are solving a problem for people who find it difficult to connect to others at large events such as trade shows. You are also making it easier for the most savvy networkers to connect with people and helping to make the most efficient use of their time. Those who make important connections will positively associate your company's name to those new relationships. You'll not just be seen as a brand, but as a company that really understands the needs of its customers and potential customers.

The "Meet" Sponsorship Bundle

If you wanted to be known as the company that helps people connect at the show, you could work with your show organizer to create a bundled sponsorship package that includes high-tech options as well as a few low-tech ones. This way, everyone has a way to connect even if they are not social media or mobile savvy. If you don't have the budget to create the entire bundle, you can always use these ideas as a starting point to create one or two connection activities.

Just keep in mind that if someone else negotiates exclusive rights to any type of attendee connection activities, you can be shut out. If you negotiate exclusivity by presenting a bundled option that covers all of the organizer's attendees, you'll be able to shut out your competition. It won't stop another exhibitor from having social events, but all your events will be promoted by the show organizer and deemed "official."

What might be included in a bundle? Here are some options:

- Online and mobile matchmaking software
- Dinner sign-up sheets in the registration area
- Special events, such as first-timers' receptions, VIP dinners with speakers, CEO cocktail parties, mixers for specific industry segments, and mentor/mentee programs
- Icebreaker games during show receptions and parties

Everyone always asks networking geniuses for tips on what helps in situations where they don't know anyone. But these people don't understand the basic fear of trying to start conversations in a room full of complete strangers. Put me in a room with 20 complete strangers, and I'm fine. Put me in a room with 1,000, and I become self-conscious. I feel like it's painfully obvious to the entire room that I am the only person without any friends. It's unreasonable, I know, but that's how a lot of people feel.

To come up with the most useful ideas like those mentioned above and others, brainstorm with people in your company who are uncomfortable at networking events and ask them what they would find useful if they were put in a room with 1,000 people they didn't know. The people who are not great at networking are your customers for this type of sponsorship, not the ones who are naturals.

Online and Mobile Matchmaking Programs

Online and mobile tools designed to connect event attendees with one another are becoming more and more popular (see Figure 20.1). As more companies enter this arena, the bar is being set higher. The tools are getting better and easier to use every day. Most tools link directly to the event registration so attendees' profiles are automatically populated with their data. All they need to do is enhance and build upon those profiles. They also connect to the attendees' social networking accounts, allowing them to easily find people they already know who will be attending the event.

Attendees can search other attendees' profiles based on areas of interest, request and set up meetings, and start conversations months before the event. They can even use the same tools to continue those conversations months after the event. And all this is done on one networking platform that not only can be branded with your company's logo, but also enables you to be part of the conversations taking place.

Many shows are starting to use these types of programs, but they are not seeing a good adoption rate among their attendees. It doesn't have as much to do with the capabilities of the applications, but more to do with the fact that these programs are not promoted properly. Many shows use the "build it and they will come" mentality. They might not have enough staff or time to promote the tool, teach attendees how to use it, and get conversations flowing.

All these problems could be overcome if the show had the right partner or sponsor to help it raise the adoption rates. I've talked to several show organizers; the problem is the same for each one. They sold sponsorship for the app, but it was less a sponsorship and more a branding opportunity. The sponsor handed over a check and a logo and that's about it. A true sponsorship requires an effort on the part of the sponsor to work with the organizer to ensure wide adoption of the app. So, do not engage in a sponsorship like this or any other for that matter, unless you are willing to put in what it takes to be successful (see Figure 20.1).

Figure 20.1   *An attendee communication tool used by EventCamp Twin Cities 2011. Pathable is the platform provider.*

If you choose this sort of sponsorship, hopefully, you have some input on what platform the show uses. Sometimes you might not have a choice if the show is under contract with a particular vendor. If you feel the platform does not provide the attendees with something that is truly useful, you might decide it's better to not be involved in this piece of the sponsorship package. It's better to walk away than have your name attached to something, at best, no one uses or, worse, leaves a bad impression on attendees.

The best platforms have several things in common:

- Integration with the registration provider to populate the attendee profile
- A way for attendees to identify one another by areas of interest
- Incorporation with popular social media platforms
- A way for attendees to protect their contact information
- A way to make the information private and available only to other show attendees
- The ability to set meetings and export that data to mobile devices
- The ability for attendees to engage in conversations before and after the event

Many platforms offer more features than this, but these are key to ensuring the tool is useful to connecting attendees with one another.

Dinner Sign-ups

One of my favorite things I've seen, and it's extremely low-tech, is *Exhibitor Magazine's* "Dinner with Strangers" program. It takes place every night during the trade show. Sign-up sheets are posted in The Square (their attendee gathering place and registration area), and anyone—attendees, exhibitors, and speakers—can put her name on a particular restaurant sheet and then just show up and meet the other dinner party guests. Yes, we are talking about sheets of paper tacked to a wall. It's that simple.

I'd love to see more show organizers incorporate ideas like this. Just like anything else, these events need to be communicated effectively. I like that these dinners are open to everyone and anyone, but I'd like to see more of an effort to market them to those who need them the most, especially new attendees and attendees who are the only individual from their company in attendance. These are the people who might not know many people at the event and who are not looking forward to dining alone every night.

However, if you're sponsoring this type of connection package, you're probably not going to want to just stick sheets of paper on a wall. You should use a more hands-on approach, like the Attendee Connect Kiosk discussed at the end of this chapter. This is where you'll tie everything together. But as a sponsor of this program, you would want to have a representative at each of these dinners to greet guests and help them mingle.

Special Targeted Events

When I go to the bigger conferences in my industry, like IAEE, PCMA, or even SISO, I am dying to connect with other show organizers who are similar to me. Sure, I can learn and get ideas from the big media companies who own several of the largest trade shows and run them internationally. But I would love it if someone would provide a way for me to connect with organizers of smaller shows who struggle with the same issues I do. I want to talk about ways to market an event with people who have budgets similar to mine, not people with seven-figure marketing budgets. Having a way for me to easily identify these people and to reach out to them would be a huge help. Just as I would like a way to connect with my peers at these events, so do many others at shows all over the world in every industry and so do your potential customers.

Many events have first-timer programs to welcome those who are new to the event (or those not-so-new but who need some extra help getting to know other attendees). They might have an orientation before the event opens or a first-timer's reception right before the opening night party. This allows people to meet one another in a smaller, more intimate setting. You could pair these first-timers with individuals from your company to escort them to the opening night party and introduce them to other attendees.

Still other shows have special programs for those who've been in the industry for 15 years or more. These people don't necessarily want help meeting new people. They find they can do that perfectly well on their own (although that study tells us they might not be as good at it as they think). But they do want someone to help them identify, connect with, and provide a place for them to meet others with the same level of experience.

There is no limit to the number of groups you can help connect or the ways you can connect them. It could get quite expensive to throw cocktail parties and dinners for every group, but the good news is that it's not necessary. All you really need is a way to help people find one another and a place for them to meet. It could be a table at lunch. It could be a cocktail party or dinner. It could be an empty room at a specified time. It could be in your booth before the show opens or after it closes. It could be at a customer site near the show's location.

Your company can be the connector of people. Just remember, you're not bringing all these people together so they can listen to you talk about yourself. You are bringing them together to meet one another. So, if you think you're going to open the party with a brief speech about your company by your CEO, stop right now. Huge, huge, huge, huge mistake. They get it—they know you paid for it because your name was all over the invitations. Just be there as a part of the group. Get to know people by just being social. Be there to facilitate introductions and to ensure everyone is having a good time. Make sure every person meets the person he came to meet. That's what will make them remember you.

Then listen to what people are talking about. You'll find out very quickly in a setting like this what the pain points are for each particular group. You'll hear what their problems are and what solutions they find most valuable. You'll know what keeps them up at night and where there are no solutions—at least not yet.

Icebreakers

Icebreakers for large events can be helpful for those who are not comfortable networking with strangers. It provides them with a way into conversation. It's best to make these types of activities voluntary. Not everyone likes to play games. It's also important not to choose silly games. These events are for professionals, and they should maintain a professional air and have a focus on the professional.

Who Done That?

This is a popular icebreaker for events focused on education within a particular industry. Usually everyone participates in a specified period of time, and prizes are given out to individuals who complete their lists.

Conference organizers make a list of 10–20 items that relate to their attendees' work life. For example, a list for a group of event and trade show marketers might have the following:

- Our company exhibits at more than 100 shows a year.
- We have a 95 percent lead follow-up rate.
- We have developed our own in-house training program.
- We performed a process improvement assessment.
- I successfully completed my CMP.
- I know what ROI is and can accurately measure it.
- I've made the transition from logistics to strategy.
- I developed a company-wide social media policy.

The list is given to all attendees, and their goal is to find someone who can sign one of the lines on the list. Each person should include her name and contact information when signing. If some of the items on the list are of particular importance to an attendee, she can collect several names and contact information for that particular item. Now you've provided her with a list of contact names for individuals who can coach her through special projects.

I like components of this game because, again, it focuses on making relevant connections for the individuals participating. I've played similar games that use a bingo format, but that included gathering irrelevant information like "has two dogs" or "likes to sail." Those tidbits are nice, but I don't go to conferences to meet other people who like to sail or have the same kind of dog I have. If it comes up in conversation, that's great; I just don't want to focus all my time there.

You could change it up and promote it not as a contest but an event-long networking tool. It should, of course, be optional but heavily promoted to everyone so people don't wonder who are the crazy people walking up to them with some strange list.

An icebreaker like this could easily be made into a mobile app or incorporated into the mobile app the show is already using. It should have a way for attendees to hunt for and share the list via social media tools like Twitter, Google+, Facebook, and LinkedIn. This type of icebreaker can also involve the wider virtual event audience as well. Someone following the event hashtag from his office in Sydney might see that @KarenFrench is looking for someone who successfully transitioned from a logistics role into a strategic one. Maybe he is a hiring manager who happens to have some great advice for @KarenFrench and immediately reaches out to her.

World Map

One way to help people connect is geographically. A large world map posted in the registration area or social lounge where people can attach their names to their locations can help people connect. It's always a plus to find colleagues who are located close to where you work so you can continue the connection after the show.

Why not create a mobile or online version of the world map where each attendee can post her picture, some contact information, and key areas of interest? This can extend to a virtual audience as well. Wouldn't it be nice to find someone who's attending the show that I couldn't attend this year and who's located near my office? I could meet her for coffee when she gets back and hear all about the show, not to mention make a new connection.

Creative Name Tags

Give people the option to include something creative on their name tags to spark conversation. They could draw a picture, include quirky facts, ask a question, or provide just the answer and make people guess the question. There should be no game or point to this icebreaker beyond helping people start talking.

If you don't want to force people to be creative, you can supply quirky badge ribbons for people to choose from. Again, it's all optional, but I've found that people seem to welcome the opportunity to identify themselves in some way other than by name and title.

Burning Question

Most people who attend a trade show have at least one problem they are hoping to find a solution for. Traditionally, they seek that solution in educational sessions and on the trade show floor. But it's possible that the woman standing next to you in line for a coffee has the answer. She just doesn't know you have the question.

I encourage attendees at my events to write their burning question right on their nametags. It helps to start conversation in hallways, at meals, on the show floor, and at networking functions. The person talking to you might not have the answer, but she might know someone who does. She makes an introduction, and now you've met yet another person. And that person might have the answer you're looking for.

A twist on that can include people who love to help others. Maybe someone at the event has just recently found the answer to his burning question. He can offer up his expertise or experience via his nametag. Perhaps he scribbles on his tag, "I just solved X, ask me how."

You might not even realize you need the answer to that question until you're standing there talking to that person. Or maybe you're trying to solve that problem and would love to get a recommendation from someone who has successfully conquered it. This type of activity encourages conversation in a way that targets finding solutions to people's problems.

You could even encourage people to post their burning questions and their areas of expertise on their mobile or web attendee matchmaking profiles. This way, if the person never crosses paths with someone who has the answer to his question, he might find the answer through the matchmaking tool.

How to Leverage Your Sponsorship

It goes without saying that you're going to need to work with the show organizer to market the bejeezus out of this sponsorship to ensure a wide adoption. As a partner, you cannot leave everything up to the organizer. You must run a complimentary marketing program of your own as well. Work with the show organizer to ensure you are both delivering a consistent message.

You need to make sure your company is featured prominently and often. But don't stop at simply telling people about the ways they can connect. Create videos and step-by-step instructions on how each component works. You can work with the mobile app provider, the software company, or both to create customized instructions with your branding—and that of the show's—for their platforms.

I also encourage you to create an "attendee connect" kiosk at the show staffed by employees of your company as connection ambassadors. This gives attendees one central location to go to for help setting up their profiles on the online application or mobile app. At this kiosk, they can also sign up for special networking events and dinners you've created. They can even go there to learn how to use the various icebreaker games you've developed. This space should not be in your booth; set it up in a central, high-traffic area of the show. It doesn't necessarily have to be on the show floor. You want attendees to have access to it even when the exhibit hall is closed.

Make sure your booth staff is well-informed of your sponsorship and have them encourage visitors to the booth to take advantage of your attendee connect program and direct them to the kiosk. You could even have special staff shirts made up with "Can I introduce you to someone?" printed on the fronts. Or have special buttons made up for all your employees at the show to wear.

Because this is a key sponsorship, make sure your staff and any of your company's attendees know that they are a part of it and that they are on duty during the entire show. Aside from the role they were assigned at the event, their secondary job is to always be connecting attendees to one another.

Networking is hard for many people, and they often leave the show feeling as though one of their main reasons for going was not satisfied. Be the company that recognizes that fact and make it easy for them to find other people at the event they might want to meet. Even those who consider themselves excellent networkers will appreciate the ease of finding and connecting with the "right" people through your sponsorship.

Summary

One of the main reasons attendees go to a trade show is to connect with others in their industry. And as we've seen with the Columbia study, it's not just the shy people or introverts who are not always making the connections they hope to when left to their own devices.

By creating a bundled sponsorship package, that includes a matchmaking program, networking events, ice breakers, and dinner signups, you give attendees several options to connect. You're helping them meet, not just strangers, but people who struggle with the same professional issues they do every day.

Work closely with the show to market the sponsorship and do your part to make it successful. You want people to go back to their offices and tell their colleagues that as far as networking goes, that show was the best they've been to. You'll be the company who provided them the opportunity to make that possible.

21

Destination Concierge

If you find yourself lucky enough to be exhibiting at a trade show in the same town as your corporate head-quarters, you might want to consider a destination con-cierge sponsorship. Your job, as the sponsor, would be to welcome visitors to your city and help them enjoy their stay. You would, in essence, become the city tour guide for the show's attendees.

A sponsorship like this is beneficial to the show organizer because it provides her attendees with useful informa-tion about an unfamiliar city while taking much of the workload of providing that information off of her shoul-ders. Show organizers often use the services of the local convention and visitor bureau (CVB) to populate this area of local content on the show website. But there is no personalization of the particular show and there is no personalization of the particular needs of the show attendees.

A destination concierge sponsorship allows you to infuse your brand with some personality. Attendees not only get to see your company as an institution, but also get to know the individuals who make up your company. And we all know that people like to do business with people they know, like, and trust.

I'm including this type of sponsorship in a book about social media because it is, at its core, very social so the use of social media tools is a natural fit. A destination concierge sponsorship is all about passing along local information to the attendees. Social media allows you to get that information into their hands at exactly the time they need it and enables them to share that information and get it into the hands of their colleagues. Incorporating social media into this sponsorship makes it easier for your company to connect with and build relationships with the attendees.

Because this is a highly visible sponsorship, I would encourage you to create special social media accounts and avatars with the sponsorship name. These accounts would be used only to share information relevant to a visitor to the city. You would not be using it to drive people to your booth. The account could be named "XYZShowConcierge," and the avatar image could be a customized version of your company logo.

You will share responsibility for making this sponsorship happen with the show organizer. While you will be creating all the content and doing some of the packaging of that content, the show organizer will also need to get the content up on their website and possibly the show app if they are using one. You'll need to work with the show organizer to ensure the sponsorship is marketed properly and the attendees know what information is available and all they ways they can access it. You'll also be working closely together on any activities you decide to do during the show. I want you to have a thorough understanding of what all is required so you can then pass that information along to the show organizer and work together to ensure its success.

This is not a linear process with a step one, two, and three. Your timeline is going to depend on which components you decide to include, how far in advance your show organizer wants things completed, and how the attendees move through the registration process. What I want to do is first tell you what kind of information you should be supplying and I'll include tips on how to incorporate social media in your communication. Then I'll show you other ways to round out the sponsorship using traditional face-to-face ideas as well as some high-tech options.

Create a Show City Guide

The information a CVB provides is boilerplate copy that show organizers can cut and paste onto their event websites. But there is no interaction between attendees and the information provider. Your sponsorship will create that interaction and provide an experience that the attendee will feel is created just for him and one that is much more personal.

One thing you can do to create a more personal experience is create a customized city guide for show attendees filled with insider tips on where to dine, shop, exercise, and tour. But don't just think of it as a printed guide. It should be available in electronic formats as well. You could create a downloadable PDF or e-book, a series of employee-featured videos where they give their favorite tips and even an interactive online database hosted on the show website. It also goes without saying you'll be using social media to spread this information.

First, you need to create a knowledge base of information that attendees will want to have access to when they come to your town for the trade show. You can get your entire company involved in this process asking them to volunteer their suggestions in the categories outlined a bit further on.

Earlier we talked about social media collaboration tools. This is the perfect place to put them to use. You could set up a Wiki outlining the types of information, including guidelines or a template of the type of detail you would like to compile. You could also use Google Moderator by creating a topic "Trade Show City Guide" and creating a question for each category. Employees could fill in their own responses to whatever question they want to tackle. I like Google Moderator for this because it lets you export the data into a CSV file when you are done which can then be imported into a show app by the application provider (see Figure 21.1 for a sample show guide using Google Moderator).

Another option would be to use a simple file-sharing tool like Google Docs or Dropbox and have volunteers add their responses to a word doc or spreadsheet.

Figure 21.1   *Sample Google Moderator topic.*

Restaurant Suggestions and Things to Do

Encourage employees to submit their favorite restaurant recommendations and suggestions for things to do about town. Let them incorporate their personalities into the recommendations with insider tips, much like employee book recommendations at the local bookstore. Here's an example:

Restaurant Recommendations

La Viola

253 S. 16th St.

(215) 735-8630

Staff Pick: Sally Snow, Finance Director, XYZ Co.

This is a fantastic little BYOB Italian restaurant located just three blocks from the convention center. You can pop into the liquor store just a block away for a nice bottle of Barolo to take with you. (Under $30)

Things to Do

Art Exhibits

Old City Area

Staff Pick: Tony Branson, Maintenance Director, XYZ Co.

On the first Friday of every month, the doors to local art studios are open to the public for a celebration of art. March's first Friday happens to fall during this year's show. I encourage you to take a stroll through old city and enjoy our local artists. (Free)

Many people have special dining needs, and it's important to include them in your information. Don't forget to mention gluten-free, halal, kosher, and vegetarian or vegan dining options on your list. I cannot tell you how often these attendees' needs are not addressed. It will not go unnoticed, in a good way, if you are smart and address these special diet needs.

Because this is information that is very handy during the show, set up scheduled tweets to go out early in the morning for breakfast suggestions and around 3 p.m. for dinner suggestions. Mix up the recommendations and always include a link to the full list or city guide.

Create a Discount Dining/Shopping Program

Why not take your restaurant recommendations up a notch? Many of the attendees at the show will have to fend for themselves for dinner at least a night or two. A lot of those attendees are on a per diem, not a sales entertainment expense account. Finding good, local spots to eat that won't cost them a fortune can be a challenge. But many restaurateurs in town would love to have this business.

So, how do you bring together the restaurant owner and the trade show attendee? You could assemble a special discount dining program. When an attendee flashes his show badge, he would get a percentage off, a free dessert, or a special prix fixe menu. You could get local retail establishments to participate as well with special offers.

Participating restaurants and retail locations could be highlighted on your city guide (printed, PDF, or e-book), on the event website, and in the mobile app. You also could promote this by creating posters with the show branding (and your company's involvement) that restaurants and retail establishments could post in their windows. Tell the attendees to look for the signs in windows around town for businesses offering a discount to dine or shop.

You could invite the chefs of participating restaurants to submit recipes for some of their dishes and post them on the show website or blog. You could also include those recipes and information about the program and participating restaurants on the show's community social media sites (Facebook, LinkedIn Group, Pathable, and so on).

Because this is a good revenue source for local businesses, you could probably get the local chamber of commerce or CVB involved to help you coordinate everything. This is, after all, why they exist—to bring business to the city in the case of the CVB and to promote business in the community in the case of the chamber. Start with the CVB or chamber PR department. If they are not the ones to help you, they can get you in touch with the person who can.

Running Routes

When friends travel to Philadelphia (my hometown) for shows, I am constantly asked, "Where is a good place to go running?" They are looking for advice not just on a scenic route, but for a loop that makes sense for where they are staying. People also need to know a route that is safe both early in the morning and at night after dark.

Map out the best routes for 3K, 5K, and 10K runs from the host hotels. I like to highlight a few points of interest when I map routes for my friends so they can combine a little bit of sightseeing with their exercise.

Yes, they could get this information from their concierge at the hotel, but it does not go unnoticed when someone thinks to provide it before they even arrive at the show so they can plan ahead. You could use social media to connect runners with one another so they have company when they go out for their run or walk. You could do this by creating a subgroup within the show or community LinkedIn group, a separate conversation on the Facebook page, or in the event community platform.

Visiting Gym Memberships

It's likely most the hotels have a fitness center, but what about attendees looking for yoga, Pilates, and other fitness classes? Many of your city's gyms, yoga, and Pilates studios offer day passes for people visiting from out of town. Another one of those extras that goes a long way is to include a list of these fitness centers for those who are looking for them.

Stick with the fitness centers and studios that are within walking distance from the convention center and the host hotels. Include pricing and class hours in the information you are providing.

An even better option would be to hire a few yoga and Pilates instructors to come to the host hotels for morning (before the start of the show) or afternoon (after the show floor closes) classes. More and more shows and conferences are starting to include these types of classes in their schedules, and they usually get 30 or more attendees participating. If you do go this route, I suggest supplying branded yoga mats for attendees to use and take home. Include this information in your pre-show communications so they don't have to pack their mats to bring with them.

This is a great place to use text message alerts. Attendees who've signed up for the early morning or afternoon classes will appreciate the reminder that they need to either wake up and get moving or change into their exercise gear. Just be sure to give them at least a half hour warning.

Emergency Shopping Tips

How many times have you been at a show and gotten a run in your last pair of tights, spilled coffee on your last clean white shirt, realized you forgot your phone charger, or found that those shoes you thought were comfortable really are not? You'd love to run out to get a replacement but only have a few minutes here and there and not enough time to hunt down the right store.

Ask your booth staffers what are the items that they commonly forget and start compiling a list. It's likely they are not the only ones who can be a bit forgetful. Putting together a list of spots where attendees can quickly run out and get replacements for what they've forgotten is a huge help.

It's likely you can strike a deal with a nearby department store for e-coupons to include with this information. Macy's, which is just a block away from the Pennsylvania Convention Center, often does this for shows located in Philadelphia. Just make sure you give yourself enough lead-time to strike a deal as the department store might have to go through several layers of approval. Your CVB membership director can help you find the right contact or go directly to the store's marketing department.

This information should be tweeted using the show hashtag all throughout the day and the entire length of the show. "Did you spill coffee on your last clean shirt? No worries—there's a new one right around the corner (link to emergency shopping tips) #showhashtag." "Forget your charger? You can buy a replacement just two blocks away (link to emergency shopping tips) #showhashtag."

Getting Around

Attendees want to know how to get around the city and where the hot spots are. Every city is different. Getting from one end to the other in New York City proper takes a lot longer than getting from one end of Center City Philadelphia to the other. Some cities have great easy to navigate public transportation systems and others require the use of taxis to get around. Other cities boast their walkability. Getting around is second nature to locals, but it's a complete mystery to first time visitors.

Start by listing options for getting from and to the airport. Although it's easy to grab a cab from the Philadelphia airport to the convention center, visitors might be surprised to find that for one-fifth the price of a cab, they can get a train and travel about the same amount of time. There are no train changes, and it's practically door-to-door service. Those on a budget might welcome the chance to save $50 going from and back to the airport by taking a train.

Give them tips on various neighborhoods in the city to visit during their off time, and tell them a little bit about why these areas are special or what they might find there. Include information on the walking distance to each spot from the convention center or trade show location as well as an estimate of what cab fare would be.

Include a map in your city guide and highlight shopping areas, historic highlights, and neighborhoods known for their restaurants and cultural spots. You could even highlight on the map your employee-recommended restaurants and places to see. Your map could be a low-tech printed version and/or PDF available for download from the show website. Or you could go a little more high-tech and have a programmer create a customized interactive Google Map that includes your list of places to see, your branding, and highlighted walking and running routes.

Where Not to Go

Sometimes giving people information on where *NOT* to go is more important than tips on where to go. Every city has its seedier spots, and the last thing you want is unsuspecting attendees wandering off into them. I like to highlight those in red on a map. For some places, I specify that going there during the day is fine, but once the sun goes down, it's best to stay away.

If your trade show is located in an urban center, you're going to have a lot of attendees who are uncomfortable. Some people see cities as nothing but crime-ridden trouble spots. And why wouldn't they? That's all they hear on the news. They don't realize that most of the city is perfectly safe and that they will be nowhere near the areas they keep hearing about on the news.

Remind visitors to take off their badges when traveling around town. A trade show badge hanging around your neck is a big flashing sign that says, "I'm not from around here and I'm an easy target." Attendees shouldn't be afraid to explore the city, but they should be on alert and take precautions.

International Visitors

If you are expecting international visitors, they will appreciate information tailored just for them. Most people use credit cards for everything to make the money situation easier, but for those who still like to have some cash on hand, let them know where they can find a currency exchange location. In more international cities, this can be easy to find, but even in Philadelphia there are only four locations in the entire city.

Talk to your CVB and local chamber of commerce. These organizations might have an area on their visitor websites with content available in different languages you can direct attendees to. Although most of your visitors will probably speak fairly fluent English, they might appreciate getting information in their native tongues.

Also ask for brochures and maps in different languages to have on hand at your concierge kiosk. I know enough Spanish to get by in Spain, but having some information and maps in English would make my visit much less stressful. Every time you do something like this, you are making a positive impression on the visitor.

Distributing Your Show Guide

After you have compiled all that information, how do you get it into the hands of the attendees? You have several options starting with the very low-tech printed guide. You could include this information as part of the printed show guides or as a printed insert that goes in the show bags. Even if you don't print a guide for every attendee, having some printed guides on hand is also nice for the attendees who prefer low-tech options. You could have some of these available at your concierge kiosk, which I talk about next.

You could also take one step up and create a downloadable PDF or even an e-book that attendees can access via the show website. Speaking of the show website—the show should set up a special page that showcases the city guide and information you are providing. It should be easy to find when visitors are on the show's home page, either through a tab on the main menu, a feature box, or banner or side-bar graphic. I prefer it be on the main menu, with a submenu for each category of information.

This information could also be incorporated in the show event app if there is one. You're going to want to work with the app provider early on in the process to ensure you are providing the information you want included in the right format. Most will send you a spreadsheet pre-formatted for you, and you just fill in the boxes with the content.

Be sure the attendees know where to find the guide wherever it is located by using social media before and during the event. Let them know where to get a printed copy and provide links to online versions as well.

Concierge Kiosk at the Show

An online show guide is a great resource but you don't want to stop there. You want the show attendees to have an interactive experience with your company. To do that you want a physical concierge desk in a central location staffed by your employees. Think of all the attendees you will reach through your concierge desk who might not have stopped by your booth. It's an opportunity for those attendees to get to know your company and interact with your employees. After all, one of the greatest things about social media is taking online relationships offline!

Many cities provide a concierge desk to show organizers at no cost if the event is large enough. The problem I've found is that it is often staffed by volunteers who are not terribly savvy about hot new restaurants and obscure yet very worthwhile activities. Nor are they savvy about the industry, the show, or the attendees. They know where the most popular restaurants are (often chain restaurants and those they might frequent), the major shows or concerts that are in town, and the major art exhibits running. They are not trained to point out the hidden gems that locals might know more about or that might be a perfect fit for the attendee demographics.

There's no one more in tune with the trade show attendees as the show floor manager. It is their job to observe everything that is going on and fix problems, sometimes before anyone even notices them. I asked Greg Ruby, one of the industry's best show floor managers and huge social media advocate, what he thinks about the concierge kiosk. "When attending a trade show in a city I have never visited before, the concierge kiosk is a must do for my first day. I like a good meal as much as the next person, and while the hotels or chain restaurants generally can offer this up, I want to experience the city I am in for a few days. Attendees are looking to get out of the 'tourist district' and experience the sights and sounds of the host city—the concierge kiosk offers this at a minimal cost to the sponsor." Greg adds, "But you also want to use social media to get this information out to the attendees. Social media enthusiasts tend to be more adventurous and are looking for insider tips and places to go that are off the beaten track."

That CVB concierge desk is also, quite often, set up in a corner of the convention center so as not to take up valuable real estate that the convention center could be charging for. In contrast, your sponsored concierge kiosk should be set up right in the middle of a common area, open throughout the show, and with prominent signage that is easy to see from just about everywhere and anywhere. Make it easy for attendees to understand what you are there for with signage that says something like, "Get all your local information from locals in your industry," or "Find places to eat, shop, run, and play."

Even before they arrive at the show, you should let attendees know about the concierge kiosk and what services they can find there. Use all your social media tools to let them know where it is located and what times it will be open. Why not let them know a little something about the people who will be staffing the desk. Perhaps staffers could introduce themselves on different social media platforms you are using and give a few of their favorite city tips.

Get your whole company involved in the show by staffing shifts with employees who might not normally get to attend industry events like these. Look for volunteers who really know the city inside out. You should see this as an opportunity for your employees to get to know your customers who use the products and services those employees help create. The kiosk should be open to anyone and everyone who is eager to participate. I even recommend having your key executives stop by to staff the booth for a few minutes during the event. Who wouldn't be just a bit pleased to get a restaurant recommendation from someone like Bill Gates? I bet she'd talk about it that night with her colleagues.

Airport Welcoming

As the official destination concierge sponsor, you should have visibility at the airport when attendees arrive. Without a doubt, banners should be hung in airport terminals (facing in to be seen by those people headed to baggage claim) and in the baggage claim areas. Most people will have checked luggage, but even if they don't, they'll be passing through baggage claim to get transportation to their hotels. If your show is a large city-wide show, the show organizer will be able to work with you to get the right contact for the airport or even arrange things for you. An alternative is to reach out to the local CVB for their assistance.

Have employees take shifts greeting attendees as they pass through baggage claim and head for the transportation hubs. They won't be looking for your company, but they will recognize the event logo and branding so make sure they appear prominently on signage your greeters are holding. You could also arrange to have a kiosk set up in the baggage claim areas with similar signage so people can't miss it. Your sign might say "Widget Congress Welcome Desk," or "Welcome to Trade Fair 2013," and include your company name and/or logo.

This is truly a very first impression—a first impression of your company, your city and the show. The person volunteering for this position represents all three. If you are using a kiosk or desk at the airport, encourage those staffing it, not to hide behind it all day. As soon as you put someone behind a counter and have them sit down, they do not look very welcoming. When it's slow, they'll be paying more attention to their smartphone or book than the people coming off the plane.

Make it easier for them by having them work with a buddy so they have company during the slow times. Have staffers sit on stools in front of the desk or just to the side. This gives them a chance to get off their feet but the height of the stool makes them much more approachable and they'll appear more welcoming. Just make sure arriving attendees will know it's your employees who are there to greet them by having employees wear branded shirts.

Your employees don't have to actually carry anyone's bags. Just welcoming them to the show and to your city sets the stage for the rest of the attendees' experience. Make sure your greeters know where attendees can catch a taxi, bus, or shuttle; board public transportation; or rent a car so they can point visitors in the right direction. Every time I get off a plane, go down the escalators to baggage claim, and see an event welcoming committee, I really appreciate it. It lets me know that I'm important to them and that they appreciate my attendance at the event.

If your event expects to draw a lot of international attendees, having someone greet them as they exit customs is important. These people are usually exhausted after a long and sometimes grueling flight. Be there with bottled water (I am usually against bottled water for environmental reasons, but in this case, there really is no alternative), mints, a snack, and a welcoming smile.

This group, more than anyone, will appreciate ground transportation help. Show them where to exit for taxis and shuttles and how to pay for them. Don't worry about translation because most international attendees coming to an English-speaking show will expect you to speak English. Just be patient and speak slowly if needed—not louder. But if you have some employees who speak multiple languages, they might enjoy the opportunity to help in this area.

For my events, I like to collect attendee travel information during the registration process. This way, I know when the bulk of people are arriving and departing and where they are traveling from and to. If your show organizer is collecting this information, it can help you know when to staff these welcome areas. You don't need to greet every attendee as they come trickling in; just find out when the rush times are.

Be sure to let attendees know to look for your welcoming committee by posting it on the website and tweeting about it on the show hashtag a couple days before the show begins right through to the first day of the event. If you will only have staff there during certain times be sure to include that information so people don't wonder where your welcoming committee is when they arrive two hours late at around 1 a.m. Although if that person is a big fish, can you imagine the impression you would make if you *were* there?

You can also post this information on the show or community's LinkedIn group or Facebook page. But don't just broadcast it, make it fun and interactive. Invite people to let you know when they'll be landing so you can keep your eye out for them. Encourage them to stop by and say hello.

Airline Check-ins, Boarding Passes, and Good-byes

Your concierge kiosk can double as an airline check-in and boarding pass hub at the end of the show. Because most people will not need dinner recommendations on the last day, you can take any laptops or computers you were using to assist attendees and turn them to face the attendees. Hook up a printer and invite people to check in for their flights and print their boarding passes if needed. Be sure to let attendees know they can access this service by tweeting on the event hashtag and making announcements over the PA system. You can also include that this service will be available in your city guide, information page on the show website, and in the mobile app.

Little things sometimes seem to mean the most when you are traveling. When I was leaving the Peabody Hotel in Orlando after one show, a bellman handed me a bottle of water as I got into the shuttle to return to the airport. Something so simple, but clearly it has left a very positive impression in my mind. Although my entire stay there was fantastic, that final interaction with the hotel was a positive one. It immediately made me think how easy this would be to do for the attendees who are, essentially, your guests. After the show closes when the rush of attendees are leaving to go to the airport, why not hand them a bottle of water and thank them for visiting your city right before they hop into their cab? Create a positive last.—and lasting—experience.

When creating the destination concierge sponsorship, think about what information and services you would find useful when visiting an unfamiliar city. Think about what would leave a lasting positive experience in your memory long after you leave an event. Having this much interaction with attendees makes you memorable—a lot more memorable than just a banner with your company name on it.

Social media is a communication tool, so use it whenever you need to communicate. Use it to poll attendees before the event to find out what kind of information about your city they want to know. Tweet out bits of information you are including in all these categories. Post mini stories on Facebook and Google+ about hot spots around town, and encourage employees to comment on them and include their own picks using their own accounts. Invite past visitors to add to the list as well.

Use social media just like you would any other communication tool to let attendees know how to access all this great information you are providing. Just be sure to actively monitor those accounts so you can answer questions quickly. There's nothing worse than a support line that no one answers. By doing this you'll also be cultivating a following and will be building a network. Keep the conversations going after the event by following up with those who contacted you for information, asking them if they found it useful and encourage feedback on the recommendations.

Summary

A destination concierge sponsorship works best when the show is in your head-quarters city. Every employee is a potential tour guide, and it gives everyone a chance to get involved in the show and meet customers and prospects. It also gives visitors a chance to get to know your company as a group of individuals instead of just a logo and a salesperson.

First, gather all the information you think a trade show attendee might need while they are in town. Tap in to your company employees for their favorite restaurants, running routes, and things to do around town. Compile all the information into a show city guide and get it out to the attendees via print, the show website, and social media platforms.

Have a welcoming committee at the airport to greet attendees when they arrive to create a positive first impression. Continue improving on that positive impression by creating a concierge kiosk in the registration area or other high traffic area that attendees can access during conference and show hours. Finally, be sure to leave them with a positive last impression as they leave the event by helping them print boarding passes and even put them in a cab or shuttle with a bottle of water or other treat.

22

Tech Sponsor

What a difference a decade makes. Ten years ago when I was on the exhibit side of shows, I was using paper exhibitor kits. Show service forms were filled out and faxed to the decorator. We carried to the show our thick binders with copies of all our service orders, shipping documents, and exhibit drawings. Shows that had converted to online order systems were few and far between. Even the majority of attendees registered for shows by faxing or mailing in their registration forms. Upon arriving at the show and checking in, they were handed show bags weighing sometimes in excess of 5 lbs. filled with exhibitor and sponsor collateral and a big thick show directory.

Now, thankfully, it seems everything is being done online. Exhibitors can order all their show services with a click of the mouse. They can upload all their collateral to the online show directory. And it's not just documents they can upload. They now have the ability to upload pictures and video and audio files. More and more shows are going high-tech when it comes to reserving space for the next year's show. Exhibitors don't even have to meet with the exhibit sales manager at a scheduled time during the last day of the show. The sales team comes to your booth armed with nothing more than a tablet computer. They just tap on your selected booth on the show floor map, and after handing over the deposit or agreeing to a contract, you've purchased your space for next year.

Attendees are not only registering online, but also signing up for educational sessions, scheduling meetings with exhibitors, and using an online matchmaking program to connect with other attendees months before the start of the show. Forget that thick, printed directory. All the information can be accessed online or via the show event app. By putting this information online, there are no longer space restrictions and no limits to what can be made available.

More and more attendees are showing up at shows with laptops, tablets, and smartphones. They are using them to access all that information the show has put at their fingertips—information like the show schedule, trade show floor maps, presentations, collateral, speaker bios, attendee and exhibitor profiles, and more. They are also keeping in touch with their offices and families via email, phone, and social media.

If you are incorporating social media components into your booth, you'll want the attendees to be using their devices nonstop. But all this great technology that helps us connect with one another or even just saves us time, puts a strain on resources. Batteries get drained at a rapid pace, and cell signals and Wi-Fi access get overloaded. The last thing you want is an attendee who can't participate in the social media aspects of your booth in the afternoon because his battery died in the morning.

Tech isn't going away when it comes to shows, and we have to start planning better for it. A good tech sponsorship does just that. To create a good tech sponsorship, you have to be able to anticipate the attendees' tech needs before they become a problem. This is a problem-solving sponsorship. It's the kind of sponsorship that leaves a lasting positive impression because attendees know who solved their problem by making sure they didn't have one.

Here again I will be telling you what is involved in the planning and set-up of a good tech sponsorship. But you will be working closely with the show organizer. Still, it is important you know what all is necessary, so you can work together to make sure the sponsorship is a success for everyone. The show might very well have this kind of sponsorship in their portfolio, but knowing what all is involved might give you ideas to improve the package. Let's start by looking at a key component, the tech lounge.

The Tech Lounge

When I envision a tech lounge, I see an area that is centrally located and open to attendees throughout the show. It's not necessarily located in the exhibit hall because it needs to be accessible to attendees even when the exhibit hall is closed. Locating it outside of the exhibit hall also gives attendees a respite from the constant assault on their senses that is the exhibit hall. It's sort of an oasis where attendees can go to recharge not just their device batteries, but their internal battery as well.

I see small groups of two, three, or four attendees comfortably seated deep in conversation about new products or services they've seen on the show floor or comparing notes on what they've learned in educational sessions. Sitting in front of them on the table are their smartphones, tablets, and laptops connected to a charging station. They are downloading session handouts, checking the show schedule, and mapping the route for their next trip to the exhibit hall via a wireless connection.

A few people who are rushing to their next appointment on the show floor or session are dropping off their phones at the phone check station (much like a coat check) to charge for an hour while they do what they need to do. Others are gathered at the tech help desk where some are learning how to create a Twitter account and follow along on the show hashtag. Others are getting instruction on how to use the attendee and exhibitor matchmaking application. Still others are printing Continuing Education Unit (CEU) certificates or their day's schedule of appointments.

All of this is provided for them and staffed by the tech sponsor. They are seeing the sponsor's branding everywhere, and they are interacting with the sponsor's employees from a wide cross-section of the company. It's not a logo that helped them understand the value of social media and staying connected with the new people they are meeting at the show; it's that incredibly helpful person from customer service or R&D. So what are the key components of a good tech lounge?

Let's Start with Power

Attendees are going to charge their batteries overnight and head to the show floor with a full battery. Although there will be a few like me who forget to plug everything in before going to bed and just get whatever charge they can while they're getting dressed. They will check email a dozen or more times before noon. They'll be on the phone several times as well. They might use the mobile app to check the schedule and speaker bios to decide where they want to be. They'll be on Twitter following along and tweeting on the show hashtag. They'll be updating their Facebook and LinkedIn status and sharing pictures. They'll also use the app to look at the exhibit floor map and get information about exhibitors they want to see. By noon their battery will be about dead. Now what?

One option is to beg for a power outlet for a quick charge while talking to an exhibitor at each booth they stop at. A second option is to find an outlet in one of the classrooms or hallways and waste half an hour trying to get a bit more charge. This is how they spend the rest of the afternoon—grabbing a charge here and there whenever they can. Then when they should be at the bar networking, they are in their rooms trying to get enough of a charge to get them through the evening. It's hopeless and frustrating.

A better option would be to offer a phone check service as part of your tech sponsorship. Attendees can drop off their phones to charge for an hour or even half an hour. They can leave their phones in a safe spot and wander off to do what they need to do, knowing they'll have a charge when they get back. There are companies who will rent you charging stations that come with everything you need to charge multiple devices at one time, including an assortment of adapters for just about every device imaginable. Rent a few of the most basic models, and you'll have your phone check service up and running.

You can also put some of these charging kiosks around the tech lounge for self service. This way, attendees can get off their feet for a while and talk to one another while their phones are charging. I've seen some that you can put customized graphics on. But that's not terribly interesting—more branded posters? So what? Instead, look into some of the charging stations available for rent that have multimedia features great for running a video loop of your customer testimonials.

So if you can put these kiosks everywhere why would you need a phone check? Not everyone wants to take the time to sit by his phone. Attendees are busy and have places to go—like to your booth. Having a phone check gives him peace of mind. Do both. But a tech sponsorship doesn't just provide a charge when attendees need one. It provides access to all those great services the show provides online, like matchmaking tools, downloadable session content, exhibitor appointment setting, and the online community.

Internet Access Stations

Despite the growing number of people accessing the Web and their email via their smartphones and tablets, some still have phones that are made simply to make phone calls. Some people prefer to use a computer because they hate working on a tiny screen. Having a few computers in your tech lounge so that people can access the Internet to check their email, update their schedules, or access any other show services will make these people happy.

There was a time when you'd see banks of up to 50 workstations connected to the Internet just for checking email. But now so many people are comfortable using their smartphones or tablets for this that 5–10 stations (depending on the size of the show) is quite sufficient if that's all they are there for. You can brand the desktop and allow access only to an Internet browser to make things simple. Computers should be rented locally to save on shipping expenses and reduce the risk of damage during shipping.

Although Internet access stations might not be necessary much longer for attendees to check email, I am seeing a growing number of computer stations at shows that use online session scheduling and matchmaking services. Many of these services are available through a mobile device, but they are a bit cumbersome because of the small screen. Having access to these services at computer stations in the tech lounge is a huge plus for the attendees and the stations are used frequently. Much of this scheduling is done by the attendee before the show, but once he arrives at the show, his priorities can shift. He might want to make changes to his session schedules or exhibitor appointments. He might discover more attendees he wants to meet with and will need access to the system to set up appointments with them.

Talk to your show organizers about including some of these stations in your tech lounge. It's likely they will want them located all throughout the show areas for easy access, but putting a few stations in your tech lounge will be convenient for the attendees and probably a place they would naturally look for them. Besides, they might want to grab a quick charge for their phones while they are playing with their schedules and downloading session handouts.

The Tech Help Desk

By now, I think we can agree that tech on the show floor is becoming more and more prevalent. If anything discussed so far in this book was new to you and sounded unfamiliar, you can be sure some show attendees feel the same way.

Even with the best instructions provided beforehand, some people would prefer hands-on demonstrations. Or even just a place to go when they have questions about how something works. They might have questions on how to use the event app, any matchmaking programs or appointment schedulers, and even how to use social media. Why not encourage people to participate in the social media platforms you are using by showing them how to set up an account and teaching them how to use it?

Some people still are not using social media. It's foreign to them, but they are often curious as to what they might be missing out on. Staff your help desk with enthusiastic employees to teach people how to set up their own Twitter, Google+, Facebook, or LinkedIn accounts. Show them how to maximize their use of social media and how to access the various platforms on their smartphones, tablets, or laptops. You can get them started by showing them how to follow your company's account, the show account, and their colleagues who may already be using it.

Teach them about hashtags and show them how to follow along with what is going on in the show by following the official show Twitter hashtag.

Many people don't use all the cool tech that is available only because they are afraid of doing it wrong. Put them at ease by giving them hands-on instruction and a friendly place to go when they get stuck. Just be aware, though, that not everyone has the patience required to do this kind of job. If your company has an IT help desk, you might want to tap into their group for people to staff your show tech help desk. They already have the skills necessary to walk people through difficult problems. Customer service is another place to find help desk staffers because these people often have an endless supply of patience.

Mobile App

In addition to the tech lounge, your tech sponsorship could also include sponsoring the show mobile app. I touched a little bit on event mobile apps earlier in Part III, "On with the Show." What was once a novelty for shows is becoming the norm. More and more shows are turning to event apps to replace all their printed material. As more and more shows are adopting these apps, more and more attendees are using them. The 2012 Shot Show reported 15,000 attendees using their event app by the end of the first day of the show. That was one quarter of the attendees for the entire event. That's a pretty impressive adoption rate for something so new.

As we mentioned earlier, a good sponsorship is not just sticking your logo on something. What you really need from a sponsorship is positive interaction between your company and your clients and prospects. Before you think about investing in this kind of sponsorship, you need to ask yourself honestly whether you have already leveraged the opportunity given to you as an exhibitor to its fullest extent possible. If you're not even taking the time to complete your exhibitor profile with detailed contact information, logo, a good description of what your company does that would interest the show's attendee base, inclusion of information sheets for download, and so on, you're not ready to take this next step.

As I said before, and I cannot stress this enough, really look at what you are putting your name on. You should put your name on something that attendees will find valuable. You want your name on an app that is easy to use and has the information that is relevant to the attendee. You should put your name on something that is a positive experience for the attendee. Perception is everything, and it's not just usability that creates that perception.

I was recently at an event that used one of these mobile event apps. The app was fine, but the show organizers dropped the ball when it came to updating the information made available on the app. They never even bothered to include a presentation title or the speaker bio for the opening keynote presentation. That entry on the schedule just said "Opening General Session." I talked to several people who were quite upset to find they slept through a speaker they would have loved to hear.

Errors like this were rampant on the app, but the fault was not with the app itself. It was the responsibility of the show to provide the content. But here is the scary part. Attendees kept referring to the app as the "abc sponsor app," not the "xyz show app." I got into a debate with a friend who felt some of the responsibility lay with the sponsor. Because its name was on the app, it was a reflection on that company, which should have done more to populate the app with the right information.

Believe it or not, at the time I disagreed. I felt it was the responsibility of the show to be sure the right content was on the app. After all, they owned that content; it did not belong to the sponsor. After further reflection, I conceded that my friend had a very valid point. If you are going to put your name on something, you must do everything in your power to make sure it's something worthy of your name. Include a list of deliverables that not only you as a sponsor agree to, but also that the show agrees to as well as what will happen if they are not met in your sponsorship contract.

I already discussed how important usability of the app is. Just as important is the information the app contains. If people find the schedule times are incorrect or there is not enough information included to decide what they want to do and when, the app is useless and will stay in their pockets. Worse yet, they will refer to it as the "useless yourcompanynamehere app" each time it is mentioned. As a sponsor, you need to work closely with the show organizers to ensure they are providing something that is of value to the attendees.

As a sponsor, it is partly your responsibility to make sure:

- The app is marketed properly so that attendees know it exists and understand its value to them.
- The attendees are trained on how the app works. This can be done via step-by-step instructions, video demonstrations provided before the show, and a help desk in the tech lounge at the show.
- The content is accurate and up-to-date. If you purchased a branding opportunity to have your logo on all the lanyards yet it was put on only half, you would not stand for that. The same goes for incomplete content on the event app.

Promoted Trends and Tweets

Another component of your tech sponsorship could be purchasing promoted trends for the show hashtag. As a show organizer, promoted trends on the show hashtag is a touchy subject for me. First, it's important to point out that no one owns a hashtag. Your show can use a specific hashtag, but they do not own it. Anyone is welcome to use it any way they please. However, because of their popularity, Twitter has found a way to monetize them through "promoted trends" and "promoted tweets."

Basically, you are buying the hashtag or trend from Twitter for a specified period of time. That purchase will put your tweet at the top of anyone's search on that particular hashtag giving you a high level of visibility. Technically, you do not have to get permission from the show organizers to purchase promoted tweets on their hashtag. But you should do so anyway and work closely with the show organizer on how you will use those promoted tweets.

There is nothing that raises the ire of the Twitter community more than when they feel a company is forcing its message on them. I've seen companies get ripped to sheds by the very community they hoped to reach by purchasing promoted tweets. I advise treading very lightly here.

If this were a show hashtag, a good tech sponsorship might include tweets leading up to the show encouraging people to register early to save money. After the show started, it might include tweets that highlighted certain aspects of the show—something attendees would find valuable as a group. The show would give its support because it is benefiting them as well. They are also more likely to be seen as valuable information rather than an invasion by show attendees.

But again, really decide whether this is worth it and be ready to take these tweets down if a backlash occurs. You could very well have the support of the show organizer but not the attendees. Other exhibitors or sponsors could potentially stir up the trouble as well.

Tweet-ups

The only thing Twitter users like to do more than tweet is attend tweet-ups. A *tweet-up* is an organized, and sometimes impromptu, gathering of people who use Twitter. Opposed to what some people out there believe, it is not a bunch of people in a room tweeting to one another instead of talking. I have found that very social people, who relish the opportunity of finally meeting in person the connections they have made online, attend tweet-ups.

These are often some of the most productive networking events you can attend. You might have spent months or even years developing professional relationships in your industry with people online. Then, you find that many of these people are all gathered at the show at the same time. Why not arrange a tweet-up so people can finally meet in person?

What's involved in planning a tweet-up? It can be as simple as just organizing the place and time and getting the word out to the community via Twitter. I've seen some companies who planned a tweet-up give one or two drink tickets to all the attendees. Some host an open bar and hors d'oeuvres. My preference is drink tickets that are branded with your company name and logo just so everyone knows where their drink came from.

However, people don't go to a tweet-up for the free food and drinks. They go to connect with their community and strengthen the relationships they have forged online. They go to finally meet their Twitter friends in person. That is far more important than a free drink or two, but it's nice to remind them who made it all possible.

Here are some tweet-up best practices:

- Hold the tweet-up in a location that has Wi-Fi and strong phone signals. The tweet-up will be a failure if attendees can't share pictures and send status updates during this event.

- Provide markers and name tag stickers for people to identify their Twitter handles. John Smith might be better known to the group as @cloudcompuguy123.

- Arrive early and greet people as they enter. Do not snub anyone. This will likely be a very social group that disdains class structure. They typically all consider themselves equals.

- Have a sign-up sheet and have everyone enter their Twitter handles. This way, you'll have all the tweet-up attendees' Twitter handles and can share these with the attendees by creating a public Twitter list.

- After the event, be sure to follow each attendee and reach out individually with a personalized thank you for attending.

Facebook Events

A Facebook event can be arranged in the same fashion as a tweet-up, the only difference is that you are using Facebook as the platform for spreading the word. Facebook has the advantage of having a tool specifically for creating events that you can use to send invitations and get RSVPs. This tool also encourages those coming to share it with their friends to grow your audience.

The reason I'm separating them into two separate events is because of the two platforms. If your audience is mostly on Facebook and that is the social media platform you are using for all your communication, it naturally follows that you would use that to promote your gathering. You could do two events with one for each audience or combine both groups on one event. Some people strongly favor one social media platform over another, although I've never seen a fight break out between the two groups. Why not invite some LinkedIn folks as well?

A tech sponsorship recognizes the fact that attendees are using their smartphones and tablets more and more at the trade show. Their devices keep them connected to the show, the exhibitors, and other attendees; but also to their friends and family at home. The tech sponsorship says, "We get that your devices are needed more than ever and we're here to help." Get the attendees off the floors in the hallways and out of abandoned classrooms where they are "jonesing" for a few extra minutes on their battery. Bring them into your tech lounge where they can carry on a conversation and continue to network while their phones are safely recharging.

Summary

When you think of a tech sponsorship, don't just concentrate on the applications. Think about how the attendees use those applications and what they might need to access them. Things like power, a workstation, and even a comfortable place to hang out with colleagues are all needed. You'll also need to communicate the availability of the services you are providing through your sponsorship in a way that focuses on the benefits to the attendees.

Include in your sponsorships social media friendly networking events such as tweet-ups and Facebook events. People who are active on social media to expand their professional networks love the chance to meet in person. By providing them a place to meet, you can in turn expand your company's social media network.

Don't assume everyone will be comfortable with the technology. As shows go high-tech, those who are not comfortable using that tech can feel excluded. They might feel they are not getting their money's worth from the conference. You can eliminate much of that feeling by providing a friendly, helpful place for them to get help using these devices, social media, and other applications. As a result of all these efforts, attendees will walk away remembering your company as one that enhanced their show experience.

23

Virtual Event Sponsor

Just as you might want to reach a wider audience by including a virtual component in your exhibit program, so might your show organizer. The fact is most association annual meetings attract only a small percentage of their membership. The American Dental Association says that less than 10 percent of its members attend the annual meeting. Many reasons factor into this, including budget cuts, increases in workloads, illnesses, family obligations, disabilities, and more. The for-profit shows have the same problem. They are able to attract a large number of quality attendees, but how many quality attendees cannot be there for one reason or another?

Yet, the annual meeting is one of the benefits of membership that associations are promoting. This is where much of the education occurs, and they are starting to realize that there is no reason why members who cannot physically attend the show should miss out. Associations are also starting to realize that it's their responsibility to provide alternatives to their members. Adding a virtual component isn't just a dream—it's now the best way to reach the broadest audience possible.

And it's not just their regular member bases associations are trying to reach. Many association and for-profit shows are trying to reach a new audience and even their student demographic. These students are digital natives who are more comfortable getting their information online. As a matter of fact, they usually expect things to be available online. Just as associations are grooming future members, you could also be grooming future customers.

Adding a virtual component to a show is something many organizations want to do, but it is yet another line item on their expenses. By putting together a virtual sponsorship package in which you are a feature sponsor, both you and the show benefit from the broader audience. The best part is that the show organizer already owns the large database for marketing. This takes a large marketing burden off of your shoulders. The benefits you receive are access to a targeted global audience, real-time interaction with customers and prospects, and another opportunity to showcase your company's talent.

If you were already considering doing a high-end virtual production as part of your exhibit strategy, you should look into this type of sponsorship. Helping to fund a show scale hybrid event will incur more expense, but the benefit increases exponentially. Now you are not just reaching an audience you have access to for marketing, but are also reaching a huge audience the show organizer has access to. While you are making a bigger investment, your return on investment (ROI) can see a huge jump due to all those eyeballs focused on you. The other benefit is that although you as a sponsor want to be part of the planning process, much of the logistical work will be taken off your shoulders.

Here again, I am giving you a lot of information, much of which will be the responsibility of the show organizer to carry out. One of your roles is to work with the show organizers to ensure they are doing things correctly. You can't stand back and cross your fingers hoping they get it right. Your name is all over this sponsorship, and if it fails, you will be front and center of that failure. This is not going to be a small investment, so I suggest making sure someone from your company is part of the show organizers' planning team. By playing an active role in the planning process, you can ensure your name will be on something you and the show organizer can be proud of.

Getting the Show Organizer On Board

If your show organizers already include a virtual component, you're already way ahead of the game. You won't have to sell them on the benefits of a hybrid event. You will still want to work closely with them to plan the virtual component, but you can skim through this bit. If, on the other hand, your show organizers are not already doing this, or if they've tried it in the past and deemed it unsuccessful, you need to get prepared to sell them on the idea. The failures of the past could be a result of poor planning and design, or just lousy marketing. That happens quite a bit, but now you can reassure them this year will be different because you are there to help them.

What you also need to do is show them how it will benefit the organizer and the attendees. Your pitch could include the following points that are important to a show organizer:

- Attendee marketing and conversion
- Increased audience and member benefits
- Increased revenue
- Expanded content creation
- Beating their competition
- Adding value for exhibitors

You already know why getting your company in front of a larger audience is worthwhile for you. A virtual sponsorship can be a huge benefit to the show organizers, but it also requires a lot more work on their end to do it right. You might have to convince them that it's the right thing to do. Let's take a look at why these benefits are important to the show organizer, so you can make a very convincing argument.

Attendee Marketing and Conversion

Some show organizers are afraid that if they add a virtual component to their event, it will cannibalize their onsite attendance. Experience shows that the opposite is actually true. Creating a hybrid event by adding a virtual component to a show actually gives virtual attendees a taste of what they are missing. Virtual attendees usually have access to only a small selection of educational sessions and keynote events. When they see the high quality of education that is being delivered, they make in-person attendance at the show next year a higher priority.

This is further highlighted by those attending virtually listening to what the attendees are saying about the show via social media. If attendees sound like they are having a great time, this sweetens the pot even more. I've attended many events virtually and had great interactions with other virtual attendees through chat tools available via the virtual platform. So I still got to do some networking, but a common conversation was how we hoped to meet in person at the event the next year.

According to an INXPO Cisco Live case study, 31 percent of their virtual attendees said they were more likely to attend the in-person event the next year as a result of participating in the hybrid event. In early 2012, the Professional Convention Managers Association (PCMA) reported that "more than 300 registrants this year indicated they were influenced to attend face-to-face by their previous participation in a PCMA virtual or hybrid meeting."

Increased Audience and Member Benefits

Ask the show organizer how many members actually attend the annual meeting. More importantly, how many members do not attend. Many member organizations have an obligation in their charters to educate their members. It doesn't specifically say only members who can attend the annual meeting. However, this is where most of the education occurs. By opening its conferences to a virtual audience, the organization is still able to deliver on that promise to attendees who are unable to make the event. It's showing members that they are important to the organization and that the organization will do everything in its power to ensure its members are getting the best education available in the industry.

Aside from the organizations current members, how many people are out there who the organization would like to recruit as members. Even for-profit shows can benefit by extending their audiences. Organizers are probably drawing only a small percentage of the people they are actually marketing to. By making some of the show's premium content open to a non-member virtual audience, they'll be giving them a taste of the benefits their members receive. They'll also be giving them a taste of the benefits of attending their show next year.

Increased Revenue

If the show organizers are providing a quality virtual event experience, there is no reason why they cannot charge for access. Although they cannot charge the same amount for a virtual show pass, because the attendees are not getting all the benefits of attending in person, they can charge its true value. Virtual attendees are benefiting from the education, after all. They can also receive continuing education unit (CEU) credits for their time online in many cases. This is a fact that should be promoted heavily in the marketing of the virtual portion of the event.

The show can also generate revenue by offering fee-based on-demand content for the virtual audience members. Fee-based on-demand content can also be offered to the face-to-face audience so they can see what they missed. The show could also make money on rebroadcast and repurposing fees.

The virtual event platform also opens up advertising and branding opportunities the show organizers can sell. Just make sure you're getting your name and message in the best spots. This becomes a more and more appealing opportunity to potential advertisers as that virtual audience keeps growing each year and word spreads beyond their members.

Expanded Content Creation

You can record the live sessions that you make available to the virtual audience and post them online throughout the year. Now you're expanding the audience even further. People who could not attend, either physically onsite or live virtually, can view these recorded sessions on-demand at their leisure. Even attendees onsite might have missed some of the sessions due to a conflicting session in the same time slot. They can catch these on-demand sessions as well. An on-demand archive is especially valuable for those seeking continuing education credits.

Recently, a conference made its sessions available a couple weeks after the conference as a rebroadcast of the event with a twist. The organizers invited the speakers back to participate in live online chats during their sessions. These sessions were shown at a specific time, and attendees were invited to log on and participate in a Q&A session right there with the speakers. I found this to be a great value-add over straight-up on-demand viewing.

Beating the Competition

No matter the industry, show organizers are all competing against other shows, and member organizations are competing for memberships. No one corners the market on trade shows. Adding a virtual component to a show puts show organizers and membership organizations in a much stronger position over their competition.

For instance, if I have my choice between two competing shows this year, everything else being even, I'll choose the show that's close to my home on the East Coast. But, if the West Coast show has a hybrid component, I'll attend both—one as a virtual attendee and one in person. If I'm trying to choose between two organizations to join, I will probably pick the one that has a hybrid event. That way, I know if I can't make the event for some reason, I can always catch it online.

Added Benefits to Exhibitors

As I said earlier, I am not a fan of the virtual trade show component of virtual event platforms. The problem is that they are trying to duplicate the live environment online instead of making a unique experience that fits an online audience's needs. Until they get this part right—and I think eventually they will—organizations are not going to be able to really profit from a virtual trade show component that many of these platforms provide.

Advise your show organizer in creating an engaging online marketplace for both the exhibitors and attendees. The more robust this component of the virtual experience, the more time potential buyers will spend there which means more buyers will be exposed to your messaging and branding. As the virtual sponsor, you will, of course, also be included in this experience. Here are some ideas to present to the show organizer to create an experience that benefits both the attendee, your company as the sponsor, and the other exhibitors.

Build in commercial breaks into the online experience, but instead of just posting a "We'll be back in five minutes" message on the screen, include one or two short videos. These videos could be marketing messages that focus on your value proposition or customer testimonials. During longer breaks, when those who are attending the show in person are at lunch, the organizer could schedule live exhibitor interviews and product or service demos. Most platforms have a networking lounge or chat room feature. Have different exhibitors sign up to moderate chat discussions. As the sponsor, you can negotiate first choice on all these different enhancements.

Ingredients for Success

Much of what I'm going to discuss here we've already covered in Chapter 13, "Live Stream Your Message," but because we're looking at it in the context of a virtual event sponsorship, it's important to understand how it relates specifically to the needs of the show organizer. The most important aspect is knowing the level of support you will receive from the platform vendor (or not receive) and the ability (or not) to customize the platform with the branding of the show and of your company as the sponsor.

It's likely the show will do most of the coordination of this sponsorship. Because your name will be attached to it, you must insist that certain key ingredients for a successful event are included. If you cannot be sure these things are going to be taken care of, I advise you to rethink your investment. You do not want your company's name attached to a product that is not up to par or is hastily thrown together. Make sure the following key ingredients for success are being addressed by the show organizers:

- **Planning approach**—Are they planning the hybrid event as one event with two different audiences, or are they just tacking on a virtual component with little thought for the remote audience?
- **Usability of the platform**—Is the platform they chose easy to access on different operating systems, computers, and devices, and is navigation once signed-in intuitive?

- **Camera crew**—Have the show organizers hired a camera crew that has experience in shooting live events where they switch back and forth between shots and zoom in on the action?

- **Streaming provider**—Have the show organizers selected a streaming provider that has an excellent reputation with immediate technical assistance should things go wrong?

- **Virtual emcee**—Will the show organizers be hiring or appointing a virtual emcee to represent and guide the online audience? Do they have experience in virtual or hybrid events, and do they have the key skills necessary to do the job?

- **Content selection**—Are the organizers using speakers with online experience? If not, do they have a training program for speakers who will be presenting sessions that will be streamed live?

Also, do you have the opportunity as a sponsor to have one of your sessions (if you are presenting) included in the live stream? If your competitor is going to be part of the live stream presentations and you are not, decide whether you still want to sponsor, or perhaps whether you can use it to your advantage in the long run.

If the show organizers have already started planning the virtual event before you were approached or you did the approaching, you want to make sure these questions are answered to your satisfaction. If they have not addressed any of these issues yet, you want to find out how much influence you can have in these areas as a sponsor. Also, decide how many resources you can devote to the project. Only you can determine whether you have the confidence the organizers will deliver a high quality, engaging event you want to put your name on.

Marketing the Virtual Event

Although you might not be immersed in the strategic and logistical planning of the virtual event, you should be very involved in its marketing. You should take your share of the responsibility to ensure as many targeted buyers as possible are attending the event so that you get exposure to this valuable demographic. Don't go off and do your own thing, though. Work closely with the show organizer so that you are putting out a consistent message.

The virtual audience is not going to need the same amount of advance time to plan to attend the event as the in-person audience does. There are no flights and hotels to book and no time out of the office to request. If there is a fee for the virtual portion of the event, it is likely not going to need the multiple levels of approval that attending an event in person would need. If there is no charge for attending virtually, even that comes off the table. Your heaviest marketing to this group will occur during the two to four months leading up to the live event.

Depending on the marketing goals of the show organizers, they might want to start promoting the virtual component closer to the event date, hoping to get more registrants to come onsite. They might be afraid that if they announce the virtual event too early, some attendees who are on the fence might opt not to attend in person but participate virtually instead. If onsite attendance is not their highest priority, they might want to start promoting the event earlier. This is particularly true if they are using the virtual component to expand their audience or provide continuing education to their membership base.

Once you and the show do start marketing, you need to be constant. Every communication the show organizers send out, every press release they issue, and every advertisement they buy should include the virtual portion of the event. And, it goes without saying, your sponsorship of this virtual event should be featured prominently in the headline. You are going to want to send the same communications out to your database of customers, potential customers, and your own media and blogger contacts. Communicate your sponsorship to all departments in your company so that they can spread the word any time they have contact with customers and prospects.

Because of the online environment of a virtual event, it is natural to promote it using social media. Create branded shortened links that people can use to quickly register for the event and then access the event at any point during the broadcast. Ways to share the experience should be built right into the registration system and platform so that the people who are attending can easily let their followers know about it. This use of social media opens the virtual event to people who might have never heard of the show.

Registration for the virtual event must be incorporated into whatever registration system the show is using. Even virtual attendees must register so you can collect attendees' contact information and any demographic information that is important to the organizer and you the sponsor, but the registration process should be much less taxing than the regular registration. Remember, people might have heard through social media that a prominent speaker is about to take the stage (virtually and literally). You want to make their registration process quick and simple, so they don't miss any of the presentation.

Be sure there is an option to share the registration link so word can spread easily through social media and email. You and the show organizers will want to attract as many people as possible to the online event. You should send registration information to your entire database of customers and prospects inviting them to join. Your sponsorship can include a certain number of "free passes" to the virtual event to give to your customers if a fee is associated with it.

Be sure the virtual event schedule is posted online and can be easily found. Virtual attendees will want to know the speaker lineup before committing. It's also good to include a time zone conversion tool on the web pages that contain the virtual schedule. If the keynote speaker goes on stage at 2:00 p.m. PST, viewers in New Zealand are not going to want to figure the time zone conversion for themselves. You need to make it as easy as possible for all your virtual attendees to arrive on time and not worry about missing a key session they were looking forward to.

Preparing the Virtual Attendee

There is no such thing as making it too easy for your virtual audience to attend the event. Upon registering, they should receive confirmation that includes a clickable link to the event platform. The confirmation should also include step-by-step instructions for logging in, where to go for technical help, a link to test their systems prior to the event, instructions for participating in the online chat, and instructions on how the Q&A feature works. As a sponsor of the event, I would also like to see a short welcome message from your company incorporated into this confirmation.

This same information should be sent to them a week before the event, then the day before the event, and then a couple hours before the event starts. Why so often? Because many attendees will inevitably lose the first email under a mountain of other emails. They will realize 15 minutes before the event begins that they need the link to log in to the event. Instead of trying to find the email buried under weeks of emails in their inboxes, they can quickly find the one sent right before the event. Again, a message from the sponsor should be included on every confirmation or reminder message. I would even include a link to a landing page on our website set up just for this sponsorship or event.

 Note

Be sure the sender of the email is the show organizer or, in other words, a name they will quickly recognize and associate with the event. That is what they will be looking for in their mountain of email, not the registration company's name.

Also be sure the organizers have an obvious link on the homepage of the event website to access the virtual event. Attendees might go directly to the event website to try to access the event. I was recently registered for a virtual event, but the organizer had sent only one email with the link to access the event upon registration. Unfortunately, the sender name was not the name of the event and I could not find it. I went to the event website, and try as I might, I could not find a link anywhere. I logged onto Twitter to ask the platform provider for assistance, and it took five hours to get a response (they did not have a virtual emcee). By this time,

I had missed half of the program and was very frustrated. I could do an entire case study on what not to do from that one event alone. As the sponsor, be sure you are watching social media and the chat stream for frustrated viewers, and jump in if their questions are not being addressed immediately.

The start time for the virtual audience should be at least 10 minutes before the presentation time. This way, when attendees log in to the platform, the virtual emcee can give the virtual audience a tour of the platform. She can show the virtual audience how to change the screen views, how to participate in the chat, and how to use the Q&A function. She should also tell viewers whom to contact if they need technical assistance. This is the first real impression the virtual audience gets of the event and shapes their opinion of it as the day unfolds. This process should be repeated throughout the event for those just joining.

She should also include an introduction to your company as the sponsor of the event. Create a script that does not just name you but includes a sentence about why you felt it was important to make the event available to those who could not attend in person. This should be a quick one- or two-sentence introduction.

By now, the online attendee has been exposed to your company as the sponsor at least 5 to 10 times. You can see why it is so important to want to attach your name to an engaging, well-run virtual event. There will be no question as to what company helped make their experience possible—let's just ensure it's a positive one.

As a virtual event sponsor, you are providing networking opportunities and education to an audience who would not otherwise attend the trade show. Your company gains exposure not just to the several thousand attendees who are at the show, but also to an even larger potential audience around the world. You are solving a large problem for many of your customers and prospects who want the benefits of being at the show, but whose circumstances have left them stranded.

You can assist the show organizers in creating something that stirs the virtual audience to the point that they do everything in their power to attend the live event next year. You are showing those who cannot attend in person that you understand their need to network and be educated and that you are going to provide them with a way to do just that.

An engaging virtual event experience is one that will leave a positive lasting impression not just of the event, but of the company who sponsored it.

Summary

A virtual event sponsorship is something to consider if you are already doing a bang-up job reaching the in-person audience through your booth participation and you want to reach an ever larger audience. It's also a great way to expand on a virtual component in your booth. If you are doing this level of engagement in your booth, you might be able to leverage this type of sponsorship to get more bang for your buck.

Just make sure you are working closely with the show organizer to ensure they are planning and executing an event you want your name on. Although you might not have a lot of say over the vendors they choose to hire, with the knowledge you now have about what makes a virtual event successful, you will know whether they are vendors you trust to carry out the job.

Be actively involved in the marketing of the virtual event. The more of your target market this event attracts, the better investment it is for your company. Part of the marketing is the registration process. This is where you as the sponsor and the show organizers set the stage for what the audience can expect. You want to make sure the registration process and the instructions for log in are as easy to follow as possible. There should be options built in all along the way for attendees to share the registration and event links with their networks, encouraging their colleagues to join them.

24

Show Floor Education

As a trade show producer, I love incorporating education on the show floor and a sponsor helps make it happen. Obviously, education should be taking place in your booth, but I'm talking about something much grander. A theater right in the middle of the show floor creates a buzz and keeps people in the exhibit hall. Many shows that have a conference component attached to their trade shows offer expo hall only passes. This brings in more attendees to visit the trade show, even if they cannot take the time to participate in the entire conference. It also allows more people to see the show floor if their budget does not allow them to attend the entire conference. But why should those attending only the expo portion be left out of an educational opportunity?

Show floor education is great for conference attendees as well. It provides them with a chance to see presentations that might not have made it into the conference schedule. Show floor presentations are usually shorter, more casual

15- or 20-minute bursts of information. They allow attendees to take some weight off their aching feet and take in a quick, targeted presentation. But it's not just an attendee benefit. It benefits the exhibitors as well by driving attendees from the education session rooms right to the trade show floor.

If you want to take this type of sponsorship up a notch, you could present it as similar in makeup to the virtual event sponsorship. You'd be creating a mini hybrid event using the show floor education sessions. You can open it to attendees around the world who could not be physically present at the event.

When you talk about education on the show floor and educational theaters many show managers have a vision that pops into their head that is horribly outdated. I'm not blaming them for lack of creativity. The problem is more one of time and resources and lack of exposure to new and different ideas. As a result their vision is a stage toward the back of the exhibit hall or off to one side with rows of chairs placed in front for the audience to listen to the presenter. The presenter is usually a sponsor or exhibitor who has paid for the opportunity to present a product or service demo or sales pitch. They see it as something to satisfy the desires of their exhibitors and sponsors more than their attendees.

For this type of sponsorship, your role as the sponsor will be much like that of the Virtual Event Sponsorship. Although you won't be very involved in the logistical aspects of the "educational theater," you will want to be involved in the planning and marketing of it. It's also very important to have a vision of what you want the show floor education to be. Included in that vision is how it will look and what types of education will take place there. After all, you're not just sponsoring a structure, your also sponsoring what takes place within that structure. But before we can talk about what your vision might look like, we first have to talk about who you are going to present this sponsorship to.

Whom Should You Work with When Planning Your Sponsorship?

An obvious answer is the show organizers or the people responsible for the trade show portion of the event. Because they are responsible for everything taking place on the show floor, it stands to reason that the show organizers are the people you will most likely work with. But there is another person you need to involve who is just as important—the education director.

A trade show or annual conference takes a small army to put together. Often one group is in charge of the trade show floor and another group is in charge of the education. Unfortunately, in some cases these two groups act as silos and barely communicate with one another. Your job as a sponsor will be to make sure you are talking to each group or silo and get them working together. You must work with the expo manager on the educational theater design, placement, and schedule. If you are adding a virtual component to the sessions, you will work with her on this and probably her general contractor as well.

But when it comes to the people who will be presenting on stage, you're going to need to work with the education director. He will work with you to choose the best speakers to bring onto the show floor. These might be keynote speakers, session presenters, or organizational leadership. You also should work with the education director on timing. It's likely his keynote speaker will not stick around very long, so be sure to get her into your educational theater right after her presentation.

You can work with both of these factions to find speakers for your innovative exhibitor speaking slots. Your expo manager might have a handle on what is new and innovative, especially if an innovation zone exists at the show. The education director will know whether these exhibitors are scheduled to speak in the education sessions as part of the conference; then you can work on getting the education director and expo manager working together to create a schedule.

You will likely not have final say on the schedule, but you can make sure you have input based on some of the best practices that follow. This is not your company's personal education theater, meaning you probably will not be the only exhibitor presenting in it. But you can negotiate in your sponsorship contract that direct competitors do not have presentation slots made available to them. That is up to you to decide if it is worth it. Arguably there will be more product and service categories at the show than presentation slots. The attendees do not want to hear from multiple vendors in the same category—they'd rather be exposed to a more complete line of offerings.

And last, but not least, you'll need to coordinate with the people who are doing the marketing to ensure your sponsorship is featured on any communications they are sending out. You'll also need to make sure there is proper signage and that the education theater is featured prominently on any show floor maps. You don't want to go to all this work and find out most of the attendees didn't know it existed.

What Does The Show Floor Theater Look Like?

Nothing says boring or low budget like a stage, a podium, and rows of folding chairs. I've also seen some show floor education theaters built as a box right on the show floor. They have four walls that enclose the theater with a door or two to get in and out. If you are going to close it off, why even have it located on the show floor? How do you attract passersby if they can't hear and see what is going on? Sure, some of these boxes are made out of see-through Plexiglas walls so people can see inside, but it still creates an unwelcoming environment. Attendees wonder what is going on and whether they are allowed to go inside.

When I've observed educational theaters on the show floor where the chairs were arranged in formal rows facing the stage, I've always seen the same thing. Attendees fill the chairs at the ends of each row, but no one sits in the middle of the rows. They don't want to commit to the presentation. Sitting on the end of the row allows for easy escape without disrupting anyone. Or people stand around on the sides of the theater or in the back. When people walk by, they see two things. One is a presentation that not too many people are interested in based on the empty seats. Two is the empty seats are too hard to get to because they are in the middle of the rows. These people either keep walking or join the crowd of standers on the edges and in the back.

You need to create an educational oasis in the middle of the show floor that draws people in. It should be open so that passersby can see and hear what is going on. It should be easy to slip in and out of, so guests don't feel as though they are interrupting something if the come in late or leave early. Seating can be a combination of theater and modular furniture that can be easily moved around to create discussion areas. When seating is arranged in a more relaxed way and you include different styles of lightweight furniture that can be moved, you create a more interesting and inviting atmosphere. You can combine cube-like ottoman seating, couches, leisure chairs, and stools that look comfortable and say to the visitor, "Come on in, take a load off, and stay for a while." Instead of being a place that people rush past on their way to somewhere else, it becomes a gathering place and drives traffic to the show floor.

You could set up this area as one large theater that accommodates only one presentation at a time or divide it into several smaller breakout areas where several sessions could be taking place simultaneously. This layout will depend on the types of sessions you will be focusing on and whether they appeal to a broad audience or a targeted group of people.

Sound

One of the biggest objections voiced when planning trade show education theaters comes from the exhibitors whose booths surround it. It's also interesting that the booths surrounding this area are one of the most coveted spots for savvy exhibitors. The reason some complain is because of the noise level coming from the education theater. Exhibitors say it distracts the visitors in their booths. Unless the sound in the theater is cranked way up, I would argue that these exhibitors are just looking for something to blame their lack of traffic on. It's much more likely that they have absolutely nothing interesting going on in their booth to hold their visitors' attention.

As far as sound goes, I've never been in an exhibit hall that was quiet. There are distractions everywhere attacking the attendees' senses. It's the exhibitor's job to be able to hold his visitors' attention amid all the distraction. Nevertheless, there are things you can do to reduce the sound to a reasonable level so that everyone is happy. You can use transparent fabric hung throughout, above, and around the educational theater to help absorb some of the sound and aim your speakers in an appropriate direction.

Like I said, savvy exhibitors love being next to all this activity. It guarantees a lot of traffic in front of their booths. Smart exhibitors piggyback on the educational sessions by scheduling their in-booth presentations right after those taking place in the theater. Attendees leaving the theater presentation are likely to wander into a booth presentation right after. As the sponsor, you're going to want to make sure your booth is positioned next to this theater.

Stage

Skip the platform stage. This is supposed to be a casual and intimate environment. If space allows, you could put in a short lift that would help audience members in the back see better without creating a barrier between the audience and the speaker. Skip the podium as well; it's a crutch and no one needs it for a 15-minute talk. However, you might need a table available if someone is doing a product demo.

If you are doing a Q&A type interview in your educational theater (highly recommended), you'll need seating for the interviewer and the interviewee. Seating is important and should not be taken lightly. I've seen setups that use low and very comfortable-looking armchairs for these Q&A sessions. And then someone sits in them and the chairs look incredibly awkward, especially for women wearing skirts. And you have not seen anything until you see people trying to politely exit from those chairs. Very sturdy stools with a back or director's chairs work best for these situations. But make sure they're not so high that you must climb up onto them. You should just be able to lean back into them from a standing position.

Your backdrop should be of a neutral color and should include your branding as well as the shows. Special attention should be paid if you plan on broadcasting these sessions to a virtual audience. A seam that is nearly unseen to a live audience will stand out on camera. You don't want lines and logos sticking out of your presenters' heads—that will be incredibly distracting to the virtual audience.

What Makes for a Good Presentation on the Show Floor?

As I mentioned earlier, short presentations are best. After all, you want people visiting booths, not spending an hour seated in a presentation. The types of presentations that work best for show floor education are town hall discussions, keynote Q&A sessions, innovative product demonstrations or product Q&A sessions, and hands-on how-to presentations.

Town Hall Discussions

At large annual meetings and trade shows, it is customary to have the incoming president of the organization give a large general session speech about where she intends to take the organization in the upcoming year. These types of speeches are designed so that the speaker talks to the audience and the audience listens. Sometimes the incoming president takes a few minutes at the end for one or two questions from the audience. This allows for very little interaction.

Why not bring the incoming leadership to the show floor educational theater for a more intimate town hall discussion? There the audience can share with her the real day-to-day issues they are struggling with and where they think the organization should be heading. This is a huge benefit to the organization as its leadership can stay in touch with the member base. It's also a huge benefit to the members because they are able to express their most pressing issues.

These sessions strip away the fanfare and tend to be much more open and honest. It's an opportunity for the organization's president to show her softer side and let her personality really show through. It comes across as much more authentic than the big opening or closing general session speeches, and the audience loves this because their voices are being heard.

As the sponsor, you should assign someone to live tweet the audiences questions and leadership's responses during the session. It's a perfect way to extend your company's exposure to the attendees and be seen as someone who provides valuable information.

Keynote Q&A Sessions

Many of the big keynote sessions are lacking in much the same way as the organization leadership speeches. There is very little time for Q&A after these big productions. Instead of taking one or two questions from the huge audience after the speech, move the Q&A portion into the show floor education theater. It's important to promote these Q&A sessions prior to the show, in the keynote description, and by announcement just before and after the presentation. Of course, social media is the perfect tool to remind people about these sessions. Like the town hall meetings, as a sponsor, you should be live tweeting the presenter's responses.

Here the audience can interact with the speaker in a much more informal setting. They have an opportunity to get their specific questions answered by experts. It's important that the organizer preps the speaker as to how the session will work. You don't want him delivering a scripted speech on the show floor. He is there to answer specific questions or expand on a point he made during his staged presentation.

I saw this fail incredibly at one such session I watched online. The speaker was a motivational speaker who clearly did not understand his audience. The difference here was that he was scheduled on the show floor the day before his big talk. The idea was that it would generate attendance for the closing session and make it a must-see event. And it could have worked, except this particular speaker proceeded to alienate his audience.

I felt like I was watching a politician answering (or I should say *not* answering) questions. The audience was sincerely interested in the speaker's topic and was asking good questions. But the speaker refused to go off script. The answers he gave were vague and canned. I have to give credit to the virtual emcee, though, who refused to get rattled. She kept pressing him for answers, and he kept refusing to give them. I thought any minute an angry mob would rise up. Vetting speakers is something the show organizers should factor into their planning.

Innovative Product or Service Demonstrations and Q&A

At every show, there are a few exhibitors who are doing something that really makes you say, "Wow!" These are must-see products or services that can really change the lives or jobs of their customers. These are the types of products and services that will do well in the show floor education environment.

It's a fine line to walk between making a self-serving sales pitch and offering genuinely helpful information in these instances. This is why I prefer the Q&A format to a straightforward product demo. The presenter can give a brief synopsis of her innovative product and then open it up to the audience for Q&A.

I saw a wonderful example of this when watching the American Public Works Association presentations in its "EXPO EXPERIENCE" through the virtual component called "Continuing the Conversation" (a concept created by The Expo Group). I had been watching most of the conversations taking place throughout the day to see what works in this environment and what doesn't. I've always been cautious of presentations by exhibitors for fear that they will come off as infomercials.

The Q&A session with Jon Hargett, president of Pavement Restorations, Inc., was a perfect example of what works when exhibitors take the stage. Jon's company has a new technology that uses infrared asphalt restoration to fix potholes. Jon briefly and concisely explained what infrared asphalt restoration is and how it differs from what most public works professionals are currently doing. Jon was talking about his product of course, but more than that, he was talking about the process.

I found myself completely fascinated—and I don't have anything to do with public works or potholes.

Clearly, the audience was fascinated as well, both the in-person audience and my online compatriots. Specific questions were coming from both audiences rapid fire. The first question was how much does it cost. Kudos to Jon for answering that question completely honestly. I was so engaged that I caught myself almost asking a question even though I was just a casual observer. You can view the YouTube video at http://bit.ly/infraredpotholes.

Keep this in mind when you are preparing presentations you will be doing in this area. As a sponsor, you should negotiate a number of presentation slots into your agreement. This is a great opportunity to get employees of your company out of the office and in front of customers. In this informal setting, the people who make the products your customers use or carry out the services you offer might be more popular than your company's executives.

How-To Presentations

Hands-on how-to presentations also work well on the show floor. Just about every industry has fantastic ways to use electronic devices, such as tablets and smart-phones, to make our day-to-day jobs simpler. Any number of software apps are available for these devices and computers that can make people more productive.

The problem lies in the fact that not everyone is adept at using these devices. That is where a little hands-on learning can be useful. A show floor learning lounge is a great place to do these demonstrations. Have the organizers schedule bring your own device (BYOD) sessions in which instructors show the audience how to download and use these great applications. They don't have to be applications cre-ated by you or other exhibitors. They can demonstrate something that is available to anyone and that can be used in any industry.

I would also suggest sessions that teach the attendees how to use social media plat-forms so they can stay connected with the people they met at the conference or that the association uses to connect with their members. Include how-to sessions for devices, apps, products, or software used in the industry of the trade show. Attendees could learn how to set up their own blogs using WordPress or Blogger as well as a few useful widgets and plug-ins. Sessions on the top 10 productivity apps for the iPad or even a session or two on how to most effectively use the show event application could be included.

Regardless of whether the session is a Q&A, town hall, or how-to, the session should be very specific. General or vague topics do not create a lot of discussion and do not get the audience involved. Only when you narrow down the presenta-tions to very specific topics will this environment work. There is no way anyone could cover "How to Best Equip Your Manufacturing Floor," in 20 minutes, but a presenter could conduct a detailed discussion on "Casters: Do They Matter? Making the Right Selection." (This was a topic I found in the show floor education program for MODEX 2012.)

Peer Sessions

Something else you could try in your show floor educational theater is an unconference format or peer sessions. These discussion topics could be crowd sourced a month before the event using social media tools such as Google Moderator. Google Moderator allows you to open topic submissions for a finite period of time and then allow others to vote on which topics they find most interesting. The most popular submissions can then be put on the peer session discussion schedule.

What is a *peer session*? These are sessions that focus on peer-to-peer learning rather than a transfer of knowledge from a speaker to the audience. I love peer sessions for several reasons. The first is that I am a firm believer in getting feedback on a problem from my peers. After all, they've been there and done that and are usually more than willing to help someone else avoid the same mistakes they've made. Why struggle through a problem when you're at a trade show with thousands of your peers who might have figured out a way to solve it? Or, even if no one has solved the problem, working through it with a group of people who are looking for the same outcome can be a productive brainstorming session.

The second biggest benefit to peer sessions is that they foster networking. When you work closely with others to solve problems, you really get to know one another. People's personalities really shine through when involved in this type of group activity. I have met mentors and mentees through my participation in peer sessions. I have also cultivated wonderful lasting friendships from people I've met at these types of events.

Peer sessions require very little planning. All you need is a moderator and a place for people to gather and work together. The education lounge on the show floor is an excellent place for this. While these sessions can be decided too late to add to a printed program, they could easily be added to the show event app. They could also be posted on a printed schedule in the learning lounge and announcements could be made on the show floor. Social media is a great way to share this information because of its real-time nature and its capability to spread information through a large group rapidly. Use social media to introduce the upcoming session, invite those struggling with the same issue to attend, and encourage those who think they might have a solution to stop by as well.

But beware. Attendees who experience the peer session learning style love it so much they rarely want to attend the one-to-many transfer of knowledge that traditional sessions provide. They find it almost impossible not to want to help fellow attendees when they think they might have an answer to someone's problem.

An educational theater or learning lounge on the show floor that is a welcome and inviting space encourages attendees to stop and stay. A schedule filled with intimate discussions with speakers and interactive learning will drive traffic onto the show floor. As the sponsor of the show floor education that is exactly what you want to have happen. But don't just rely on your branding to make your presence known as the sponsor. Participate in educational sessions by presenting, live tweeting sessions, getting ideas for future content, and just networking with the crowd.

A show floor education sponsorship helps attendees network and allows them to take advantage of great interactive educational opportunities they might not find in formal sessions. It gives them a chance to have their voices heard and interact with presenters and association leadership. It allows them to easily connect with their peers in an informal setting. It also positions your company as one who is in tune with the day-to-day issues of your customers and potential customers.

Summary

An educational theater on the show floor does not need to be dull, drab, or boring. You can create a relaxing oasis that encourages conversation between the speakers and the audience. It should be a welcoming place where people want to gather and exchange information and ideas with their peers.

Work with the expo manager and education committee to create a schedule that targets specific solutions to problems attendees might be having. The more specific, the better. Give people a forum in which to ask questions of keynote speakers, industry thought leaders, and organizational leadership. Create a space in which it is fun to experiment with hands-on learning of tools that will make attendees' lives easier. Show them you are in touch with their needs by giving them a way to suggest the topics they think should be addressed.

And open the learning to a wider audience by creating a hybrid event that broadcasts the learning to a virtual audience. Let those who could not attend in person ask questions of the speaker and have their opinions heard in order to bring both audiences together.

Conclusion

It's Not the End . . . It's the Beginning

After a couple hundred pages of talk, talk, talk, we're right back to where we started. I spent a half a billion words saying it, but really it comes down to this one idea: Social media is just a tool. What is really important to your exhibit program's success is designing an incredibly solid strategy. Then, and only then, do you choose the tools that are right for the strategy.

Just before I started writing this conclusion, I got a request from someone who wanted me to write a blog post arguing for the use of augmented reality in trade shows, and he'd write a post arguing against it. He had heard me mention once that I saw some potential for the use of augmented reality in exhibit booths and trade shows, and he thinks it's a gimmick.

I politely declined the offer because he just doesn't understand basic strategic planning. How can you possibly be either for or against a tool? How on earth can one argue against a drill or a saw completely on its own? The argument would have no point. It would be irrelevant and just plain idiotic. Unless I know what the goals, objectives, and strategy of the exhibitor or show organizer are, how can I possibly know whether augmented reality is a tool that should be used? It would be like saying armed guards serve no purpose at a trade show without knowing what show you are talking about. Sure, they might not be necessary at a puppeteer convention (I don't know a lot of puppeteers, but I imagine they are nice folk), but those responsible for security at the G8 summit might feel differently. I stay out of most general discussions that focus on social media tools. I see no value in them. Social media is a communication tool—how you use it depends entirely on your exhibit strategy. There is no one-size-fits-all solution; every exhibitor is going to have its own strategy and will use social media in ways that will fulfill that strategy. You need to set goals and measurable objectives, and then design your strategy around them. Only when you work in this order—goals first, objectives second, then strategy, and finally tools— can you have a successful exhibit program.

Some people might say, "Just give me ways to use social media. I'm too busy to worry about goals and strategy. I just want the solution." To them I say, "Sorry, there is no magic bullet and there never will be. You will never get out of the weeds if you build your program around tools. You will be starting over from scratch every time you exhibit at a show. You will never get ahead, and you will never see the kind of success you should be seeing."

You will also never get ahead in your career because you will be easily replaced. There will always be someone else who can upload photos to Flickr, post videos on YouTube, and run silly contests on Facebook. If that is the only value you add to your exhibit program, when budgets get cut, your job will be one of the first to go. After all, any intern can do these types of tasks.

You need to understand your company's overall business goals, objectives, and strategies, and then make sure the goals and objectives of your exhibit program are aligned with them. You need to prove you are not just a line item in the expense column—you must be able to show that you are a profit center. People who are an integral part of their company's strategic vision are the people who hang on to their jobs, and they are the employees who rise through the ranks. Companies desperately need more strategic thinkers in their exhibit marketing programs.

Beware of so-called social media experts who talk only about social media. A real social media expert will talk mainly about strategy. Someone might come along who has previously used social media, and a specific tool for another exhibit program, and it might have been wildly successful. That is no indication it will be successful in your program. It would be like putting solar panels on your roof because someone told you they saved tons on their electric bill. The only problem is you live in the middle of the woods, and your roof never sees a ray of sunlight. Posting photos of everyone having a great time in your hospitality suite is not the right answer if those who are there are extremely private individuals who think there is way too much exposure already on the Internet.

If someone comes to you and says, we should do Foursquare check-ins in our booth, ask them why. How it will help you achieve your objectives? Even if it appears as though it might make sense, ask yourself whether it fits in your strategy, or is there a better tool you should be using. Ask if you have the manpower to handle such a project, or if there is a better, simpler way to meet your objective.

I love show event apps. I think they are fantastic for some large events. But I wouldn't spend $40,000 on one if the only things I'd use it for was a mobile schedule of events that could more easily be printed on a 4" × 6" piece of paper. That little piece of paper is a much easier and more cost-effective way to accomplish my goal of letting people know when they need to be where.

It's a good practice to get out and see what other people are doing. It's great to see how they are implementing new technology into their exhibit programs, but it's not a good idea to simply duplicate their efforts in your own programs. What you want to do is see how and whether you can adapt their ideas to your own unique strategy. Think strategically, not logistically, and you'll see the bigger picture, and possibly come up with something others will try to adopt down the road.

Finally, use social media as a conversation tool. Don't just broadcast your message to the widest audience possible. Create and cultivate relationships with customers, prospects, partners, and industry thought leaders. Provide your network with valuable information—not just information created by your company, but information you've found from other sources that they will benefit from reading. Connect people. Introduce people you've met on social media to other people they will benefit from knowing.

If you do these things, you will become the go-to source for the information your customers need and are looking for. Your company will be on their must-see list of exhibitors at the show. They'll get to know your company by the employees that make up the organization instead of just a corporate logo. They'll be sure to bring their colleagues with them when they come to see you because they'll be proud of their discovery. And social media can help you do all this without giving away a single iPad in your booth.

So, to sum it all up, remember this: Goals, then objectives, then strategy, and finally, the tools that will get you there. Okay, begin!

Index